The Ethical Vision of
Clint Eastwood

The Ethical Vision of Clint Eastwood

SARA ANSON VAUX

William B. Eerdmans Publishing Company
Grand Rapids, Michigan / Cambridge, U.K.

Published 2012 by

Wm. B. Eerdmans Publishing Co.

2140 Oak Industrial Drive N.E., Grand Rapids, Michigan 49505 /

P.O. Box 163, Cambridge CB3 9PU U.K.

Printed in the United States of America

17 16 15 14 13 12   7 6 5 4 3 2 1

Library of Congress Cataloging-in-Publication Data

Vaux, Sara Anson.

The ethical vision of Clint Eastwood / Sara Anson Vaux.

p.   cm.

Includes filmography.

Includes bibliographical references (p.   ) and index.

ISBN 978-0-8028-6295-2 (pbk.: alk. paper)

1. Eastwood, Clint, 1930 — Criticism and interpretation.

2. Motion pictures — Moral and ethical aspects.   I. Title.

PN1998.3.E325V38   2012

791.4302′8092 — dc23

2011019094

www.eerdmans.com

Contents

Foreword

This study of Clint Eastwood by Sara Anson Vaux has been long awaited in many corners of the world. Trained in religion and literature at Rice University and versed in theology and film studies through the University of Chicago, Northwestern University, Cambridge University, and the seminaries of the Chicago area, her voice is one of the clearest we have in analyzing film technique, discerning theological and ethical implications, and assessing cultural significance. The book displays her flair for uncovering the implicit theological and ethical themes that surface in the work of the great filmmakers. Showing an impressive mastery of the history of film, this book has an enthusiasm for the genial work of Clint Eastwood that is visible on every page. Vaux has shared these insights in courses in religion and film at Garrett-Evangelical Theological Seminary and North Park Theological Seminary, and she is presently doing so at Northwestern University, where her courses attract flocks of creative students.

Vaux's analysis is solidly grounded in contemporary biblical and ethical studies, but she does not burden the reader with academic jargon. By detailed analyses of film after film, she demonstrates Eastwood's long-standing concern for the state of the American soul. She uncovers his passion for justice and kindness to the oppressed and persecuted, his concern for the transfiguration of violence into reconciliation and peace, and his incessant search for the inestimable human dignity of all persons, whatever their gender, ethnicity, nationality, or circumstance. Although she does not claim that Eastwood is a consciously religious director, her work allows readers to understand that these traits reflect a universal endowment in the image of God. Her work will be called on by many as we search for alternatives to our warring madness, our tendency to degrade others, and our apathy toward those in need. To quote the preface to Victor Hugo's *Les Miserables,* "So long as there shall exist, by reason of law and custom, a social condemnation — which creates hells on earth — so long as the problems of the age — degradation by poverty, the ruin of women by starvation and the dwarfing of childhood by physical and spiritual night — as long as social asphyxia is possible . . . books like this cannot be useless."

ROBERT JEWETT,
Guest Professor of New Testament
The University of Heidelberg

The Intent of the Book

One stormy eve more than a dozen years ago, I received a call from Robert Jewett, fierce biblical scholar and even more ferocious sailor. Would my husband, Ken, my daughter, Sarah, and I like to go for an evening sail on Lake Michigan? The sky over Lake Michigan the night of our sail grew dark, the lake almost empty of boats, and the wind alternated between breeze and gust. We were not supposed to be out there. Yet what a perfect atmosphere for two theologians, one film critic, and one culture-savvy teen to venture into the testy waters of art and apocalypse! *Unforgiven* had burst upon the movie scene only a few years earlier, fodder for a burgeoning religion-and-film industry. Jewett, who had written early and well on religion and movies, cautioned against the seductions of redemptive violence in Clint Eastwood's films, this one in particular.

In response to Jewett's concern about the movie's high body count, I countered with a plea to consider the actual plot: what transpires on screen, the ways that words, images, and sounds steadily undermine a usually proviolence narrative template that was shaped during the western genre's B-movie heyday — from the twenties through the end of the fifties. As Eastwood himself has reflected, "*Unforgiven* is less a study in violence than an ironic meditation on its costs."

At the end of a perilous sail, during which the winds — but not our debate — turned hostile, we agreed to publish our arguments in *Christianity and Literature*.[1] Over the past sixteen years, my Eastwood project has taken

1. See Robert Jewett, "The Gospel of Violent Zeal in Clint Eastwood's *Unforgiven*,"

on a life of its own alongside my interests in French, Scandinavian, Belgian, Iranian, and Polish cinema. The current American political scene — and my concern for the survival of a welcoming, generous, and spiritually vibrant American social order with inclusion and healing for its citizens and guests — has fueled my interest in and study of the ways an icon of power honors the least among us with his art. In the following chapters I mention some of the atmosphere in which my ideas took shape: a family with its door always open to strangers; a palpable contrast between winters in a bustling and chaotic northern industrial city after World War II and summers in a hot, sleepy Southern town where the Confederacy still lived on; and a father whose love of American history was seasoned by his trenchant criticism of religious intolerance. The debate with Robert Jewett pulled me toward American movies like *Unforgiven*, movies that took a critical look at the dominant Hollywood model of the superhero in a superpower.

Few critics venture to think about Eastwood's moral agenda. Jewett, Eastwood biographer Richard Schickel, writer Laurence Knapp, and critic Dave Kehr have come close. Kehr was an early admirer of Eastwood's work. Bruce Ricker, director of a PBS American Master Series on Eastwood, says: "Dave [Kehr] and I [have been] raised as Lutherans, which creates a moral stance about things. And the one thing that Clint does bring out is a sense of morality, but you're not hit over the head with it." Ricker also notes Eastwood's "sparse aesthetics."[2] In recent years, Richard Locke and David Denby have tackled the wider dimensions of Eastwood's movies, and A. O. Scott and Manohla Dargis, both of *The New York Times*, have written astute analyses of his later films that acutely capture their familiar and yet deeply unsettling ethical implications.

The best work on Eastwood as a philosophical, ethical, and artistic voice has been done in French by critic Noël Simsolo and in English (the United States and Britain) by Kent Jones and fellow critics Karina Longworth, Ed Gonzales, and Kevin B. Lee.[3] Michael Henry Wilson, whose sage film analysis

---

Christianity and Literature 47.4 (1998): 427-42, and my reply, Sara Vaux, "*Unforgiven*: The Sentence of Death and Radical Forgiveness," *Christianity and Literature* 47 (1998): 443-60. The latter article expands on my chapter on the movie western in Vaux, *Finding Meaning at the Movies* (Nashville: Abingdon, 1999); see also Jewett, "The Disguise of Vengeance in *Pale Rider*," in *Religion and Popular Culture in America*, ed. B. Forbes and J. Mahan (Berkeley: University of California Press, 2000), 243-57.

2. http://www.pbs.org/wnet/americanmasters.database.eastwood_e_interview.html.

3. "Eastwood Critics' Roundtable," hosted by Evan Davis, presented by the New York Film Society, January 3, 2009: http://www.youtube.com/watch?v=gWun9zSQYvg.

and interviews with Eastwood I cite frequently in this book, cuts to the heart of Eastwood's remarkable artistry and offbeat social and cultural criticism. Otherwise, apart from Schickel's comprehensive and immensely readable biography, many books and articles simply recite the plots of the films and production details, information easy to find on IMDb (Internet Movie Database), the format followed by Marc Eliot's *American Rebel: The Life of Clint Eastwood.* That book is a fun read but offers little that Schickel's excellent biography or Patrick McGilligan's questionable one, *Clint: The Life and Legend* (HarperCollins, 1999), did not cover first. Christopher Frayling's analysis of Eastwood's movies is wonderfully thorough and appealingly written, in both his book *Clint Eastwood* (1992) and his discussion of the genre entitled *Spaghetti Westerns* (2006). My book will not unpack every movie in the detail that Frayling does; after all, his major work tackles the origins, narratives, décor, and cultural currency of Spaghetti Westerns. But I aim to inform my own analysis with the verve and scholarly accuracy that he displays.

I plan to address this relative void by focusing on Eastwood's unfolding moral agenda in order to grant him his proper place in intellectual and film history, and to expand our knowledge of the complexities of his major movies. In the chapters that follow, I analyze Eastwood's best-known, iconic films from narrative, artistic, and thematic perspectives. Eastwood deserves to be placed alongside Robert Bresson, Martin Scorsese, Carl-Theo. Dreyer, Claire Denis, and Luc and Jean-Pierre Dardenne as a director who (in his personal movies) intentionally engages the moral nature of humanity, mediated through visual art.

Seen along a forty-year continuum, Eastwood's movies reveal stages in an unfolding moral ontology — a sense of being in the world. They become more sophisticated and nuanced in tone and narrative exploration even if the basic motifs — justice, confession, war and peace, the gathering, and the search for a perfect world — remain the same throughout his career. But the films far exceed any elaboration of set themes, even as they studiously avoid or deliberately distance the trappings of religious symbolism or practice (in part the liberating legacy of his mentor, Sergio Leone). For those who might search Eastwood's movies for endorsements of a particular religious system, Bill Murphy's words may warn them to look carefully: "Religion too often provides a language and a cosmology for defining certain categories of people who should be excluded, subordinated, mistreated, and killed."[4] Karen Armstrong, in turn, probes the misuses of

---

4. Bill Murphy, "Violence and Obscurity: Religious Cosmology of Seeing and Hearing

religious language and practice by highlighting its positive uses: "[T]he essence of religious experience is not 'accepting dubious propositions,' but showing compassion toward other living creatures. 'All the world religions say that it is compassion that brings you into a state of transcendence, by dethroning you from the centre of your world and putting another in your place.'"[5] These two thinkers' insights capture the heart of Eastwood's cinematic practice. Armstrong's quote applies to Eastwood, who in his movies argues against exclusion of the weak and marginalized and for compassion, charity, sanctuary, and justice. Love the neighbor, welcome the stranger, treat others as you wish to be treated, and seek justice for all.

This book proceeds to examine Eastwood's iconic movies in four sections, loosely grouped into westerns, mysteries, war movies, and healing narratives. A number of central motifs assert themselves throughout Eastwood's work.

- *Justice, mercy, and the angel of death.* The angel of death can resonate with either an apocalypse (blind, violent, unreasoning fury) or "with healing in her wings." Eastwood explores multiple kinds of justice, from a judge in the west seeking to "bring justice" to a massive territory (*Hang 'Em High* [1968], the first film produced by Malpaso, Eastwood's new production company) to the corruption of the agents of justice themselves *(Pale Rider, Unforgiven, Changeling, Invictus)* to institutional assaults on universal justice itself, as the powerful prey on the weak. The search for "justice" assumes that something in creation or in the evolution of human institutions has gone wrong and must be put right. The term shifts meaning from film to film and within films, most plainly dissected in *Unforgiven*: Little Bill's full-fledged assault on a divinely ordained justice that respects human life.
- *Confession* lies at the heart of Eastwood's iconic films. The past, confronted and shared with another person, becomes central to transformation. Variations in setting, lighting, and ritual resonance infuse the physical with the spiritual. Confession may lead to self-discovery and healing, as in the campfire and death scenes in *Unforgiven* and Walt's confession to Thao in *Gran Torino;* or it may be driven by dark forces,

---

in the West African Rainforest," in *The Theology of Light and Sight: An Interfaith Perspective* (Eugene, OR: Wipf and Stock, 2011), 62-77.

5. Karen Armstrong, quoted by Alice Clegg, "Through Troubled Times to the Spiritual Life," *Oxford Times* 37, vol. 20, no. 3, Trinity 2008.

as in the saloon shootout "confession" in *Unforgiven;* or confession may be made up of false confessions, as in *Mystic River* and *Gran Torino. Invictus* works its way to ritualized public confession directed toward forgiveness and reconciliation.

• *Eternal war versus the dawn of peace.* The tension between apocalyptic and redemptive or reconciling views of human nature and the social order appears not only in the "war movies" but also, more subtly, within the others. "Eternal war" assumes that humans are inexorably doomed to make war on each other, to "get even" for real or feared wrongs (a Hobbesian vision of human nature). The idea of the dawn of peace arises from the biblical books of Jeremiah and Micah; Jesus' teachings on love and peace; and biblical references to the possibility of the kingdom of heaven in this earthly life and for all nations.

• *The gathering, particularly the meal,* provides an arena for flawed and suffering characters to transcend borders and construct a "new life." Theologically, a shared gathering means the formation of a holy people who envision and move toward a better, if not a perfect, world in this earthly life. The institution of the Lord's Supper weaves together meal, confession, and communion. *The Outlaw Josey Wales, Unforgiven, Million Dollar Baby, Gran Torino,* and *Invictus* (among others) resonate with the Gospel of John via Dostoevsky's *Crime and Punishment* and *The Brothers Karamazov* and Bresson's *A Man Escaped.* New life can lead to personal, political, and social reconciliation. The final chapter of this book will pull together the threads of gatherings across films as disparate as *Josey Wales, Bridges of Madison County,* and *Gran Torino.*

• *Reconciliation:* the wish for a perfect (or at least better) world, a "paradise," provides the backdrop of many an Eastwood story and the ultimate goal toward which his characters yearn. A shared gathering represents a movement toward the way things are meant to be: wholeness of the person and healing of the wounds of dispute, discrimination, and war.

Shakespeare in *King Lear,* Dickens in *Little Dorrit* and *A Christmas Carol,* and Dostoevsky in *The Brothers Karamazov* and *Crime and Punishment* measure palpable human tragedy against the transvaluative vision of the Sermon on the Mount: "Blessed are the poor in spirit, for theirs is the kingdom of heaven." So also does Eastwood hint in his movies of an earthly kingdom that inspires the downtrodden and weary. In a better world, children, men, and women would not die young. Immigrants, people of color, women, and wayfarers would all be welcome; nations would not make war against each other; hierarchies would disappear; the poor would not be disdained. Empires would cease.

The wish for a better world is implicit in *High Plains Drifter*, as the new town that has arisen has been fueled by greed and sprinkled with blood. *The Outlaw Josey Wales* opens with an image of paradise as mother, father, and child till the earth. Violence destroys the dream, and the young farmer is driven out of Eden. Years pass before he comes to know a somewhat less perfect kingdom of heaven, a precariously positioned new family of outcasts. Gus and Ben in *The Gauntlet* dream of the home they'll make together; Maggie and Frankie in *Million Dollar Baby* speak of the little cabin where they can care for each other; Walt in *Gran Torino* stews in the wreckage of a blasted dream, but when he gathers an expanded and unexpected family around him, he widens his vision of what that dream can include.

In Part I, I explore the ways that Eastwood breached the boundaries of a genre that had dominated American moviemaking for generations, the western. Robert Jewett and John Shelton Lawrence are correct in slotting the majority of American westerns (and a good deal of other popular literature and film) into the template of "the American monomyth" and the "myth of the American superhero."[6] Like Jewett and Lawrence, I have tracked the proliferation of violent heroic redemptive figures (asexual men in love with violence) and watched with alarm as the model of American power and arrogance (America as the savior of the world) has repeated itself in political and international policy even as it saturates novels, films, TV, and video games. Although "the hero" is an enduring literary and mythological figure, when the character is linked to stories of conquest and domination of lands and peoples at the expense of community and peace, the model must be challenged. Eastwood's iconic westerns challenge the model in every sequence, with the help of cinematographer Bruce Surtees and his successor, Jack Green, who took over until 2003.

Part II moves away from westerns, with their tension between hero and community, justice and mercy, and apocalypse and reconciliation set in the destructive aftermath of the Civil War. *Mystic River, Million Dollar Baby*, and *Changeling* (all shot by cinematographer Tom Stern) stand on

6. John Shelton Lawrence and Robert Jewett, *The Myth of the American Superhero* (Grand Rapids: Eerdmans, 2002); see also Jewett's discussion of *Pale Rider* in dialogue with Romans 12–13 in *Saint Paul at the Movies: The Apostle's Dialogue with American Culture* (Louisville: Westminster John Knox, 1993), 118-33.

the meditative narratives of *Bird, White Hunter, Black Heart, A Perfect World,* and *Bridges of Madison County,* movies I refer to throughout the book. The undergirding motifs echo those of the westerns. But each film takes a different approach to human suffering caused by individual actions, institutional structures, and the possibility of cosmic instability than the ones before. The confession, a regular feature of each western, becomes at once more central to and more fraught and misleading within the unfolding narrative. Each movie in this section ends in uncertainty and ambiguity as foggy as the mists into which the Stranger and the Preacher disappear, the mountains or the dark night that swallow Josey Wales or Will Munny, or the cloudy windows of the diner that may obscure Frankie Dunn's solitary figure in *Million Dollar Baby.*

Yet hints of a better world weave throughout the movies' textures, even if by negation in *Mystic River* (one small reconciliation in a wash of death); tight-bound physical contact in health and illness redeemed by steadfast love in *Million Dollar Baby;* and a hope for a sweet reunion, mother and son, that outdoes even vindication and execution in *Changeling. Bird,* one of the Eastwood team's most radical undertakings, features another man of light and darkness, Charlie Parker, and underscores Eastwood's lifelong love of jazz.

Part III confronts four films that surely portray Eastwood and his creative team at their boldest. They tackled location shooting and battle scenes in the extreme; institutional betrayal by the American and Japanese governments at its most cynical; and the fissure between America's image as the world's protector with open arms and its treatment of immigrants and poor at an unacceptable level. I treat the three movies *Flags of Our Fathers, Letters from Iwo Jima,* and *Gran Torino* as three panels of a triptych steeped in religious symbols, religious ritual, and the promise of reconciliation. Walt Kowalski's sacrifice to redeem his fractured community may fit this description best, but the suffering of all the soldiers referred to in the three films resonates with Dietrich Bonhoeffer's and Garry Wills's equation of torture and other war crimes as akin to the scourging of Jesus. Alive or dead, their bodies, hearts, and memories have been rent by what they have seen and what they have done. The hint of a better world lies in the ways the movies are presented to be absorbed, discussed, and meditated on — not passively consumed — by audiences. *Invictus* relates the postconflict tale of Nelson Mandela, former terrorist turned prisoner, philosopher, and peacemaker.

Part IV considers three dimensions of Eastwood's iconic movies that are not included in the "violent gunslinging amoral savior" hero image touted in the publicity for reissues of the Spaghetti Westerns, *The Outlaw Josey Wales*, or the *Dirty Harry* movies. In the westerns the Eastwood character moves uneasily between past and present, his existence as a creature of legend and his role as a human being caught between apocalypse and redemption. The figures in *High Plains Drifter* and *Pale Rider* are coded with horror-movie lighting and music, which undercuts any "realistic" spin the spectator could put on their actions. Josey Wales and Will Munny tread uncertainly between two worlds. Josey's life story becomes swept up in a major reprisal drama, a microcosm of the thirst for revenge that consumed the former Confederacy after the end of the Civil War. But, unexpectedly, Eastwood and his team begin to construct a counternarrative, a story of rebuilding a life and a unified country that refuses the language of exclusion. Josey finds love and builds a new family. Lighting, music, and framing signal the shifts from one story to another.

The three chapters in Part IV unspool the movements from apocalypse toward reconciliation in the iconic movies. The second chapter focuses on the gatherings, particularly the meal, in which bonds form and reconciliation blossoms. *A Perfect World* and *Bridges of Madison County* prepare the way for the grand feast of *Gran Torino* and the earth-shaking British tea in *Invictus* as they offer two of Eastwood's most beautiful and complex renderings of the human experience.

In the final chapter, entitled "Another Clint," I explore music, sound, and silence in *Unforgiven*, as Will Munny is reborn, first as a purified sinner and then as a man of property (allegedly).

Finally, I have devoted a short chapter to the latest Eastwood film, *Hereafter*.

A word about Eastwood's film technique:

Beyond the gratifying visual consumption of an Eastwood feature, the various technical aspects of his films are to be "read" rather than watched. Eastwood always insists that he only wants to tell a good story. But what can we observe of his film technique, the ways he and his creative team tell those stories? Particular styles of lighting, framing, distance, and sound establish connections between his characters, the films' larger messages, and his audience. The opening and closing frames of *Unforgiven*, for instance, anticipate the film's multiple audiences, but they also create merciful distance from Eastwood's explosive inner tale to allow the spectator to meditate on the film's multiple meanings.

We connect with Scrap's soothing voice-over in *Million Dollar Baby* (2003), the thoroughly ordinary yet somehow reassuring babble of the son and daughter of Francesca (Meryl Streep) in *Bridges of Madison County* (1995), the sparring among Eastwood's and Laura Dern's characters and the mindless FBI agents in *A Perfect World* (1993), the droning voice-overs of *Flags of Our Fathers* (2006), and the archaeologists' discovery of buried letters in *Letters from Iwo Jima* (2006).

Kent Jones, in one of the best books on film criticism in years, locates the search team in *A Perfect World* and the clueless siblings in *Bridges* as "surrogates for the average viewer, a phantom creature asked to participate in polls, marketing surveys, focus groups, and test screenings for which the world is a perpetually happy, stable place."[7] In his iconic films, Eastwood does not play to this audience. The movies may contain buffering characters for calming or comic effect: the ridiculous sons in *Gran Torino* offer another such example of theatrical overkill, a *commedia dell'arte* holdover from the burlesque of the Spaghetti Westerns. Harsh lighting, mismatched planes, and shallow depth in a shot, as in the scene with the plastic birthday cake, disorient the viewer and emphasize the absurdity of the actions of the sons and daughters-in-law.

Despite the side characters' antics, Eastwood is going for the heart. Without the buffers, the spectator could not process the unruly passions and social dysfunction of a movie like *A Perfect World* or *Million Dollar Baby.* The buffer characters may be acting in an ordinary Hollywood movie, all smiles or sobs and no substance, but they free Eastwood to go as deeply as he wants in his "real" movie, an inner tale of human emotions set against the backdrop of eternity. The compelling meditative narrative poetry of *Unforgiven, Million Dollar Baby,* and *Letters from Iwo Jima* releases complex layerings of meaning within their "realistic" settings: the gift of voice-over and the protective buffer frame stories that bookend the films. By contrast, the hypnotic, addictive, and visually brilliant *High Plains Drifter* and *Mystic River* plunge the viewer into the fire without a narrative guide or protective cushions to ease the shock of too much truth.

---

7. Kent Jones, *Physical Evidence: Selected Film Criticism* (Middletown, CT: Wesleyan University Press, 2008), 185.

Eastwood Story Time

C lint Eastwood — actor, director, and cultural icon — is everywhere these days. The British Film Institute (BFI) in London hosted a retrospective of his movies in the summer of 2008; the Museum of Modern Art (MOMA) includes *The Gauntlet* (1977) in its April-September 2008 "Jazz Score" festival; Spain is celebrating the Spaghetti Western trilogy (*The Good, the Bad and the Ugly* and its predecessors), the movies that launched Eastwood's international career in 1964; MGM recently released restored versions of that trilogy; and *The Good, the Bad and the Ugly* played in Paris in June 2009, and again in 2011. Warner Brothers released a thirty-five-film boxed set in early 2010. Meanwhile, Eastwood had the foresight to cast Angelina Jolie as the star of one of his recent movies, *Changeling*, and that casting ensured its thorough (and constant) coverage, along with photos of Brangelina's blessed offspring. Before long, the ambitious director had filmed the magisterial *Invictus* (2009) and had undertaken to explore *Hereafter* (2010).

As two final sweet touches, the Summer 2008 issue of *The American Scholar*, dean of general/literary scholarly magazines, featured an article on the enduring significance of the American western, beginning with *3:10 to Yuma* (2007), and including *The Assassination of Jesse James by the Coward Robert Ford*, John Ford's *The Searchers*, the Spaghetti Westerns. It finished with Eastwood's *High Plains Drifter, Pale Rider,* and *Unforgiven.* In addition, David Denby claimed Eastwood for *The New Yorker* in a thoughtful piece in March 2010.[1]

---

1. David Denby, "Back Issues: Clint Eastwood," *The New Yorker*, March 1, 2010, posted

"Eastwood" is not simply Eastwood, of course. The man who escorted Angelina Jolie at the Cannes film festival in 2009 evokes a wide range of associations, some of them hard to shake, such as "Dirty Harry" Callahan with his .44 Magnum; the "Man With No Name" in the Spaghetti trilogy; and "the Stranger" in *High Plains Drifter*. A five-disk boxed set of the *Dirty Harry* movies was issued in 2008; and a thirty-five-disk set of Eastwood movies appeared in 2010. Furthermore, the seductive but misleading trailer for *Gran Torino* played heavily on the Harry Callahan persona.

Other attachments, however, seem to belong to a film director far removed from Hollywood's tidy plots and easy answers. Eastwood has directed small, idiosyncratic films such as *Honkytonk Man* and *Bronco Billy*, as well as unlikely romances such as *Blood Work* and *The Bridges of Madison County*. And there are more: the acute social and emotional analysis of *Bird*, *Unforgiven*, *Mystic River*, and *Million Dollar Baby*. And, of course, the westerns, including the superbly crafted *The Outlaw Josey Wales* (to be taken up shortly in this book), fit all three categories and "also display an unusually expressive feeling for landscape," as the British Film Institute (BFI) introduction to Eastwood's movies notes — the emotional landscape as well as the natural terrain.

To confound matters further, in 2006, Eastwood — long a master at capturing a sense of place, the look, sounds, and feel of American spaces — directed two politically charged movies that are not so much antiwar as deeply humanistic and compassionate testaments to the tragic waste of young lives in wartime. Could this be Clint Eastwood, mayor of Carmel, California, directing *Flags of Our Fathers*, an exposé of racism and government propaganda during World War II? Is this the hard-bitten patriot of *Heartbreak Ridge* directing *Letters from Iwo Jima*, a war movie in the Japanese language set on a Japanese island that portrays Japanese fighters sympathetically?

Indeed it is. For from the beginning of his career as a movie director, Eastwood has addressed fundamental questions such as these, placing his iconic identity of rugged American masculinity in tension with a broader vision of individual and social wholeness. How should we live together? How do we define the "good"? What is family? What does it mean to be human? And who belongs to "the human family"?

When Eastwood exerts full control over a film, he engages with justice,

by Jon Michaud at: http://www.newyorker.com/online/blogs/backissues/2010/03/back-issues-clint-eastwood.html.

violence, and war memory, as well as the vital dimensions of human experience that those questions raise. Through a disciplined use of genres such as the western and the war film, ritual structures such as call-and-response and antiphony in *The Gauntlet, Bird,* and the war diptych *Flags of Our Fathers* and *Letters from Iwo Jima,* and the innovative use of his own musical compositions in *Unforgiven, Mystic River,* and *Million Dollar Baby,* he displays emotional as well as artistic empathy with the people he portrays: outcasts and pariahs and all the marginalized men, women, and children who have been left outside the gates of the paradise they had so passionately longed to enter.

Eastwood unspools tales of endless journeys across America's magnificent landscape in the South and the Far West, journeys undertaken by pioneers and slaves (or their descendants) who pushed west or south after the Civil War, or by those who migrated to the cities in a quest for identity or peace. Movies like *The Outlaw Josey Wales, The Gauntlet, Pale Rider, Unforgiven, A Perfect World, The Bridges of Madison County,* and *Million Dollar Baby* present different but equally poignant tales of these forgotten men and women. In 2006 he brought that empathy for outsiders, unusual in a Hollywood director, to its logical extreme with *Letters from Iwo Jima.*

How are we to explain this radical disjunction? On the one hand, Eastwood the actor embodies, perhaps more than any other, the iconic force of the vengeful American killer, machismo at its most remorseless and violent. On the other hand, we have the focus of Eastwood's cinematic direction on forgotten lives, storytelling marked by eloquence and compassion. That split naturally invites the question of how he used his early experiences not only to populate his artistic worlds, as had novelists John Steinbeck in *Cannery Row* (1945)[2] or Harper Lee in *To Kill a Mockingbird* (1960), for instance, but also to shape works with a distinctly ethical — even theological — edge, which ultimately must be reckoned as those of a revolutionary thinker, though that is a role usually not assigned to him in the public imagination. What is his own story, and how has it influenced his remarkable artistic output?

Perhaps Eastwood built on his own memories of living on the edges of mainstream American society to construct these various communities and give their inhabitants distinctive personalities, quirks, and backstories. Richard Schickel's *Clint Eastwood: A Biography* and *Clint Eastwood Inter-*

---

2. Thanks to my colleague Steve Hill, Northwestern University Office of Fellowships, for the Steinbeck reference (2009).

views by Robert E. Kapsis and Kathie Coblentz describe how, during the grim years of the Depression, a young man and his wife, with a son and daughter tucked into the back seat of their Pontiac, roamed the Pacific coast searching for work to keep the family fed and moving. After Eastwood's father found a stationary job in 1940, the family settled in Piedmont, California, near Oakland, where over the next eight years the young boy began to develop as an athlete and a piano player at the Omar, a local jazz club.[3] Fleeing Piedmont High School for the more diverse economic and ethnic atmosphere of Oakland Technical High School, where he felt more at home, Eastwood lived off and on with his grandmother in the mountains, but he preferred to be on the move.[4] Young Clint survived on "a lot of instinct and a little luck."[5] The draft disrupted the musical career he had planned, and he came close to dying in a water accident during army training. After the army years, he held down odd jobs and, urged by his army buddy David Janssen,[6] rattled around Hollywood for years in any minor roles that were accessible to an actor who was too tall or too quiet, with teeth too jagged, to be a star.[7]

Christopher Frayling describes how Eastwood, cast as a second-string lead in the long-running television show *Rawhide* (1958-1965) as the lady-loving yet hotheaded cowboy Rowdy Yates, was spotted by Italian director Sergio Leone.[8] Leone, who would become one of Eastwood's mentors in

3. Robert E. Kapsis and Kathie Coblentz, eds., *Clint Eastwood Interviews* (Jackson: University Press of Mississippi, 1999); Richard Schickel, *Clint Eastwood: A Biography* (New York: Vintage Books, 1996), 29ff. Schickel, the director's close friend, was allowed generous access to interviews and materials. Reliable sources for biographical information, in addition to the above, are: Noël Simsolo, *Clint Eastwood: Un passeur à Hollywood* (Paris: Editions Cahiers du Cinéma, 2006); Michael Henry Wilson, *Clint Eastwood: Entretiens avec Michael Henry Wilson* (interviews with Eastwood) (Paris: Cahiers du Cinéma, 2007); and Christopher Frayling, *Spaghetti Westerns: Cowboys and Europeans from Karl May to Sergio Leone* (London: I. B. Tauris, rev. ed., 2006). Patrick McGilligan published a tell-all unauthorized biography, *Clint: The Life and Legend* (New York: St. Martin's, 1999); Eastwood sued him. For an excellent discussion of Eastwood's work up to 2003, see Deborah Allen, "Clint Eastwood," *sensesofcinema* online: http://archive.sensesofcinema.com/contents/directors/03/eastwood.html.

4. Schickel, *Clint Eastwood*, 27-28; Michael Henry Wilson, *Clint Eastwood*, 58.

5. Kapsis and Coblentz, *Clint Eastwood Interviews*, 4.

6. Janssen went on to star in the popular television series *The Fugitive*. The detail about odd jobs is from Kapsis and Coblentz, *Clint Eastwood Interviews*, 108-9, and Schickel, *Clint Eastwood*, 45-46.

7. Schickel, *Clint Eastwood*, 51-55; Kapsis and Coblentz, *Clint Eastwood Interviews*, 4.

8. Frayling, *Spaghetti Westerns*. The story is backed up by Schickel, *Clint Eastwood*, 102-15.

the craft of directing, cast him in the magnificently operatic *A Fistful of Dollars* (1964) and its even more baroque sequels, *For a Few Dollars More* (1965) and *The Good, the Bad and the Ugly* (1966). The Spaghetti Westerns turned the young actor into an international star. When Don Siegel's *Dirty Harry* appeared in 1971, Eastwood had become America's leading box-office draw.[9]

The Eastwood character of the Spaghettis exhibited the trademark poncho, the cheroot clinched in his teeth, the six-gun, and the unflappable cool. This foundational image fused in most moviegoers' minds with the considerably more tortured Dirty Harry, a detective at war with punks as well as his own police department, and it anticipated the "meaner than hell, cold-blooded damn killer" we find deconstructed at the end of *Unforgiven* (1992). Yet despite the popularity of films like *Rambo, The Terminator,* and *Superman,* it seems obvious that American men resemble the down-and-out dreamer Red Stovall in *Honkytonk Man* or the muddy pig-farmer side of Will Munny more than they do the cool, fast-drawing, invincible one in *The Good, the Bad and the Ugly.* They are more Llewelyn Moss than Anton Chigurh, the golem figure in *No Country for Old Men* (Coen brothers, 2007).[10] They are more likely to go on for hours about football scores over beer and sausage than walk coolly into the middle of the street with a big gun and a half-eaten hot dog to shoot bank robbers, as Dirty Harry does.

Eastwood the director, I contend, loves those tax collectors and prostitutes, those schmucks, more than he loves the clever men he portrays in the Spaghetti Westerns and the *Dirty Harry* series. A lesser man with the same magnificent gifts might have turned his wandering years into a hunger for power and an obsession with belonging, letting his fame, fortune, and cinematically enhanced invincibility infect his inner being. After all, many Hollywood stars have chosen that path. But Eastwood had a different idea. He decided instead to celebrate the journeys of the losers, the immigrants, outcasts, and vagrants who made the winding journeys, those whose poverty or race or country of origin increasingly has excluded them from a so-called successful American life.[11] These were the men and

---

9. Schickel, *Clint Eastwood,* 102-15.

10. In Jewish narrative, the golem is a creature fashioned by a rabbi to do the rabbi's bidding. Predictably, as in the story "The Monkey's Paw," the human desire to control nature goes terribly wrong. Chirgurh physically resembles the figure in the 1936 Julien Duvivier film *The Golem,* where the golem is represented by a lumbering, square-bodied creature.

11. See Wilson, *Clint Eastwood,* prologue: "With maturity, Eastwood enlarges his empa-

women among whom he lived and worked from childhood, which makes their later cinematic appearances more powerful and wrenching.

Furthermore, early on in his film career, Eastwood began to identify not simply with poor vagabonds and African-Americans, but also with Americans of Indian, Chinese, or Mexican heritage, women, persons with disabilities, prostitutes, children, people past their prime, and accused criminals. *Breezy's* hippie, *Bronco Billy's* vanload of misfits, *A Perfect World's* escaped convict and a little boy reared in a religiously restrictive household, a broken-down cop (played by Eastwood), and a nerdy female psychologist — all travel the same dusty road. Despite the almost continuous rumors that he had another Dirty Harry installment in the works, Eastwood starred in *Gran Torino* as a cynical Korean War veteran who becomes enmeshed with a family of Hmong immigrants — barely visible Americans ripe for corruption or for rescue and redemption. And *Invictus* moves its viewers to South Africa, once known as the skunk of the world for the government's racism and oppression.[12]

It will not be lost on seekers of spiritual wisdom that Eastwood's journey toward embracing empathy for outcasts and pariahs, the disposition to wrest power from the mighty and elevate the weak comes from the Bible: the Virgin Mary's *Magnificat*,[13] the Beatitudes, and the Gospel writer's references to the wisdom of folly (Luke 1:52-53): "He has put down the mighty from their thrones, and exalted those of low degree" (RSV). The apostle Paul exhorts the church at Corinth to remember that God in Jesus Christ has redefined the terms of this world: "Let no one deceive himself. If any one among you thinks that he is wise in this age, let him become a fool that he may become wise. For the wisdom of this world is folly with God" (1 Cor. 3:18-19, KJV).[14] In interviews with Michael Henry Wilson, East-

---

thy for outsiders to embrace all victims." See also, on 39, Wilson's exchange with Eastwood on *The Outlaw Josey Wales,* and n. 32: "Like the archangel (in *High Plains Drifter*), Josey sympathizes only with the marginalized" (my translation).

12. From Nelson Mandela's inaugural address: http://www.wsu.edu:8080/~wldciv/world_civ_reader/world_civ_reader_2/mandela.html.

13. A midrash on 2 Samuel, the *Magnificat* is a war text turned toward reversal of power that privileges the equality of all human beings regardless of social class or wealth. The *Magnificat* forms a link between war and peace.

14. The wisdom of folly and the folly of wisdom relates to Eastwood's empathy for social and political outsiders but also extends to his respect for people without guile. One of the sweetest sequences in all of his films occurs in *Bronco Billy,* when Billy (Eastwood) and his little traveling Wild West show ask his friends in an "insane asylum" to help make a new performance tent. Wondrously, the inmates design and sew up a massive tent made from

wood has commented on his fascination with "the biblical stories and their correspondence with the mythology of the Western."[15]

Yet, while critics talk about the "Christ figure" in George Stevens's 1953 western *Shane*, Eastwood never attempts to construct the hero as a savior. In fact, he distinctly challenges this time-honored — though now formulaic — cliché.[16] Rather, as he absorbs scriptural debates about community in Genesis 22, John 3:16, and John 17, he chooses instead to create the sights and sounds of men and women, huddled around a sputtering campfire, telling each other their dreams and nightmares, as in *Pale Rider, A Perfect World,* or *Unforgiven*. Or he has them dancing to tunes they remember from happier days, as we see in *Josey Wales* ("Rose of Alabamy") and *Bird* ("Moonlight Becomes You"). Notably, he crafts echoes or reflections of those scriptural debates, as in the Dardenne brothers' forgiveness drama, *The Son* (2002), or their meditation on Jeremiah 31, *The Promise* (1996), or on the holy Trinity in *The Child* (2005).

In *Million Dollar Baby,* Eastwood focuses an attentive eye on Maggie Fitzgerald (Hilary Swank), trailer trash turned boxer, and Frankie Dunn, a poetic Irishman down on his luck. He remembers Delilah, the innocent prostitute, and the simple Davey in *Unforgiven;* failed country singer Red Stovall in *Honkytonk Man;* the escaped convict Butch and his surrogate son in *A Perfect World;* and the powerless miners in *Pale Rider*. Yet, even as he has a soft spot for ordinary people, Eastwood is no sentimentalist. American aspirations for land, wealth, and recognition prove illusions that must be stripped away to make way for new life. Eastwood's vagabonds have been deceived by the "conquest of the west" mythology, which required ethnic cleansing; by the romantic aura that surrounded the Southern lost-cause stories, which masked the profound moral horror of slavery; and by the propaganda that extols victory at any price over the real-life cost of broken bodies in wartime.

In *Unforgiven,* Eastwood's images open our hearts to sorrow and hope, to a brilliant winter sky and hope for a new birth when Will Munny awakens from his death-stupor. Will's shocking relapse into the world of myth and murder is framed and shot like a horror film, and his sad ride through

castoff American flags! *Bird* and *Changeling* also refer to the misuse of an "asylum" to lock the politically inconvenient out of sight.

15. Wilson, *Clint Eastwood,* 58 (my translation).

16. Lloyd Baugh, *Imagining the Divine: Jesus and Christ Figures in Film* (Kansas City, MO: Sheed and Ward, 1997).

the darkness and rain at the movie's end reveals the aging man's profound sadness. In *Mystic River,* we grieve with Jimmy (Sean Penn) as he tries to break through the police line to see his daughter's broken body, a sacrificial circle mirrored visually later in the film as Jimmy and his gang surround their childhood friend Dave (Tim Robbins) in the darkness before they kill him. *Million Dollar Baby* gives us Maggie, the "girl" boxer, lovingly silhouetted against the grey-green walls of the Hit Pit gym or driving through the darkness with tough old Frankie (Eastwood), her trainer, their faces merely points of light.

We shudder in *Flags of Our Fathers* as Doc Bradley (Ryan Phillippe), one of the flag-raisers in the famous Iwo Jima photograph, is served an ice-cream sculpture sundae covered with strawberry syrup at a state dinner. He sees not a mound of confection but rather a hill covered with blood, rivers of blood spilled over the raging hot island, which for Japan symbolized its mystical essence as a nation, a people, and a divine power in the world. To the young Japanese boys trapped in the island's hewn thermal caves, or to the young American boys who rushed up those rocky beaches and cliffs, neither the divine sheen of Japan as an imperial idea nor the concept of a just war waged by a divinely blessed America saved their arms, eyes, or sanity.

The deeply humanistic and spiritually compelling themes of inclusion, repentance, and rebirth thread through all the scripts Eastwood has chosen to direct. This is startlingly so in *High Plains Drifter* (1973) and *The Outlaw Josey Wales* (1976). Indeed, these two films alone reveal far more about Eastwood's ethical and spiritual concerns than we ever would uncover by checking his church attendance or a marked catechism book. Neither movie glorifies violence, despite the catharsis of *Drifter*'s refining fire. Rather, both reflect on the fragility of the social order and the resilience of goodness despite the inherent violence of human existence. They anticipate Eastwood's continued dissection of nationalism, fratricide, and greed; the theme of equality against kingship; honor, not shame, for the poor. They honor generosity of heart, which prepares us for the rich reflections that flourish in *Unforgiven* and reach into his recent antiwar films, *Changeling, Gran Torino,* and *Invictus.* Both *Drifter* and *Josey Wales* begin with John Locke's *tabula rasa,* a clean slate and a pure heart, then offer their characters a chance to construct an ethical system from scratch.

Throughout his career, then, Clint Eastwood has continued to temper justice with mercy. In *Unforgiven,* building on the insights of *High Plains Drifter, Josey Wales,* and *Pale Rider,* he further reveals the profound sadness of a post–Civil War world in which the men and women he understands, values, and loves seek a new start but become trapped in an endless cycle of vengeance. By the time he directs *Million Dollar Baby, Flags of Our Fathers,* and *Letters from Iwo Jima,* Eastwood's leanings toward peace, reciprocity, and clear-eyed social analysis have become even more intense and his movies less commercial, a move that is unusual among American directors. Who else would underscore the dawning love of a washed-out alcoholic cop and a hard-nosed prostitute — the dregs of American society — with the gospel classic "Just a Closer Walk with Thee" and set this redemption tale against a barren concrete cityscape, as in *The Gauntlet*? Who else would dare to show competitive sports as licensed human sacrifice or show the ending of a cherished life as undertaken with anguish and unqualified love, as he does in *Million Dollar Baby*?

Who else has told the sorrowful stories of one immigrant neighborhood with such unvarnished clarity as Eastwood tells of the Boston Irish in *Mystic River*? (Perhaps Martin Scorsese's *Gangs of New York,* though *Goodfellas* might come closer to the sense of individuals trapped in an unforgiving past.) This dark movie is strangely devoid of the unconditional forgiveness Eastwood offers his characters in other films. Yet Jimmy, Sean, Dave, Celeste, and Annabeth, the characters in *Mystic River,* are the more dearly loved — and forgiven — despite their messy and tragic lives. And what other filmmaker would dare to enter the daily lives and sorrows of a historical "enemy" of America, as Eastwood did with the young Japanese soldiers in *Letters from Iwo Jima*? This is Eastwood the director, theologian, and ethicist — a "man on fire."

PART I

The Angel of Death
(The Avenging Angel)

The book of Revelation, that most cinematic of biblical texts, has furnished generations of filmmakers with imagery that reaches deep into ancient thought and literature: humans passionately wish for transcendent validation of their hopes, attention to their miseries, and righting of perceived personal and societal wrongs. At the end of history (or perhaps before that, through a human or divinely sent angel of death), "the crooked shall be made straight" (Luke 3:5).

"Angel of death" suggests an agent of apocalypse, more vengeance than reconciliation and rescue. Both dispositional poles are connected metaphorically with the "Son of (the) man" sayings that pepper Hebrew Scripture (Dan. 7:13) and the Christian Gospels (e.g., Matt. 16:27, 28; Luke; Mark 13 and Revelation). Earthly injustice (failure to love the neighbor) brings forth curse, flood, or end times. The Son of man comes as rescuer, but also as judge. Matthew turns Jesus' teachings (for instance, peace as the partner of justice) toward apocalypse and a theology of vengeance, even as he emphasizes the necessity of works of love for the marginalized.

Cinematically, the "angel of death" provides convenient shorthand for the historical church's preference of remorseless judgment to Jesus' compassionate forgiveness. It is a short hop from Dostoevsky's "Grand Inquisitor" *(The Brothers Karamazov)* to Carl-Theodore Dreyer's *Day of Wrath.* The Inquisitor angrily rebukes the Jesus who has come again, not in expected imperial glory but rather as he first appeared, humbly and without fanfare, healing the sick and raising the dead. Likewise, the Protestant leaders in Dreyer's tale of cruelty believe themselves angels of death who are divinely appointed to uncover the works of Satan: their religious uncertainties inflame their torture, as though they desired to wrest the secrets of the universe from torn flesh.

Luis Buñuel (*The Exterminating Angel*, 1962), Ingmar Bergman (*Seventh Seal*, 1957), Robert Bresson (*L'Argent*, 1983), and Andrei Tarkovsky (*Stalker*, 1979) created worlds where apocalypse (and thus the angel) enters human time. It was the time of a decadent Europe; the time of the Crusades and the Black Death; France in the grips of amoral capitalism; and a postindustrial wasteland of unspoken horrors and ever-present watchers. Bergman and Tarkovsky explicitly set their narratives in the fiery yet eternal moments when time ends, locating the ending squarely within humans' self-created disasters. More recently, the world of *Children of Men* (Alfonso Cuarón, 2006) pulses with apocalyptic dread, yearning for a savior but finding only the death angel.

The American western has offered an endless parade of angels of death, suspended between human and heavenly realms. Clint Eastwood's westerns confront the confused narrative identities of western gunslinger-saviors, capturing the Bible's interlaced divine judgment and compassion for forgotten peoples. *High Plains Drifter* (1973), *Pale Rider* (1985), and *The Outlaw Josey Wales* (1976) unabashedly harness the angel imagery even as they challenge the genre's pervasive nationalism. *Unforgiven* (1992) turns the mythic redeemer-gunslinger William Munny into a human whose (alleged) past murders torture his conscience. When Will emerges as a reborn angel of death, his actions must be read within the context of grief over the death of his beloved friend and the corruption of a "perfect world," a kingdom of heaven lived in contemporary time, envisioned in the Christian vision that his wife had taught him and that he longed for.

Mystic River (2003) revives the demonic force of the angel of death metaphor as the film moves relentlessly from wrong to wrong: Jimmy becomes the avenging angel, shedding blood for blood. Redemption is absent from the film, a testimony to the seriousness with which Eastwood regards the abrogation of justice by a vigilante. In *Million Dollar Baby* (2004), Frankie Dunn takes on the role of the angel of death, but in love and sorrow, not in vengeance. Eastwood's war films, *Flags of Our Fathers* and *Letters from Iwo Jima* (both 2006), ask whether any nation is ever justified in seizing the role of angel of death, for innocents on all sides will be destroyed.

Gran Torino (2008) and *Invictus* (2010) explicitly reject vengeance for peace and reconciliation. The director and his artistic team bypass the clear-cut Hollywood template of good (gunslinger) versus evil (stereotypical villain) for much more nuanced worlds in which evil has many faces and powers, but "good" (though sometimes faced with compromised choices, as with *Million Dollar Baby, A Perfect World,* and *Gran Torino*) firmly embraces relationships and communities of welcome and comfort.

High Plains Drifter

What would you do if you could start all over — escape your past, choose your friends, and select a spot of natural beauty to create a perfect world in which you would become happy and wealthy? The debate over "happiness" continues in our time: a recent conference in France, advised by Amartya Sen and Daniel Cohn-Benedict, deliberated about whether it is possible or desirable to devise social programs that maximize human flourishing. The debate has not died down despite the horrors of modernisms in the twentieth century — Nazi and Communist programs, for instance — or the failure of utopian communities through urban "renewal" schemes in nineteenth- and twentieth-century America.

The millions of people who poured out of Europe into the New World from the seventeenth through the nineteenth centuries literally banked on a vision of an actual physical paradise and a new life. The land companies sold to those who had money. Individuals with no money sold themselves or a child into servitude. Land grants, ironically made during the Revolutionary War, allowed communities to stake out territory where they could live together in harmony, free from war. The great uncharted West beckoned with its promise of wide-open lands. The United States government periodically opened up its purchases to summon restless and hopeful men and women to stake out their bit of paradise: a perfect — or at least a better — life than they had known back across the ocean.

Clint Eastwood's high plains drifter rides down from the mountaintops into such an oddly static town that has been freshly built alongside a vast body of water, all fluid motion set against the townspeople's icy stares.

14

Opening with a wide shot, the camera cuts across the horizon and exposes the eerie newness of a small settlement: Lago, an anagram for "goal" (but also the word for "lake" in both Spanish and Italian), is perched along the edge of a vast lake that is scooped out of the endless desert. The camera settles on the immobile face of the rider in a series of complex shots that involve the viewer in the unfolding action even though no shots include a frontal close-up to establish the lead character's point of view.[1]

The town's peculiar location and construction underscore its falsity, an allegorical theatrical set located on every level, between its false-paradise, magazine-perfect externals and its internal hell. By 1973, when *Drifter* was released, Eastwood was already an international star, *Dirty Harry* was in the air, and serial westerns such as *Gunsmoke* still played almost nonstop on television in reruns. The Paris Peace Accords had been signed. American troops were pulling out of Vietnam, and United States citizens could begin to fantasize once more about peace, equality, and justice.

High Plains Drifter, like its follow-up, *Pale Rider*, offers a reflection on justice that reimagines *Shane* and *High Noon*, "without the arty self-importance of those earlier films."[2] In Eastwood's version, the sheriff is dead; the deceased is resurrected and mad as hell; the prosperous new town is burned down; and redemption is scarcely whispered. In several interviews Eastwood has noted that this is a "what if" film: What might have happened if the Gary Cooper character in *High Noon*, who single-handedly stood up to his town's apathy, had been killed?[3] The high plains drifter rides into such a town, now plagued by evil and its own guilt.

"What-if" hardly conveys the horror of the film's two flashback sequences, in which we watch in a drawn-out close-up the excruciating pain of a young man being whipped to death. Make no mistake, the in-

1. Comment by filmmaker Alex Schwarm, in Northwestern University Eastwood class, Winter 2009. The film, written by Ernest Tidyman of *French Connection* fame, was shot at Mono Lake, California, in the Sierras, with some shots done in Inyo Forest, California. The town was built from scratch and burned for real. Note the shimmering image of the rider, as though he arose from the heat of hell. "The cinematographer creates the illusion of heat by holding a flame under the camera" (filmmaker Mike Smith in an email to author).

2. Richard Locke, "Grand Horse Opera," *The American Scholar* (Summer 2008): 134.

3. Eastwood offered the proposition in a number of interviews. One appears in Kapsis and Coblentz, eds., *Clint Eastwood Interviews* (Jackson: University Press of Mississippi, 1999), 99-100. See also "Old West and Reality: A Showdown," *The New York Times*, July 23, 1997, online: http://query.nytimes.com/gst/fullpage.html?res=9A07EFD8133BF930A15754 C0A961958260. Eastwood spoke about this with critic Caryn James and earlier with Michael Henry Wilson.

Legacy of the Civil War: Strangers are not welcome.

terpolated sections function the same way Raskolnikov's dream of the little nag functions in *Crime and Punishment:* as the torture death of an innocent, even to the whip lashes across the victim's eyes. As Dostoevsky describes Raskolnikov's dream, the animal serves as a displaced human sacrifice.

> He runs past the horse, runs ahead of her, sees how they are lashing her on the eyes, right on the eyes! He is crying. His heart is in his throat, the tears are flowing. One of the whips grazes his face, he does not feel it. . . . But the poor boy is beside himself. With a shout he tears through the crowd to the gray horse, throws his arms around her dead, bleeding muzzle, and kisses her eyes and mouth.[4]

The bystanders in Raskolnikov's dream — the few who shout that the murderer is "no Christian" — are replaced in *Drifter* by the innkeeper's wife, Sarah Belding (Verna Bloom), and Mordecai, the town dwarf (Billy Curtis). However, the young child who runs up to the nag to kiss her bleeding eyes and lips has no counterpart in the movie's flashback. In the film, the role of moral arbiter belongs to Eastwood himself and to a version of himself as symbol of protest, the Stranger. The viewer does not need the novel's commentary that the nag's owner (or the murderer of the young marshal) is "no Christian"; nor does the plot require the little

---

4. Fyodor Dostoevsky, *Crime and Punishment,* trans. Richard Pevear and Larissa Volokhonsky (New York: Vintage Classics, 1992), 57-58.

child's intervention. The camera tells all in the flashback. In the movie the Stranger (as a ghost of himself) avenges the death of the defenseless man.

With no establishing shot and no backstory to tell us otherwise, the first flashback belongs firmly to the memory bank of the Stranger, who, stretched out on his hotel room bed, has locked us in for the duration of his nightmare. He winces as the dream sequence unfolds: the shots of a brutal whipping are juxtaposed against his sleeping face, his jerks visually echoing his sharp reaction to the sound of a whip in the movie's second sequence. When he awakens, the Stranger checks his own face in the mirror as if to look for scars. He is surprised to see none; we are surprised to see any reflection at all, because, even as early as this sequence, he reeks of the netherworld, though the tight shots and brutality of the flashback murder encourage us to identify with his physical, human suffering.

The movie's allegory packs a distinctively theological punch, as we might guess from its allusions to Dostoevsky. Mordecai, an abused holy fool who is crowned king (sheriff) when the Stranger is appointed town rescuer, serves a god, as his name implies. The Stranger operates in a distinctly apocalyptic zone, where he wields supernatural powers. The whore's gunshots don't wound him; he appears and disappears at will; yet he satisfies his human appetites for sex, food, fine wine, and pretty boots with a Mephistophelian flourish.

The Stranger's pursuit exceeds the elimination of the men who murdered him or the humiliation of the bystanders who passively observed the drawn-out death shown in the movie's flashbacks. He is no savior of embattled townsfolk. Rather, he is the avenging angel whose words of judgment recall those of Jesus, who overturned the money-changers' tables in the Temple and seared the consciences of the men who stoned the woman for adultery despite their own sexual sins (John 2 and 8).[5] He claims the right of reversals: he literally elevates the despised Mordecai and distributes riches to the dispossessed, the Native Americans who mysteriously appear in this white town of the invisible poor. The angel asserts equitable distribution of goods, regard for the weak, hospitality for the homeless, and freedom from fear (some of the early episodes of *Rawhide* highlighted these virtues). Eastwood's strange angel destroys this town that has been

5. As an additional gloss on the purifying actions of the Stranger, Robert Jewett notes that the money-changers' sin lay in appropriating the court of the Gentiles, not in selling ritual items. The word of the Lord was meant to be open to "all nations," not simply to the Jews (Jewett, channeling Joachim Jeremias). Conversation with Robert Jewett, October 2010.

built on fraud and fueled by murder. As the town of Hell, formerly Lago, burns to the ground, the harsh overhead lighting makes the buildings look like they are dripping with blood.[6]

The Stranger in *High Plains Drifter* attacks an even larger target: the lynching of so-called rustlers. *The Virginian's* frontier justice earned critique as a desecration of the rule of law and human decency. Both the 1902 novel and its 1929 film adaptation (with a young Gary Cooper) glamorized lynching: until the rule of law arrives in this godforsaken territory, just string 'em up, guilty or not.[7] (This idea would reappear in Ted Post's *Hang 'Em High* [1968], the first production Eastwood chose for Malpaso Studios and a star vehicle for him following the Spaghetti Westerns.)

Martha Nussbaum offers a context for this tale of a new settlement gone bad. Writing on the necessity of justice in social order, she says that "people need norms to guide them, in both personal and political life. And it seems reasonable to suggest . . . that we ought to deliberate together about the principles that guide us. Philosophers have traditionally played a part in that public deliberation. Kant, for example, saw philosophers as important agents in reducing herd-like public behavior and promoting deliberation."[8] As a director, Eastwood suggests that such herd-like public behavior dominates political discourse, because the desire for wealth and power shapes the enactment of the law, as well as what its sterile words become when people are free to design their own rules from scratch and practice physical cruelty in the name of theoretical justice.

Eastwood thus addresses not only an American and biblical past but also his America in the mid-twentieth century. The relevance not only for last century but also for our time is hard to ignore. "Help me," which we see and hear the victim utter in the second flashback, recalls the highly publicized death of Kitty Genovese outside her Queens, New York, apartment in 1964. As many as thirty-eight people may have heard that attack, which took place over a thirty-minute period, but no one intervened. The flashback also recalls Shirley Jackson's notorious 1948 short story "The Lottery," which recounts an ancient annual rite of hu-

6. Comment by Adam Dorsky, Northwestern University Eastwood class, Winter 2008.

7. Owen Wister, *The Virginian: A Horseman of the Plains* (New York: Macmillan, 1934), 436-39. Robert Jewett has observed that *The Virginian* was required reading in English classes all over America during the 1930s.

8. Nussbaum is commenting on the work of philosopher John Rawls. Martha Nussbaum, "The Enduring Significance of John Rawls," *The Chronicle of Higher Education*, July 20, 2001, p. 1 of online posting: http://chronicle.com/free/v47/i45/45b00701.htm.

The town of Lago ("Goal") has been painted Hell-red.

man sacrifice in a small New England village, again punctuated by the bystander effect.[9]

In *High Plains Drifter,* there is never a doubt how appeals to humanity to do the right thing will stand up in the face of money's corrosive influence. The normal response in the face of someone else's disaster is to do nothing. The balance of power is stacked from the outset against Rawls's "purity of heart" — and in favor of the power structure. Rawls's full sentence is: "Purity of heart, if one could attain it, would be to see clearly and to act with grace and self-command from this point of view." Eastwood holds a darker position: in this new town everyone defers to those who wield power. His lighting and camera positions in each flashback suggest that a deeper flaw — love of the spectacle of public bloodletting — afflicts each person, except for Mordecai and Sarah Belding, who emerge from the film unscathed and self-aware.

The wealth that generates the mine owners' power comes from a morally reprehensible violation: they have stolen the land from its original inhabitants, the native Americans, and that robbery has been justified by Manifest Destiny.[10] Businessmen have gained control of federal lands. The

9. The story was printed in the June 26, 1948, issue of *The New Yorker* magazine. Nicholas D. Kristof has written about the bystander effect — the willingness to save one drowning child and unwillingness to reach out a hand to aid groups that attempt to save many children (*The New York Times,* July 9, 2009, A25). A counterargument was made by Feinberg School of Medicine student Prajwal Ciryam that same day in a program about the expanding eye clinics now flourishing in parts of India and East Africa.

10. The term "Manifest Destiny" was coined in 1845 by journalist John Louis O'Sullivan

wealth generated from government mines that might benefit all the citizens of the republic — the federal land's owners — in the form of railways, postal and telegraph service, and roadways funnels instead directly into the pockets of a few moguls. It is a subtle but perceptive touch that neither railways nor telegraph wires appear in any shot of this town.

High Plains Drifter also confronts the lynching of blacks across the South. Eastwood would have remembered the savage murders in June 1964 of three Mississippi civil-rights workers who had been registering blacks to vote, the "crime" for which the three young men were accused, tortured, and executed. Beatings, torture, and murders of blacks by whites were common in the 1960s, a hundred years after the end of the Civil War. The white preachers and other citizens who flocked to the South in solidarity with the blacks who wanted to vote were treated as "foreigners" and "outside agitators." As Martin Luther King, Jr., wrote in *Letter from Birmingham Jail,* How can you be an outsider in your own country? What affects one affects all.

Kenneth Vaux, my husband, one of those idealistic and patriotic young preachers, was arrested in April 1964 in Hattiesburg, Mississippi, and thrown into jail for registering black citizens to vote. He lost twenty pounds before his wife was able to raise bail, and he, like many other white preachers who protested injustice, lost the church he was serving when he returned home. The blacks who remained behind could not escape; some of them lost their lives. As one black Hattiesburg resident told Rev. Vaux when they passed a local lake, "That's where the bodies are." Vernon Dahmer, one of the persons arrested with Vaux, and the president of the Hattiesburg NAACP, was murdered eighteen months later when white men from Hattiesburg firebombed the family's home. It was not until 1998 that Sam Bowers, formerly the Ku Klux Klan's imperial wizard, was convicted and imprisoned for Dahmer's murder.

Twenty-two years after he made *High Plains Drifter,* Clint Eastwood connected whipping with race hatred in *Unforgiven:* the murder of Ned (Morgan Freeman) at the hands of Sheriff Little Bill Daggett (Gene Hack-

---

to encapsulate the view of "America's providential calling and mission," which suffused the sermons and writings of the earliest colonizers, the land companies, and many of the Founding Fathers. As Rosemary Ruether points out, "O'Sullivan coined the phrase first to justify the annexation of Texas as a state of the union." He wrote then and later that American had the right to expand "by the right of our manifest destiny to overspread and to possess the land." Ruether, *America, Amerikkka: Elect Nation and Imperial Violence* (London: Equinox, 2007), 72.

man), a man determined to bring his version of justice to Big Whiskey, Wyoming. Ned's death visually resembles the whipping death of Marshal Duncan in *High Plains Drifter*. In both movies the camera alternates between close-ups of the sufferer's face and the torturers' distorted faces. Although *Unforgiven* never mentions Ned's race during the course of the movie (though he is played by a black man), the allusion to the lynching deaths of blacks after the Civil War could not be clearer.

Will the survivors of the Stranger's refining fire in *High Plains Drifter* now live blamelessly by the side of their lake, their sins washed clean? Will the Union heal its wounds and shape its rule of law according to the architecture of the Founding Fathers? Or will the shadow narrative of the American experience, the conquest of the West, assert its glorification of power? How can the divided peoples of our land live together in peace? Eastwood reflects on those questions from new angles in the next western he directed, *The Outlaw Josey Wales*.

The Outlaw Josey Wales

B lood-bound, brother-bound, and boundary-shattering, *The Outlaw Josey Wales* offers a first-class tale of precious bloodshed on the lush green grass and rich soil of Union and Confederate territories: largely Missouri and Kansas in this movie, but by metaphorical extension all the territory that led from "bleeding Kansas" through the Indian nations, down deep into Texas and back again. Eastwood would explore this terrain further in *Unforgiven* (William Munny, out o' Missouri, who tries to become a Kansas farmer) and *Million Dollar Baby* (Maggy, trailer trash out o' Missouri, who succeeds in becoming a boxing champ). Made in a year of national bicentennial celebration, 1976, *Josey Wales* exposed the fault lines opened up during the Civil War that reappeared with the long war in Vietnam and have never quite healed.

The Outlaw Josey Wales, which on its surface (and on its DVD cover) appears to be nothing more than a genre film, actually engages transformation on a social as well as an individual plane. It breaks most rules for classic westerns, making its frequent labeling as a revisionist western almost euphemistic. Eastwood, unlike most of the directors of American westerns from 1903 on, refuses to glorify the Civil War or its aftermath, or to submerge the race and class conflicts of those years (almost always ignored in the sanitized accounts of that conflict), or to forget the acres of rotting corpses and the postwar resurgence of racial hatred that engulfed the country. Like its predecessor, *High Plains Drifter,* and its heir, *Unforgiven,* the movie explicitly reveals the price of any civil conflict: premature and lingering death (Jamie); amputated limbs (the postwar Texas border town); displaced persons (Lone Waitie, Little Moonlight, and the Comanche); and killers on the loose (the series of bounty hunters who pursue Josey). As David W. Blight puts it in *Race and Reunion: The Civil War in American Memory,* the Civil War was reconfigured in narrative and memory to erase its foundational origins (slavery) and to eliminate black soldiers from the noisily prominent "reunions" of soldiers after the war.[1] The South cast itself as the "Lost Cause," which was endlessly romanticized in books and later movies, a mythology perpetuated today via symbols such as the Confederate flag. Frank Rich (following Blight) talks about the "long trajectory of the insidious campaign to erase slavery from the war's history and reconfigure the lost Southern cause as a noble battle for states' rights against an oppressive federal government."[2]

Eastwood's apprenticeship under Sergio Leone in the "Dollars" trilogy served him well. Although, like Leone, he had absorbed the elements of the western genre (the lone man with a gun, wide-open spaces, the embattled town), Leone's irreverent treatment of the American western's conventions allowed Eastwood to take artistic and thematic risks with *High Plains Drifter,* as I have described in the previous chapter. That is, the characters Eastwood the actor plays carry around but reverse the "codes" of the Man With No Name. The Stranger in *Drifter* takes over the explicitly biblical assignments of the angel of death (the purifier) and comforter (help for the marginalized) that the town's corrupt preacher has abandoned. As for Josey Wales, a man with a name and a tragic history, the hero veers between isolation and community — "Lone Man versus Family Man," as my students like to say.

The Outlaw Josey Wales provides a powerful example of Eastwood's willingness not only to tamper with the formulas of the western, subverting them outright (reworking showdown scenes, celibacy, racism, sexism,

---

1. David W. Blight, *Race and Reunion: The Civil War in American Memory* (Cambridge, MA: Belknap Press of Harvard University Press, 2001), passim. Blight digs under the mythologizing of "reunion" that sought to mute the bitter divisions between North and South. He discovers not only that the "lost cause" was a carefully orchestrated campaign, but also that blacks lost almost everything they had gained. Black soldiers were excluded from the garish reunions held on ceremonious occasions, and few on either side — North or South — were prepared to acknowledge the unspeakable horrors of the slaughter. Narratives of war from the Confederacy side expunged all mention of slavery as the major cause of the war.

2. Frank Rich, "Welcome to Confederate History Month," *The New York Times,* April 18, 2010: http://www.nytimes.com/2010/04/18/opinion/18rich.html.

and the myths of the celebrity of the hero), but also to offer correctives to his Hollywood macho killer image. As the British Film Institute Retrospective of 2007 comments, he is willing to "undercut and play with his heroic screen persona."[3] However, "playful" correctives certainly apply to *The Gauntlet* in the following year (1977), where the cool Man With No Name and handsome if unhappy Dirty Harry are replaced by the failed alcoholic cop Ben Shockley.

Or perhaps less playful is the detective in *Tightrope* (1984), Wes Block (played by Eastwood), who is both a loving father and possibly also a psychopathic killer. The "heroic" personality inhabited by Eastwood in *Josey Wales* is also precariously split between two story selves: the man dehumanized by loss and constantly haunted by flashbacks from the original trauma, seen to be a killer, and the suffering man who barely holds onto life and gradually reclaims his humanity through compassion for others. As Karli Lukas argues in "On Hell's Heroes Coming to Breakfast," Josey carefully lives within this dichotomy, the instability of his identities alternately signaled in the film by changes in lighting, sound, and camera work.[4]

Lukas sees the changes in personality as commercially motivated, from the "good" (read "weak") Josey to the Eastwood-as-star Josey, the violent one viewers have come to love. But a close look at any of the flashbacks reveals the icy grip of the Civil War's posttraumatic stress disorder and asks what it might take to overcome the past. That is, the film, in all its palpable beauty, sets up an immediate tension between violence and vengeance, and forgiveness and reconciliation, a tension that exists between the surface of each of its narrative movements, even as it initially seems to fit squarely into the wronged man formula that fuels an alarming amount of gratuitous slaughter in American movies.

How does *The Outlaw Josey Wales*, with its rootin'-tootin' gun-totin' DVD cover (a film endorsed recently by a prominent social critic as a top "vengeance" movie), become Eastwood's "first true anti-war movie," as writer Drucilla Cornell has argued?[5] The short answer engages the stub-

3. British Film Institute program notes, London, 2007.

4. Karli Lukas, "On Hell's Heroes Coming to Breakfast," sensesofcinema (February 2004): http://archive.sensesofcinema.com/contents/cteq/04/outlaw_josey_wales.html.

5. Stanley Fish, "Vengeance Is Mine," online with *The New York Times*, December 28, 2009. Fish completely misreads both *Gran Torino* and *The Outlaw Josey Wales*. See also Drucilla Cornell, *Clint Eastwood and Issues of American Masculinity* (New York: Fordham University Press, 2009), 139.

born nature of mythic stereotypes, which underlies an equally compelling "realistic" look. Then again, perhaps there is no short answer, since both myth and realism in this movie depend heavily on cinematography (particularly lighting) and Jerry Fielding's magical soundtrack (fife and drums; jazz; scant orchestration) to convey deeply human experiences under the shadow of eternity. But first, let's take a look at the myths.

As a companion piece to *High Plains Drifter, The Outlaw Josey Wales* alludes to the love affair between an audience and its christened heroes. For international viewers, the tall, athletic Eastwood of the Spaghetti Westerns incarnated the ultimate warrior: the knight who could leap on his steed with a flourish and brandish a battleaxe like Beowulf, a lance like Lancelot, or a six-gun like W. S. Hart. While that warrior does reappear in *Josey Wales,* Eastwood steadily dissects the myths that perpetuate egoism and greed. To replace national protectionism, racism, and class hierarchy, he models generous, tolerant, border-free communities where all can live in peace. He creates such a human family in *Josey Wales,* but not without addressing the deadly heritage of revenge.[6]

What can such a "model" do to change our social order? Not much, to judge from the continued conflicts in 2010 that disrupt national unity: the perpetuation of insidious racism and anti-immigrant sentiment; the continued marginalization of the American Indian (whom Eastwood champions in *Josey Wales*); and the domestic and international resistance of vengeance to the spirit of reconciliation. Although *Josey Wales* was produced about thirty-five years ago, Eastwood has been countering the vengeance script since that time with movies like *Gran Torino* and *Invictus.* Yet not much seems to have changed in domestic or international politics.

Indeed, Eastwood once commented: "No film is able to change the world, or make it more just" (MHW, 47). He also has said that he does not make movies as social analysis (MHW, 52). Nonetheless, we should believe what he shows us, not what he tells us, and in *The Outlaw Josey Wales* he shows us both cosmic injustice — the deadly slaughter of brother by brother, with the cause of the original hatred (slavery) — rejected and eventually erased, and *ways to live and love differently.* The tension between

6. Eastwood took over as director from Philip Kaufman, whose directing style seems to have irritated the efficiency-conscious actor, according to biographer Richard Schickel in *Clint Eastwood: A Biography* (New York: Vintage Books, 1996), 326-27. Eastwood told Michael Henry Wilson that, though he himself had hired Kaufman, the latter had a different plan for the movie than did Eastwood, who wanted to tell the story he envisioned (quoted in Wilson, *Entretiens avec Michael Henry Wilson* [Paris: Cahiers du Cinéma, 2007], 39).

revenge and reconciliation makes *Josey Wales* a timely and urgent movie for today.

As for the connections between *Josey Wales* and Vietnam, Eastwood commented: "In the case of the War of Secession, there was something particularly traumatizing: Americans combating other Americans. The same people tearing each other to pieces. And according to the state or county where you found yourself living, you were put into one camp or the other. It's the same absurdity today in Northern Ireland, where the same community kills its own members in the name of God and religion" (MHW, 35). The debate between Martin Buber's "I" and "thou," hatred and love, continues in every frame of this spiritually rich and provocative movie.

After moving through the mythic elements of the film, we now move toward *Josey Wales's* "realism," infused with spiritual resonance by way of its lighting and soundtrack and its steady antiphonal alterations of call and response.

Josey, a young Missouri farmer who is content with himself, his family, and his land, turns over the sod on a late spring afternoon in the early 1860s, his smiling face turned toward his little son. The setting sun filters through the trees and over the stream, a scene laid out in hues of soft brown. After the scorching inferno of *High Plains Drifter,* we are soothed by the stream's soft ripple; the image of mother, father, and child; and Fielding's music on the soundtrack. The father wears a hat of soft brown felt — the gear of a farmer, not a warrior. This is the paradise any young family might have hoped for at the beginning of that terrible decade: a place of lush fertility and spiritual tranquility far from the crowded Eastern cities or the foul mines of Wales.[7]

The astute viewer of westerns expects change — the sound of hoofbeats, an arrow in the shoulder, the high-pitched whoops of an invading force. However, even seasoned viewers could not have predicted the cinematic cataclysm about to engulf the young Wales family. Color and sound suddenly shift, as mother, child, and homestead are ravaged in economical strokes: a wisp of smoke, the flash of horse hooves glimpsed through the brush, blonde hair streaming over a woman's partially

---

7. Battles raged along the Kansas-Missouri border well before this, at least back to 1854. Some feel that the Civil War originated with the Missouri Wars over slavery and land. For the moment, Josey seems safe from the bloody conflicts. See Drew Gilpin Faust, *The Republic of Suffering: Death and the American Civil War* (New York: Knopf, 2008).

Josey (Eastwood) and Ten Bears (Will Sampson) choose life.

stripped body, bright flames devouring a sturdy farmhouse. In a series of shots reminiscent of the warriors' rush into action in Akira Kurosawa's *The Seven Samurai* (1954), we follow the young man's panicked dash as he cuts through the saplings toward his home. The camera immediately plunges the spectator into the unfolding death scene, as we experience the horror through Josey's eyes.

The cartoonlike torching of the corrupt town in *High Plains Drifter* takes on hellish urgency here, for *Josey Wales* is anchored in the earthy substance of real lives, not in archetype, parable, or myth. The homage to Kurosawa's masterpiece signals that Eastwood plans to depart from the terrain of the B-western to capture the desperation and beauty of the ordinary — not mythically or heroically glamorous — lives. In the film's second sequence, the camera hovers near a mounting pile of earth in a ghastly replay of the earlier pastoral shots. As Josey drags a body bag toward the fresh grave, a little hand pops out of the seam and the father tenderly puts it back inside its burlap winding sheet.[8]

In *High Plains Drifter,* Eastwood's scriptural knowledge, theological wisdom, and ethical mandate sizzle with apocalyptic fury. But *Josey Wales* begins at the point of grief and sorrow, where the young father marks the grave of his wife and child with a cross and a fir tree. He ends his graveside blessing with "Ashes to ashes, dust to dust," not with "Blessed be the name of the Lord," and with his own long, anguished sobs. The camera shows his farmer's hands digging a gun and holster out of the rubble.

8. Elizabeth Lewis Pardoe, historian of colonial America, offered this telling detail.

The subsequent shots intercut between target practice and a series of warmly lit single shots of what the young man must now leave. The gun and the clean hits are sharply in focus, but Josey's face and body are obscured. (A similar sequence appears in *Unforgiven*, when Will Munny prepares to go on a bounty hunt: the latter film is saturated with references to the actual physical act of killing. Will's face and body, clearly visualized as inseparable from his deadly actions, are witnessed by his incredulous and judging children.)

We see the ruins of Josey's homestead, the grave, a small fir tree, his donkey, and the rich brown soil he so recently has coaxed into fertility. Anchored firmly to the earth and to Josey's life story, these images will float timelessly in the memory of a man with no past except suffering, no name except legend, and no future except wandering. Eastwood ends the interlaced shots and cements the reference to Job's despair with multiple views of Josey sitting on the freshly turned earth with his hat pulled down, bathed in the dying light, his back to the camera. Whatever happens next in the movie's plot will resonate with the human desire to rage at heaven for allowing the unthinkable: the murder of innocents.

When the Missouri bushwackers, sympathetic to the Confederacy, appear over the horizon, they offer Josey a tempting appeal. Revenge on the Union slayers, they seem to urge, is the only answer, and it's time to inflict a Kansas bloodbath. As viewers we ask, will Josey become another figure not simply of legend (e.g., Jesse James, Billy the Kid, Will Munny) but also of American literature — the American soul that D. H. Lawrence defined as "hard, isolate, stoic and a killer"?[9] Well, to paraphrase Dirty Harry, will he?

Now that Josey's backstory has been laid out and he has signed on for vengeance, credits begin to roll over images of thousands of corpses. Lest the fetching fife and drum music that runs under the shots seduce the viewer, the images are shot in muted and distancing blue tones like the early glass photographs of the period, with burnings, hangings, and beheadings obscured by the fog of war. Two years before *Josey Wales*, the celebrated French director Robert Bresson opened his movie *Lancelot du Lac* (1974) with a similar montage: knights riding in quest of the Holy Grail who burn, torch, lynch, and behead, whose lances sweep across holy altars in desecration of the spiritual symbols the men seek to validate. The

---

9. Ezra Greenspan, Lindeth Vasey, and John Worthen, eds., *Studies in Classic American Literature*, Cambridge Edition of the Works of D. H. Lawrence (Cambridge: Cambridge University Press, 2003), 65.

killers in both movies are shot from a distance and appear nearly faceless: the Knights of the Round Table shrouded in armor, the guerrillas nearly invisible behind the legs of hanging bodies or the smoke of burning barns.

Eastwood need not have known that movie to portray the supposedly purifying quest of the bushwackers as a descent into hell. Fletcher, who leads the band and lures Josey to join, speaks in scriptural language: "Let's set things aright," a reference to "make straight the highway of our Lord" from Isaiah. As this scene plays out, we realize that *The Outlaw Josey Wales* became a theological meditation on justice and revenge the moment Josey's wife and little boy died.

Whether or not Eastwood intended to give homage to Bresson, both *Lancelot* and *Josey Wales* deal with the quest for revenge increasingly cut off from an original fault. The bushwackers, exhausted at war's end and willing to surrender, are betrayed, the oldest of human vices, according to Eastwood in a 1984 interview with Michael Henry Wilson.[10] Josey, a lone holdout from postwar "amnesty," sees their slaughter from afar and rides in to avenge his friends' deaths in an immediate and horrific burst of matching Gatling-gun fusilade that should satisfy the fans of superhero comic fare everywhere. Not surprisingly, Josey finds himself pursued by Union law enforcement (or rather by the renegade Red Legs, who, at the end of the Civil War, had insinuated themselves into the Union Army like Blackwater contractors in Iraq). Josey turns his now legendary killing skills toward survival.

But this is survival of a different kind from the average story line of *The Fugitive,* the television show (1963-1967) starring Eastwood's friend David Janssen, the Harrison Ford movie of the same name, or any prison-break movie. It is more like Eastwood's own prison-break movie, *A Perfect World* (1993), where the hero is on the run, but danger and escape make up only a small part of what unfolds during the film.

Josey Wales is a far richer film thematically and visually than a plot summary indicates. Eastwood himself said in an interview that, given different circumstances, the movie could have been as successful — commercially and critically — as *Unforgiven* was. He considered it an equally revolutionary take on American history and his own persona crafted from the Spaghetti Westerns and *Dirty Harry.* The transfer of violence from the Civil War and solitary revenge to commerce occurs in *Unforgiven,* but only at the end, as the narrative frame helpfully leaps from the point of view

10. Wilson, *Clint Eastwood,* 39.

and judgment of the heroine's mother to that of the cool, detached, impersonal, and thoroughly unreliable narrator. In the scrolled material in the closing frame, we read: "It is said that Will Munny moved to California and succeeded in dry goods." Commerce threads through the movie and leads us to this moment: the main characters' names all refer in some way to currency, as Patrick McGee helpfully observes.[11]

The dark monetary undercurrents in *Unforgiven* had their precursors in *Josey Wales*. As Josey flees farther and farther south, and as the episodes with assorted fools become stranger and stranger, the movie increasingly diverges along two distinct narrative paths: the pursuit of money (which subsumes even the desire for vengeance), and the haphazard and completely free acquisition of "worthless" castoffs from the great American Dream. If a human being is only "worth" what he or she can bring in cash or horses, what do we make of the costuming of Lone Watie (Chief Dan George) once he burns his black-tie getup and top hat; or Grandma Sarah and Laura Lee wearing tattered remnants of their elegant dresses; or the patchwork duds of the rest of the gang Josey picks up once he gets to Texas? They defy stereotypes with their mobile faces, growing affection for each other, and disregard for social boundaries.

The buyers and sellers of human flesh are sharply drawn: they are figures of dark comedy closely allied with the mercenaries who pursue Josey. The antiphonal structure of the movie is carefully constructed: the two-faced boatman paired with the charitable old woman on the one shore, and his metaphorical mate, the white-suited carpetbagger peddling false goods, whom he ferries to the other shore. The initial betrayal of Fletcher, who sold his own friends for a bag of gold, becomes a chorus of nascent capitalists: the backwoodsmen who crow "I got me the Josey Wales," to the two "pilgrims" and Zukie in the trading post, who wheedle, "I saw him first," to the carpetbagger and the dry-goods salesman who would be "glad to share in any reward." The two bounty hunters recall Blondie's and Tuco's scams in *The Good, the Bad and the Ugly,* just as they anticipate *Unforgiven's* Will Munny and Ned: "A man's gotta do somethin' to make a living" — especially when the war is over and the pig farm fails.

It would be easy to dismiss the episodes — "interpolated tales," as literary critics call them — as comic relief along the desperate vengeance trail followed by the picaresque fugitive Wales. The Missouri boat ride in-

---

11. Patrick McGee, *From Shane to Kill Bill: Rethinking the Western* (Oxford: Blackwell Publishing, 2007), 195. McGee refers to Peter Krapp, 595.

cident, after all, introduces all kinds of charlatans and fools who seem just a bit over the top for a well-dressed middle-class audience. Instead of escaping on his swift steed, Josey drags along a mortally wounded child soldier, Jamie. To get to the Indian nations and safety, the fugitives must cross the river (the Missouri or the Mississippi, whichever lies between them and the South), watched over by the aforementioned two-faced ferryman, who is reminiscent of Charon and the river Styx, a character more like the slippery trickster Tuco in *The Good, the Bad and the Ugly* than a savior.

They depend on the charity of Granny Hawkins, an old crone who watches over supplies. Framed by low-hanging vegetation at the river's edge, she takes pity on the wounded boy and his protector and gives them food and bandages for free. The white-suited carpetbagger's sleazy and florid speech as he grubs for profit will be mirrored in the figure of the television announcer in *Invictus*. Always shot in harsh white light, the squat little man's false face oozes evil, like Herman Melville's confidence man, the opposite of Granny Hawkins's plain speech and penetrating assessment of Josey's character. (Granny's truth-telling will reappear in the characters of Sue and the Hmong shaman in *Gran Torino*.)

Expectations of regular viewers of westerns rise again as the ferryman, his harshly lit features distorted by a raffish grin, abandons the fugitives and hastens to deliver the pursuers to Josey's side. The camera pulls away as Josey refuses to slaughter the approaching soldiers, spotting his victims through the branches of his sheltering tree and shooting out the ferry rope instead (yet another reference to *The Good, the Bad and the Ugly*). In Leone's great antiwar masterpiece, Blondie ("the Good," played by Eastwood) remains aloof, disdainful, and generally unaffected by what he sees around him. The disparity between his low affect and the chaotic bloodletting around him underscores his comment about war's enormous waste of human lives.

Not so with *The Outlaw Josey Wales*. Josey may seem detached, almost paralyzed by "what he has seen, what he has done," a phrase that is to be echoed by the war-damaged men in *Flags of Our Fathers* and *Gran Torino*. But the movie is anything but detached. It presents one furious critique of war and greed after another. The double-dealing ferry boatman may be a figure of comedy, but like the white-suited charlatan, his duplicitous nature bottom-feeds off the Civil War's bloodshed and the dregs of postwar violence. The entire movie takes place during the years when millions of citizens, North and South, were teetering on the edge of extinction. This added to the deliberate destruction of the country's Indian tribes and the

Josey (Eastwood) and Laura Lee (Sondra Locke) dance with their new family.

return to virtual slavery of its newly "freed" black citizens. Even though (following the source novel) the movie appears to demonize the North and praise the South, Eastwood the director spreads the judgment. Loss was not the property of the "victimized" South: every family in the vast expanse of the country had been ravaged by the loss of a husband, father, or other breadwinner.

To paraphrase the original question in this chapter: How does a movie that supposedly celebrates vengeance become a movie about peace and reconciliation? When you have been grievously wronged — when you have lost all that you cherish, as Josey Wales has — in what ways should you respond? How do you learn to lay hold of the past's corrosive memories and move into the future? Here is where the angel of death trajectory established in the early sequences of the film yields to the powerful narrative pull of the angel of mercy.

The regenerative path of this film is already well under way when Josey rescues Jamie, his war companion (Sam Bottoms). It continues appropriately enough with a sewing story. Josey has carefully shepherded the wounded Jamie away from the pursuers, despite the boy's weakened state and the threat to his own life. There's nothing here about a crisply square-jawed hero wandering around with a bleeding, singing adolescent who blathers about how his daddy embroidered linsey-woolsey shirts for him. Any notion of a monolithic masculine model is completely undone by the appeal of the image: the father, in Jamie's fevered memory, sits and sews as he sings "Rose of Alabamy" to his motherless child. Word and image are duplicated for our eyes and ears as Jamie now sings the old ditty to Josey.

The older man quietly assumes the role of father and caregiver to his simple charge, just as early in the movie he smiled down at his own little boy.

The careful student of Eastwood who looks back at this 1976 movie's understated tenderness after seeing *Gran Torino* must consider the rich embellishment of the father-son theme between 1976 and 2008. Josey acquires a son to cherish after his own little boy has been burned alive, but he has already accepted Jamie as "kin." Walt Kowalski, having reared two despised sons who want to file him away in a retirement home, is also given a second chance to become a father — not to a kid who resembles him in looks, history, or life experience, but to a Hmong teenager named Thao, who has been thrust into an alien culture without a guide. Walt becomes that careful and loving guide through gardening, woodworking, and a dubious but hilarious education in what it means to be an American man. *Gran Torino* radically recasts "sonship" to supersede violence as part of masculinity — a reconciliation model that redefines kinship in human rather than ethnic terms.

When Jamie dies, Josey pronounces words of parting free of the husks of ritual that attended the deaths of his wife and child, which was a reference to an absent God as disturbing as the bedside sermon of the pastor in Ingmar Bergman's *Cries and Whispers*. For the orphan Jamie, he speaks simply of loyalty to kin and friends, unknowingly taking a step toward the family he will form during the remainder of the film.

The reconciliation strand of the narrative strengthens with each episode that follows. The instances of crass commercialism multiply with venal variations, but the strength of weakness becomes ever more prominent. What Karli Lukas calls the shift in the film from "Eastwood as weak" to "Eastwood as star" makes a catchy theory, but in the overall plan of the movie, the "weakness" in the eyes of the powerful (an armed, commercially driven, postwar society) becomes transvalued, or redefined, as strength. What matters is not power or money — a glimpse of the Texas town full of regulators and amputees tells what became of the men caught in the war's bid for power and gun-running wealth — but rather shelter for the displaced, cheated, violated, dispossessed, and homeless.

Lone Watie, odd even by the untutored Jamie's example, enters Josey's world almost as a classic illustration of the movie's embrace of the dispossessed. If Jamie's speech rhythms seemed almost too unsophisticated to be true, if his anecdotes seem to slow the swiftly paced pursuit narrative, Lone Watie's tales take the seemingly random, alternate narrative pattern even further. As Josey snores away, the aging chief treats the audience to a much-needed history lesson on the human costs of land acquisition, a story largely omitted from textbooks in American classrooms until recent decades, but a story that needs to be told to give historical background and context for the rest of the movie. Here's another man whose monumental losses — his wife, his sons, his home, his culture, his place in the natural world — would surely seem to demand violent revenge. The chief is an older version of Ten Bears (Will Sampson), the Comanche chief who dominates the reconciliation narrative toward the end of the movie.

Lone Watie's role in *Josey Wales* switches quickly from that of sidekick and occasional protector to that of a reborn man who falls in love. Will Josey similarly open his life to love and rebirth? The scene at the trading post probes that question even as it explores Josey's conflicted selves through lighting and music. It further embellishes the postwar robbery motif (here identified with adulterated goods and rape), and it introduces the "imperiled woman" theme even as it displays Josey's wildly theatrical killing skills.

This is not just any showdown scene between the hero and the bad guys. It takes place not in a saloon but in a trading post, supposedly one site (like a nineteenth-century lunch counter) where human beings should be able to purchase food and supplies free of discrimination. The scene is constructed to be almost devoid of natural light, and the intimacy of the enclosure allows the cinematographer to manipulate the space and emphasize Josey's emerging darkness. As Josey and Lone Watie approach the post to buy a horse, we see the building from Josey's point of view, a tiny speck at the bottom of a valley. Its owner, Zukie, cheats the two Indians who want to sell pelts. He beats his Navajo assistant, Little Moonlight (Geraldine Keams), for breaking a bottle, then allows two roughnecks to rape her for money.

Suddenly Josey enters, silhouetted in the doorway (in a reference to the John Wayne character Ethan Edwards in John Ford's *The Searchers*). For the rest of the sequence, only a strong edge light outlines his form and part of his face, as Matt Mckenna has written. The silhouette and darkness cloak Josey "in an element of mystery and danger," a "moving force of darkness, a violent shade of a man."[12]

Yet the compassion that Josey has shown the dying Jamie resurfaces as he and the young woman exchange glances. Josey takes over from there, and the "pilgrims" are history. Once the liberated Little Moonlight catches

12. Matt Mckenna, Northwestern University Eastwood class, 2010.

up with Josey and Lone Watie, she weaves her way into their male friendship and into Lone Watie's heart.

More evidence of Josey's dual nature appears with the rescue of the Kansas women; the superhuman defeat of their captors, the savage Comancheros; and his shooting of the bounty hunter even as he adds five new family members (survivors of a silver mine, another "new" American commercial venture). Slowly, the past is being left behind, as the soundtrack underscores the arrival of the ragtag family at their new Texas home, an abandoned ranch.

Significantly, the former owner of the ranch, Tom, died in a skirmish along the Kansas-Missouri border. But the tragic past is forgotten as the little group rounds a bend and enters the grove where the house lies. An extreme long shot unites the voyagers visually as a group when, one by one, they spot the small house. The camera darts around, looking for reactions. Is this really the "paradise" Grandma Sarah had predicted? Joy bursts out from the "birth of the new collective," as Hayley Schilling has written.

The music that accompanies their entrance, the tune of "The Sweet Bye and Bye," will be repeated in the service of thanksgiving that follows their first settlement. For now, there's work to be done: Grandma bustles around inside the house to bring order and prepare to feed everyone; the men begin to repair the fences. What about Josey in this domestic scene? When he tries to enter the doorway, he is framed for a moment by light in another echo of the opening and closing shots of *The Searchers*. The camera cuts to an over-the-shoulder shot that for a moment makes Josey and Grandma appear to be the same height, signaling "the shift in power" from Josey the trailblazer and protector to the older woman as the organizer.

One of the most powerful scenes in the movie occurs later that night. It begins with an intimate conversation between Lone Watie and Josey that will be echoed in tone by Scrap and Frankie Dunn in *Million Dollar Baby*. As Jesse Anderson-Lehman has written, "We get a treat: a classic Eastwood shot, the frame dominated by darkness, with only Wales's face lit by the flickering fire." Lone Watie assures Josey that he has his home with this ragtag group, and he must seize his joy. In response, Eastwood places a meditative Josey above the bustling homestead as the rest of the family repairs, reshapes, rebuilds. As Schilling has written, the scene has a

> powerful intensity that derives from tight editing and sound design. As each individual chops wood, fixes a fence, or beats a rug, the sound of each of their activities combines into a single, synchronous rhythm — a

harmony of separate parts as one whole. The rhythm's emotional connotations catalyze a flashback reaction within Josey's psyche (similar to the effect of the crack of the whip in *High Plains Drifter*), where the sounds of domestic chores become the drumming of raiders' hooves or the crackling of his flaming home.[13]

Schilling continues by noting Eastwood's use of extreme close-ups to Josey's eyes, rare in a movie where Josey's face is almost always shrouded by the brim of a hat. "The camera's agitating proximity and its time-travel capabilities through the magic of editing" bring the intractability of Josey's memories close to the spectator — a jarring vision that makes his love scene with Laura Lee the more poignant and the sensuousness of the fiddle music, singing, and dancing the more compelling. The movie has yet to work out its tensions: vengeance or reconciliation? New love and new life, or a future forever observed from a distance, with Josey's body blacked out in shadows against a cloudy sky as he is here and as he will be when he finally corners Terrill, the murderer?

Josey falls in love again, not with a kind-hearted prostitute or a schoolteacher, as in the classic western *High Noon,* but rather with Laura Lee, a fellow sojourner given to otherworldly flights of fancy. Both lovers have been marked by heart-stopping loss, but how refreshingly she begs the sorrowing giant to dance and how generously he smiles and stumbles as he joins in the family's celebration. The colors are bright, as each of the family members expresses a differing dance style. The sequence is drawn out for pleasure. We detect hints that "come spring," Josey's sweetheart might add a baby to the little family of outcasts (and so she did in the source novella).[14] No cowboy celibacy (a common trope in the western) for Josey! With the addition of the prostitute Rose, a saloonkeeper, two Mexican workers, and a fiddler, Josey's world is now complete. And the world of the film is also complete.

The composition of Josey's family group overtakes the destructive

13. Hayley Schilling and Jesse Anderson-Lehman, in Northwestern University Eastwood class, Winter 2010.

14. Imagine my happiness when I read the novella that the film is adapted from and confirmed that Laura Lee does have Josey's baby and that they live happily with him after he is wounded. Imagine my distress (the same as Eastwood's and his team's) when I discovered that the book's author was a former Ku Klux Klan member. But Eastwood has a way with stories. Just as he transformed the male-focused bodice ripper by James Waller into the cinematic and female-centered jewel *Bridges of Madison County* (1995), he turns the Josey Wales novella into a plea for peace and reconciliation of warring peoples.

vengeance of the Cain-and-Abel drama in the rest of the movie, vicious reprisals against men and women not too different from ourselves. Instead
of excluding people, the family bears witness to the love of the neighbor,
which in the words of Matthew 22:37-40 flows from the love of "the Lord
your God." (Both Matthew 22 and Luke 10 elaborate on the Torah, on the
Decalogue, or Ten Commandments: "You shall love your neighbor as
yourself; I am the Lord.") Honor the poor and the sojourner, revere your
parents, respect servants and the deaf and blind, honor old persons, and
welcome the stranger. These commands are borne out as Josey shelters
Jamie, then the displaced and "worthless" old man Lone Watie, then a rape
victim, then his former enemies, the Kansas "pilgrims," then the refugees
from a failed mining venture, all poor and homeless — including two
Mexican-American men! "The stranger who sojourns with you shall be to
you as the native among you, and you shall love him as yourself, for you
were strangers in the land of Egypt; I am the Lord your God," as it is expressed in Leviticus, the text from which Matthew and Luke draw.

Proof-texting has its dangers, though. It is fine to see Leviticus as a
source for ideas of generosity, but Luke (noting Jesus' parables) radically
expands them. Luke no longer envisions "the neighbor" as other Israelites,
as in Leviticus and Deuteronomy — your own kind — but rather people
who appear to be totally different from you in ethnicity and history. With
the parable of the Good Samaritan, which seems foundational in *Josey
Wales,* you rescue another person without even caring about that person's
ethnicity — Jew or Gentile? Another Samaritan or your former enemy?
You support him with your body, you pay for his care, you fold him (or
her, or them) into your own life in compassion. As Jack Miles has written
of the Samaritan story, "This is not random kindness for a random enemy.
It is 'uniform treatment of all.'"[15]

The Man With No Name finally has a name and a home — even if,
when Josey rides out of town, the viewer is not sure whether he is returning to his little family in Texas or whether the new, all-embracing social
model we see at the end of the movie (a commune with ethnic, gender, and
economic parity at peace with the neighboring Comanche) ever spread to
other parts of America. Even if he did return, could he ever forget the war
traumas that engulfed him? Eastwood's later war movies, at least *Flags of
Our Fathers* and *Gran Torino,* suggest that war's injuries endure far beyond

15. Jack Miles, *Christ: A Crisis in the Life of God* (New York: Vintage Books, 2001), 180-
81.

the media flurry that reports or distorts them. A recent flood of war articles and films (*Newsweek* May 31, 2010) supports this view.

Eastwood deliberately leaves the ending of this movie ambiguous, as he told interviewer Michael Henry Wilson. Even more outrageously, *The Outlaw Josey Wales* dares to model peace, bane of the traditional western and enemy of the American imperialism inherent in endless land grabs and exterminations of native peoples. In a magnificent set piece framed against a glorious blue sky, Josey offers Ten Bears, the chief of the Comanche, "life" rather than death. They cement their bond in blood. Josey's promise to supply food for the Comanche journeys (which we see fulfilled later in the movie) recalls the biblical meals of fellowship in Genesis 18 and the Gospels, where strangers are welcomed and food is provided for all, rich and poor.

The peace pact is the more startling because in the antiphonal structure that marks this and other Eastwood films, the repeated oppositions of Kansas and Missouri, North and South, brother against brother, Cain and Abel are now elaborated in a complex response to treatment of another human being. In *Josey Wales,* Eastwood highlights not only the ways that Josey releases the demons of wrong done him by his own people, but also the question of how survivors of the Civil War will embrace the peoples both sides had excluded from the American family for centuries — Indian tribes, former slaves, women, and the poor.

Josey Wales signals a rejection of the culture of death — including the ravages of capitalism — in favor of new life, human dignity, and expanded definitions of "family." He must find a way to bring the paradise of the little homestead back out to the wider world, but for now, this beautiful movie has looked vengeance in the eye and has turned toward the sun.

Pale Rider

At the end of *Harry Potter and the Order of the Phoenix,* the chief villainess, headmistress Dolores Umbridge, is lying in the Hogwarts Hospital, uncharacteristically silent and fearful. Gone are her simpering swagger and vindictive construction of laws to forbid everything, particularly actions that threaten her power in Harry's school or that smack of adolescent high spirits. Spoiler alert: despite her students' devising of colorful ways for this killjoy to be brought to justice, she has been immobilized simply by a little trip into the forest, followed by her former students' imitation of the clip-clopping of horses' hooves. (Long live the power of allusion!)

Pale Rider begins with this precise order of terror, a feeling stimulated by sounds that call forth images of the four horses of the Apocalypse and the end time, when all shall be judged — and either damned or redeemed. As with earlier Eastwood movies (e.g., *High Plains Drifter, The Gauntlet*), movie "realism" is permeated with hints of worlds beyond. As the credits roll, hooves thunder in frightening sonic counterpoint to the pastoral sounds and sights of daily life in a small mining camp. Mirroring the crosscutting of rescue and attack sequences made famous by *The Birth of a Nation,* the camera flits anxiously between the contented, industrious miners and the horde of demonic pursuers tearing down the mountainside.[1] The horsemen we see on the screen and hear on the soundtrack ride

---

1. Tom Gunning, *D. W. Griffith and the Origins of American Narrative Film: The Early Years at Biograph* (Champaign: University of Illinois Press, 1999). Gunning notes here and

toward death in a goal-driven herd. The small miners — men, women, and children — work pebble by pebble against the sparkling palette of a clear stream, blue skies, and lush background forest, their shacks propped against welcoming trees, their wash hung out to dry in the gentle breeze.

Within a few screen minutes, Eastwood has established the unbridled power and wealth behind these horsemen, their probable place in the nineteenth-century struggle between competing modes of settling the west, and the distinctively religious set of references that will characterize this film. He plunges viewers into a drama *in medias res,* caught under the driving wild hooves, while in the blink of an eye he allows them to savor the pure air in the miners' camp.

We have returned to Eastwood's western country after nearly a decade's absence, wondering (if we can catch our breath) where along the spectrum of this resilient genre the canny director will touch down this time. The pounding hooves of the movie's opening conjure up the threat of attacks on settlers by Indian tribes, one of the staples of the western genre (*Red River,* 1948; *The Searchers,* 1956), or North against South, or the thousands of head of cattle movin', movin', movin' along trails such as the Sedalia, from Texas to the markets in Kansas, and from there to the East *(Rawhide).* The opening sequence of shots also revives memories of the Manichean schemas of thousands of westerns from 1903 right up to today: the evil versus the (apparently) good.[2]

A young girl darts into the middle of the gang. Will the director launch into a captivity narrative, as John Ford does in *The Searchers*? And who has sent these riders? The most frequent villains in cowboy movies are greedy ranchers who seek to drive out homesteaders, as in *Shane,* the classic western that *Pale Rider* seems to allude to the most. Will this movie demonize Indians, corporate ranchers, gunfighters, or rich, cynical men from the East (as in *My Darling Clementine*)? Will *Pale Rider* tackle class warfare, the Civil War, the evils of capitalism, individual revenge, or justice

---

elsewhere the moral implications of editing, where the meaning of images changes according to shots that precede and follow them.

2. When I recently rescreened Kurosawa's *Seven Samurai,* I noticed the correspondences of the movie's opening sequence with the opening of *Pale Rider.* Marauding bandits swoop into a terrified village; the seven samurai rescue the villagers. In *The Outlaw Josey Wales,* the context differs. We see bandits and murderers from two perspectives: the close-up, "realistic" murders of Josey's wife and son by the Kansas Red Legs; and in response, the visually and perceptually distanced murders and burnings along the other side of the Kansas/Missouri border by the Missouri guerrillas.

in the abstract, frequent themes in Eastwood's movies?[3] Is it anything at all like his earlier westerns, which set the genre and the explosive events within them in a broad political and theological context? Or, as Robert Jewett has suggested, does Eastwood intentionally "demystify all elements of American mythology"?

The two westerns that Eastwood directed in 1973 and 1976 took distinctively different paths. *High Plains Drifter,* austere and severe, dismantled the myth of the noble gunslinger with a Christ-like aura, dismembered any thought of the new settlements in the west as utopian, and moved handily between apocalyptic parable and justice discourse. *The Outlaw Josey Wales* dissected the Civil War and its unending legacy of bloodlust, while it explored the possibility of establishing new communities and new neighborhoods freed from the need to seek vengeance for searing wrongs. In both movies, the steely efficacy of the protagonist (fueled by otherworldly hellfire in the first and grief and mourning in the second) was tempered by the presence of fools and charlatans, pock-marked villains, and otherworldly dreamers. The ghostly rider in *Drifter* leaves the brittle town of Lago in shambles, but *Josey Wales* creates a new community out of the dregs of towns for which Lago is an allegorical model, towns laid waste by exhausted minerals (silver), war (fratricide), and migrations (forced by poverty or near-extermination).

Pale Rider seems an odd and unsettled combination of *Drifter* and *Josey Wales,* with its multiple apocalyptic yet reconciling themes. Like *Drifter* and *Josey Wales, Pale Rider* constructs different kinds of neighborhoods (staked-out spaces), or communities, formed by a sense of belonging, where men and women can test the constraints and freedom of the law. This time the communities are being formed in and around the gold mines of the west during the 1860s. But, as viewers, we must ask: Does the movie's continual slippage into alternating realms of mysticism, judgment, and revenge detract from our sympathy for the men and women with whom we identify from the first frame forward? Christopher Deacy asks: "Does *Pale Rider* represent a step backwards rather than forward after the tenderness of *The Outlaw Josey Wales*?"[4]

Since the movie's "device," the uncertain identity of the Preacher

---

3. See Patrick McGee, *From Shane to Kill Bill: Rethinking the Western* (Oxford: Blackwell, 2007), 225-34, for a discussion of class warfare in the westerns of Eastwood and others. Sadly, McGee overlooks the rich visual texture and interlocking subtexts of Eastwood's western movies.

4. Christopher Deacy, message to the author, November 24, 2010.

(played by Eastwood), hovers just beneath the surface of every human interaction, the viewer justifiably watches with a fair amount of confusion and anxiety. Does the Preacher's presence (more accurately, his frequent absence) detract from the director's commitment to peace, community, and supportive neighborhoods fostered in the last half of *Josey Wales*, and in two sweet small films from the early eighties, *Honkytonk Man* and the genial *Bronco Billy*? If westerns offer a forum for discussing current war issues (such as Vietnam in *Josey Wales* and Iraq in *Gran Torino*), what is at stake in *Pale Rider*? Viewers may well leave the movie entirely puzzled about what they've just seen, particularly since Eastwood added a vengeance backstory to the original script.

On its surface, however, *Pale Rider* presents a perfect example of a "religious" movie, or at least one permeated by biblical references that can be and have been mined by pastors, theologians, and teachers of religion and film. Critics have seized on one or another element of the film, lured perhaps by its lush cinematography and seductive combination of sexiness and disembodiment. Eastwood is loath here, as he was in *High Plains Drifter*, to completely disembody his mystical figure. As he shows us, it's more fun to deconstruct and reject the myth of the celibate cowboy who never gets the girl than to play an ethereal ghost or man with no human desires. Will the Preacher serve as the director's agent for embodiment within the community, stimulating spiritual regeneration that permeates and dignifies human affairs? The early signs indicate that he might. Yet the attentive viewer also senses trouble simply by listening to the soundtrack.

The Preacher arrives onscreen after the opening disasters as though he were conjured up by the young girl's desires, as though she were motivated to ask for a miracle by Jesus' words: "Ask and it will be given to you; seek and you will find; knock and the door will be opened to you" (Luke 11:9).[5] Images of mountains are juxtaposed against her shadowed figure as she prays her version of the Lord's Prayer over the body of her dead dog, which she has buried in the forest near the miners' settlement. When she says the words "we need a miracle," mountain, clouds, and man come together in our field of vision. Furthermore, in keeping with popular ideas of an apocalyptic visitor, the Preacher's appearance is imaged almost literally as coming "out of the clouds," the biblical poetic image of the Son of man.[6]

---

5. Thanks to Alex Schwarm, Northwestern University Eastwood class, Winter 2009, for the Luke reference, as well as for the comment on score and editing.

6. For a full discussion of the Son of man motif in Scripture, see Walter Wink, *The Hu-*

The lone figure riding out of the distance into full view, cutting across the screen, may be one more well-worn convention of the western, echoing the opening of *Shane*. But, whereas in other movies the hero is summoned by the director to solve narrative problems or appeal to audience expectations, in *Pale Rider* the figure appears to respond directly to Megan's prayer for rescue. Several scenes later, when Megan and her mother are enclosed in the domestic space of the family kitchen, the young girl reads from chapter 6 of the book of Revelation, and, lo, a mysterious Preacher (seemingly the same person we saw earlier) rides into view. (Eastwood confessed to amplifying the supernatural elements to develop the biblical parallels.) In both cases, Megan appears to summon the Preacher in what in witchcraft trials was called *vocatio*, the call.[7] Is this a second coming — that is, not simply rescue, but also judgment and extermination of evil, what we would today call a media event? Who or what has Megan summoned?

Here we have the first clear clue that the Preacher may not be the heavenly creature that either miners or critics may have wished. However satisfying it may be to see Eastwood the actor arrive on stage (viewers are always looking for the Man With No Name or Dirty Harry), if the movie aimed to make some kind of savior argument, his entrance undercuts it. The score and editing heighten his menacing nature. Horror-movie music anticipates his arrival and rumbles under the shot every time he materializes in various cutaways. Who or what has sent him?

Eastwood the director has stirred up a stew as uncertain as the Bible's apocalyptic texts themselves, which becomes further complicated when one looks more closely at Megan's prayer. The sequence establishes location: mountain and dense forest, both religious symbols. As Megan recites the Lord's Prayer over the grave of her dead pet, her adolescent rebellion surfaces as she punctuates every line of the prayer with theological doubt. In the movie's context, the prayer for a miracle may be spoken to an empty heaven. The incident articulates the theological unease and challenge that shudders beneath any western worth watching: Why is it so painful simply to live on this earth? (And why, as Rachel Koontz has asked, is the western a fitting venue to explore such questions?) The image of the Preacher, a fig-

---

man Being: Jesus and the Enigma of the Son of the Man* (Minneapolis: Augsburg Press, 2001), 166-70.

7. Joseph Klaits, *Servants of Satan: The Age of the Witch Hunts* (Bloomington: Indiana University Press, 1985). See also Carl-Theo. Dreyer's *Day of Wrath* (Denmark, 1943), with its interlocking movements of fanaticism, viciousness, religious doctrine, misogyny, and magic.

Preacher (Eastwood) investigates a crime.

ure seemingly drawn from every lone savior figure who ever rode into town to calm viewers' anxieties, hardly reassures us.

Rather than deifying his Preacher character, Eastwood takes pains to emphasize his liminal state. Do we see him or not? The camera may be tricking us. Is he dead or alive? Or is he the living dead, like the Stranger in *High Plains Drifter*? Naturalistically low-lit sequences that emphasize his physicality, like the display of a hearty appetite at his first meal with Megan's family, alternate with sudden appearances and disappearances, like his apparitional vanishing from the train station when the main mining villain comes to town. Even more disorienting, his presence on screen is accompanied by texts riddled with death, not life. "His name is death" and "hell followed with him" cue his first appearance in the mining camp. The scars from seven bullet holes in his back are displayed for the filmgoers but surprisingly ignored by Hull, leader of the miners, who actually may expect his preacher-rescuer to walk the thin line between here and the netherworld.

The scars, however, are those of a dead man — a dead man who nonetheless enjoys his food, has sex with Hull's fiancée, and doesn't possess much real power until he reclaims his gun from Wells Fargo about midway through the film. Despite the Preacher's supposed resemblance to the "saintly" Shane, he is not celibate, peace-loving, or heaven-sent. This hero may come from the underworld, but his own powers depend on technology and a good deal of camera sleight-of-hand and trompe l'oeil.

Stripped of a savior-gunfighter we can believe in (or who feels as familiar as an old western boot), what are we to do with the texts from Revelation? One possibility is to turn them on their head and consider the Preacher of dynamite and gunplay an alter ego for the ineffectual Hull. Or we could pay closer attention to the light side of the biblical verses so popular among a contemporary crowd that is hell-bent on making the end of the world happen sooner rather than later. After all, the apocalyptic references of Revelation 6 are shared by Matthew 25, the book of Daniel, Mark 13, and all the "Son of man" sayings. On the one hand, they set the stage for human vengeance on enemies. Indeed, people live by revenge myths. The hint that the Clint figure will take out the evildoers — sweet satisfaction! — keeps this movie popular after more than a quarter century. Just observe the buying public's response to the Dirty Harry–style trailers for *Gran Torino*.

Then consider what Eastwood the director actually did with the seductions of revenge in *Gran Torino:* he overturned them. In 1985, with *Pale Rider,* Eastwood seems to want something else out of his Preacher figure and the "revenge" motif: he wants to challenge revenge as a natural accompaniment to religious belief and practice. The counter to the vengeance instinct ("Vengeance is mine, says the Lord") characterizes Judaism, Christianity, and Islam — regardless of the bloodthirst of some of its orthodox practitioners. The Matthew 25 text, for instance, explicitly links the judgment of the Last Days, not to the fiery wrath of Revelation, but rather to acts of mercy: feed, clothe, visit, and do not abandon the "other." By what criteria will we be judged in the Last Days? The Matthew text says that if we have given food, care, and comfort to the needy and despised of the world, we are identified with the Lord.

A recent television advertisement for an Eastwood and James Bond retrospective helped me shape a more radical interpretation: *Pale Rider* as a critique of vengeance. Unfortunately, in their efforts to market the series as movies that glamorize violence and style, the trailer writers misread *Pale Rider.* At the deepest level, Eastwood's western is a film about "righteousness." But righteousness does not appear in the advertisement either as a concept or as a narrative marker. The buildup for the *Pale Rider* ad features scenes from the movie that the promoters believe are its key themes: blessed are the poor in spirit (the fool figure Spider gunned down by six armed men dressed like something from *Men in Black* or *The Matrix*); blessed are the peacemakers (the Pale Rider in his preacher's collar); and blessed are those who hunger and thirst after justice (the ragtag gold miners embattled by industrial competitors).

The thematic progression of the preview (poverty, peace, and rescue) appears to work nicely as a tidy summary of the movie's plot. The miners have certainly fled poverty for the promise of gold and a better life, and they want to live in peace. As Eastwood told an interviewer, "One is invited to sympathize with a living community [of worthy people]."[8] The small miners need a justice figure to intervene to protect them from violent attacks and displacement by a powerful mining company that covets their land.

But the thematic rhythm of the trailer reveals a problem that has dogged the movie's critical reception ever since it showed at Cannes in May 1985. Eastwood constructed the film to draw forth multiple viewer responses: rescue, retribution, and reconciliation. Undeniably, the tiny pastoral community works precariously on the good earth, vulnerable to nature's assaults: storms, blizzards, droughts, locusts, and illnesses such as the cholera that nearly wiped out the settlements in the Midwest in the early 1850s. They have weathered all of these natural assaults, but they cannot stand up against rampant capitalism, the assaults that rip into the verdant mountainsides and crush trees, animals, and wildflowers with the force of their monstrous equipment. The missing element in the advertising promotion is *righteousness*, not justice: righteousness as stewardship of the land and of each other (*dikaiosune*, serving others, balance).[9]

We need to reexamine the apocalyptic texts to which the movie alludes. The mythic structure carved out in the film preview collapses the message of the Beatitudes, from which the phrases are drawn (repeating

8. Michael Henry Wilson, *Clint Eastwood* (interviews), (Paris: Editions Cahiers du Cinéma, 2007), 63 (hereafter, page references to Wilson appear in parentheses in the text).

9. The Beatitudes, which constitute part of the Sermon on the Mount, appear in the New Testament in Matthew 5:2-12 and Luke 6:20-26. They present a full-blooded view of the "kingdom of heaven" as reversing earthly power structures. "Righteousness" is used in Matthew's version. Righteousness, an ethical term but also an attribute of the divine, means "rightness with God," and it carries the expectation of service to others. It is used 500 times in Hebrew Scripture (the Hebrew root *tzadik*) and 200 times in the Greek New Testament (as *dikaios*, from which we get the word "deacon").

the phrase "blessed are the . . ."), with the biblical text that Megan reads. The actual Beatitudes, Jesus' restatement of the heart of the Decalogue (the Law), advance from "poor in spirit" to "righteousness," not justice. Two contrasting biblical images collide in the movie: the avenger (the angry God: Jesus in the Temple driving out the money-changers) and the community organizer (Jesus and the outcasts).

Eastwood may be doing something more sophisticated than setting up a western rescue with a predictably violent ending. Is the pastoral role of the Preacher the most vital angle of the narrative? Is his community organizer role (based on biblical peace texts) more important than his avenger god role (lifted from the angry God texts)? It is a bit difficult to tell where he stands from his reply to interviewer Michael Henry Wilson, who notes that the stranger becomes the miners' pastor and obviously "shares the aspirations of the gold miners." Wilson comments: "The character of Michael Moriarty evolves with contact with the pastor and finishes by becoming the chief of the community" (pp. 61-63).

The cinematography helps create the feeling of a living community that the viewer comes to love. The movie opens with shots of men, women, and children tending animals, hanging clothes, and singing, and later spotlights the unrushed conversations about what has brought them to this lush part of the world. Why, then, inject horror elements into a movie that on one level could be interpreted as the miraculous appearance of an effective community organizer? Even the signature Eastwood meditative campfire confessional is mediated by a figure who is so low-lit as to resemble a Halloween lantern head bobbing in a sea of darkness: this is the director's chiaroscuro lighting (used so effectively by Eastwood's mentor, Sergio Leone), here taken to an extreme. This sequence, where the small miners consult with the Preacher about the industrial company's offer to buy them out, calls attention to the dark side of the coming of "the law" to the west in the mid-nineteenth century. As the Preacher comments to the frightened community, the mining company has summoned a ruthless marshal and his men, vigilantes emboldened by badges but paid to murder. "They uphold whatever law pays them the most," says the Preacher of the as-yet-unseen marshal and his six gunmen, who have been hired by the hydraulic mining operation to ruin the small miners. If the Preacher sides with a deeper law (i.e., he is not for hire because he opposes killing), should the viewer be comforted when a "dead" man shoots down seven men (evil or not) without benefit of trial by a jury of their peers, as happens at the end of this movie?

With so many themes in play, the viewer seeks a larger message that might hold all the parts of the film together. The Preacher actually fits uneasily into the little settlement of small-pan miners, almost as though his character chose them only to draw the attention of the man he intends to kill, rather than the other way around. Perhaps he lurked in the shadows of a number of small settlements until he found one suited to his real goal: to avenge himself on his murderer. Has he found in Megan a convenient agent of his vengeance?

When Michael Henry Wilson posed the question of Megan's role to Eastwood, the director gave only an equivocal response: "Perhaps it's a dream, perhaps not. She prays, and the pastor descends from the mountains. Many interpretations are possible." Her age is no accident. (In *Shane*, the movie that Eastwood supposedly pays homage to with *Pale Rider*, Megan's character was a young boy of around nine.) She has never known her father, so the Preacher is a perfect substitute. On the other hand, at almost fifteen, she is already thinking of love and marriage — or at least of sex. Her mother and her grandmother both married at fifteen, as the movie takes great pains to inform us.

To begin with, then, even before we notice Megan's skin color and are told that her grandparents disapproved of her mother's marriage, her presence introduces several additional doubts about the "meanings" in this movie. How much of the plot is her imagination — related to us by her and filtered through her thoughts? Further, is she a force for good or for disruption? The movie implies that her father was a gunfighter, perhaps one of the men who roamed the country after the Civil War, unable to stop killing and hired by large ranchers to murder their competitors — someone like the Preacher himself when he was alive. Is Megan infected with her father's insatiable desire for vengeance, like the burning passion for revenge of the prostitutes in *Unforgiven*? Will she end up destroying her family and her community? Or did Eastwood deliberately turn her into a young woman of color and then just as deliberately not call attention to this, as he forgoes commenting on "difference" with Ned in *Unforgiven*, with Graciella Rivers in *Blood Work*, and with Scrap in *Million Dollar Baby*?

And who exactly is the creature she calls forth? Here, too, Eastwood hedges, saying that his character inspires courage in the desperate miners. Yet he also notes the personal backstory of the preacher — "the forces of good and evil that manifest themselves in the struggle between the Trust and the independent miners" (Wilson, p. 59). Regardless of the Preacher's

48

Preacher (Eastwood) enjoys home cooking.

identity, apocalyptic judgment hangs in the air from the film's opening. But who judges? And what exactly is at stake? What apocalypse does Eastwood the director want us to consider: the murderous henchmen and the rapacious mining company, the complete destruction of the small community, or the evil marshal and his six hit men? The three disasters require at least three separate responses.

First comes the thundering, unthinking herd, the mounted robocalls who intend to instill fear. Mighty on their powerful steeds, they bravely kill a calf and a little pet dog, knock over the miners' shacks, rip up laundry lines, and terrify women and children — all symbols of the domestic life that threatens the all-male corporate structure. This narrative line is situated solidly in the realm of (possible) history, as the opening so thoroughly shows the specific identities and multiple ethnicities of the small miners. The henchmen expose the little settlement's vulnerability and the fragility of its social structure, and this is designed to make us care about the fate of the individuals whose faces are caressed by the camera and whose voices we hear throughout the movie.

The threat to a community posed by an outside force is stock western fare, of course: *High Noon,* for instance, or *The Man Who Shot Liberty Valance.* Fearsome as they appear initially, the henchmen are only minor players in a larger and long-term destruction of the earth. Ecological disaster was hastened by destructive hydraulic mining, a practice that began in California in about 1853, resumed in earnest in the mid-1860s, and only stopped in 1884, after decades of protest from farmers whose land downstream was ruined by the companies' dumping. Greed unleashed massive destruction. Westerns usually ignored the devastation of the land that the homesteaders, cattle barons, and cowboys roamed. *The Searchers* and Jim Jarmusch's *Dead Man* (1995) are outstanding exceptions.

Regard for the land may make up the larger agenda that holds all the movie's parts together, greater than the personal revenge angle or even the survival of the small mining community. Eastwood told Michael Henry Wilson what he found when he scouted locations for the film:

> My grandmother lived at Angels Camp, in the heart of the gold country, in fact very near to one of the places where we filmed. I also had filmed certain episodes of *Rawhide* there, and it's there, at Sonora, that I shot the sequence of the train. During the course of scouting, I traveled to the north, in Idaho, where many mining exploitations had used hydraulic means. One still finds the vestiges of their machines, but we finished by reconstituting everything ourselves. Happily, this proceeding was forbidden in California shortly after the period evoked in the film because that ruined the earth. (p. 58)

Perhaps the larger backstory of environmental degradation pulls all the plot threads together. The small apocalypse figured in the shots of hydraulic mining at work might lead to a larger disaster shortly afterwards: the destruction of the fresh waterways and forests in that area, for instance, and the poisoning of the rich farmlands downstream.[10]

In *Pale Rider,* then, the extensive attention given to hydraulic mining

---

10. Eastwood refers to the film's story as taking place shortly before the practice was stopped in 1884: "It's a classic story of the big guys against the little guys, little guys versus the big guys, the corporate mining which ends up in hydraulic mining, they just literally mow the mountains away . . . the trees and everything . . . . [A]ll that was outlawed in California . . . way back, even before ecological concerns were as prevalent as they are today. It's kind of an ecological statement — the fact that this corporation is moving fast because they're afraid laws against it will come along" (Wilson, 134-35).

itself — not simply to the greedy men who run the company and hound the little community — argues that science and technology are not value-free. The land becomes an "industrial commodity." The near-rape of Megan alludes to the by-products of unfettered power: human tragedy is unleashed beyond the power of its possessors to contain it, like Prometheus or Frankenstein or the golem-like creature in *No Country for Old Men*. The creators cannot control their creatures.

Is one of the roles of the mysterious Preacher perhaps to stop hydraulic mining? By the end of the movie, it certainly appears that the LaHood mining company will close. Eastwood the director may think he has created a film in which viewers come to share the aspirations of the miners, but what lies deeper? Shall we engage the world with the aim of improving it? The film certainly does seem to set us up for ethical conversations. What kind of world do we want? Is it one where, "instead of savage exploitation of land, water, and air, he seeks a gentle synergy of human endeavors within our sister earth and all creation" — redemption and discipleship?[11]

Despite the horror-movie music that rumbles whenever the Preacher appears, his near silence and shadowy lighting when he is with the miners, and the operatic orchestration of discordant music and drumbeats during the final showdown, the most striking visuals and sounds during the movie swirl around the corporate mining operations. The link between the near-rape of Megan by LaHood's son and the rape of the land is established by the extensive screen time given to sights of the hydraulic machines at work. Eastwood dwells on the details: the majestic trees are torn up by their roots and felled, the chasm is dug into the earth, and the foul sludge is washed into the stream. The sequence begins with a shot of a deforested mountainside, the giant trees toppling off the edge and the denuded land separated only by a fragile line of firs and water pipes in the foreground.

Shockingly, in the middle of a sequence of brutal destruction, the shot turns grey. Two men are silhouetted for seven long seconds against the cascades of water. One bears the outline of the cowboys who run this operation. The other, dressed like a Chinese worker, refers to the role played by the hundreds of thousands of Chinese who built the railroads, which in turn fueled increasing American prosperity. The men stand precariously on a sterile wasteland devoid of color and life in almost eerie anticipation

11. Rosemary Radford Ruether, foreword to Kenneth Vaux, *America in God's World* (Eugene, OR: Wipf and Stock, 2009).

of the barren rock that becomes the tomb of Japanese soldiers in *Letters from Iwo Jima* (2006).[12] The cinematography creates an image of the earth after life has been extinguished, similar to the landscape of *Children of Men* or *Apocalypse Now* (1979).

Perhaps, then, critics have been stingy with their appreciation of the movie: too harsh with their assessment of *Pale Rider* as "a triumph for naked gunpower" (Robert Jewett), too dismissive of its mystical aura (its reception at Cannes), or too quick to see it as story of spiritual conversion. Yet, whatever archetypal western sheen *Pale Rider* possesses (the Preacher trades his collar for a gunbelt), the film's fabric, like that of *The Outlaw Josey Wales,* is woven from dozens of small connective moments that, taken together, present a fresh vision of human community, a new "family" or "neighborhood" that expresses the righteousness of living together in wholeness. If justice is interpreted only as vengeance, then it fails as the basis for human interactions. *Pale Rider* does contain slick gunfighter and savior elements, but community wins out in the end, thanks to the breathtaking, life-affirming visual compositions and the repeated undercutting of the Preacher by horror music, silence, and backlighting.

Is it permissible to cut into the earth if you do it responsibly? We cannot forget that even the pastoral miners whom we have come to admire have staked out wrongfully acquired lands. Compared to the ravaging claws of the industrial mining operation, their modest mining methods seem positively saintly — in harmony with nature, like Thoreau. Take a bit of gold from the earth and live in peace, they seem to say. Yet, as the episodes with Hull and Spider and their nuggets show, the small miners are also seeking wealth. They may be tired and poor, but their search for gold nonetheless mirrors the rapacity of their competitors. Another quick comparison with *Shane* underscores the violence inherent even in the small mining operation: the two central male characters in the older film bond when they remove a tree stump to allow Joe, a farmer, to plant more crops. (As if to highlight the craziness of this partnership, though, a triumphal score accents that sequence in *Shane*.) In *Pale Rider,* the Preacher and Hull split a boulder to find gold.

Eastwood seems to be responding to the whole western canon by say-

12. The subject of the Chinese workforce, yet another terrible injustice that has stained the story of America's progress, is brought up and almost passed over in *Unforgiven*, with English Bob's offhand remark about shooting Chinese people. *3:10 to Yuma* also images this, as it does torture. *Tombstone* (George P. Cosmatos, 1993) contains a throwaway line by one of the characters that refers to the "anti-Chinese society" of Tombstone.

ing that the lone strong man is an illusion. He exposes the mystery in *Shane*, where the protagonist is deliberately coded as a savior with angelic hero lighting, a wound in his side, and adoring worshipers. How can we regard a gunfighter, so haunted that he must roam the earth forever, as a "savior" figure? The Preacher may inspire the small miners to pull together as neighbors, rescue Megan, and exercise quite a bit of fancy gunplay to the rhythm of drums and oboe and cymbals, but he is a man caught between earth and eternity, eternally damned by whatever he did in his early life. He warns Megan not to love "a man like me" — words that jar in the romantic setting (background strings and woodwinds) in which she proposes to him.

But Eastwood does not mean for the Preacher to be emulated, despite the super-cool way he dispatches the bad guys. His skill with weapons is neither representation nor modeling: it is flashy filmic style displayed by a semidead man. The community that Eastwood so vividly images in all its fearfulness and poverty and warmth is worthy of love. Sadly, the pioneers have been caught in the snare of greed that has harmed the land and killed its original inhabitants. The social conscience that emerges during the ecological disaster sequence is not the Preacher's. It is the director's: Eastwood uses the Preacher and his interactions with this group to reveal one more troubled episode in the ongoing move to "conquer" the west. He exposes greed and rapacity as a threat to human values.

Furthermore, if we consider the true provenance of Megan's prayer scene at her dog's gravesite, the movie may be seen as stimulating rather than stifling theological doubt. The scene is visually echoed later in the movie when the young girl proposes marriage to the tall stranger. More significantly, the rhythm and elaboration of Megan's commentary on the Lord's Prayer echo a scene from one of the few war movies Eastwood admired, *Bastogne* (*Battleground*, William Wellman, 1949). The examination of easy spiritual comfort in the darkness of suffering will play out in Eastwood's own war movies, but as an underlying philosophy, not a direct address to the audience, like Megan's commentary or that of the conscripted soldier in *Bastogne*, a man reflecting on the ironies of religious practice as he meditates on Isaiah 40:31.

In the Wellman film, Christmas approaches and the men, weary and low on food and ammunition, make their way toward Bastogne, a small town in Belgium. One man reflects ironically on the biblical text the pastor is reading for the makeshift Christmas service: "They that wait upon the LORD shall renew their strength; they shall mount up with wings as eagles;

they shall run and not be weary; they shall walk and not faint." After every phrase of the text, the disillusioned and frightened soldier comments bitterly in voice-over on the expectation that a just God protects the innocent. The young soldiers will "mount up with wings as eagles" — "if the fog lifts." They "shall run and not be weary" — "unless they have frozen feet." "They shall walk and not faint" — "if they don't lose too much blood before the medics come." The rhythm of the recitation and the tone of the rejoinders almost duplicate Megan's interrogation of her ritual text. Clustered at the edge of a small but key village in Belgium, dreaming of blueberry pie and home, the young soldiers have just discovered that they have been abandoned. *Bastogne* is shot in black and white, with intense close-ups, no star power or glamour, and no glorification of war, much less of the much-vaunted Battle of the Bulge.

In 2006, more than twenty years after he directed *Pale Rider,* Eastwood made *Flags of Our Fathers* and *Letters from Iwo Jima,* lacerating views of the mismanagement and human sorrow of war, in which he sets human suffering in dialogue with a vision of a peaceful world. In this message lies the key to *Pale Rider:* it challenges a theology of human history that deifies conquest and allows great human wrongs to be committed, a challenge to American exceptionalism and manifest destiny. The possibility bears close scrutiny. Does Eastwood aim to highlight a dialogue between weakness and power — power along all fronts, including the theological — and finally reject all? The last sequence of *Pale Rider* recalls the operatic bullfight at the end of *The Good, the Bad and the Ugly,* with the fighters facing each other in a corrida for the final act.

The director's use of music in *Pale Rider*'s earlier slaughter sequence (the death of Spider, the fool) alludes to *The Seventh Seal,* where the fool figure, Jost, is forced to imitate a bear as the lead-up to being lynched as an "outsider." When the marshal and his deputies — seven in all, a ritual number — line up to kill Spider, strings and a circular bass line are suspended as a prelude to the music of the dance of death: their gunshots. Conversely, when the Preacher arrives to avenge Spider's death (and his own), drums, an oboe, and a clarinet prepare his way. The actual shootout is scored with amplified ambient sound, continuous drumbeats and cymbals, heightened sounds of spurs and gunshots, and wind — again reminiscent of the Spaghetti Westerns.

What does the "end time" flavor of this movie's script say about the ways we should live life today? We live not in apocalyptic fury but in eschatological hope that together we can fashion a better (if not a perfect) world.

The words of theologian Rosemary Radford Ruether could well be adapted to interpret *Pale Rider* and many of Eastwood's other movies. Instead of American exceptionalism, she says, we need to seek "cooperative reciprocity of nations." Instead of a security state, we should support human rights in the United States and worldwide. We should build a "creative community of nations through mutual service." Interfaith cooperation and the redevelopment of local economies reflect our scriptural heritage better than do destructive wars between religions. She summarizes: "Instead of savage exploitation of land, water, and air, we should seek a gentle synergy of human endeavors within our sister earth and all creation."[13]

Pale Rider does not yield to simplistic or convenient analysis. Ambiguity invades its images, music, and narrative structure. However, the questions it raises, particularly about "the flaws in our religious and civic dogmas,"[14] continue to make it a rich and satisfying film to watch and reflect on more than twenty-five years after it was made.

---

13. Ruether, foreword to Vaux, *America in God's World.*
14. Robert Jewett, correspondence with author, November 24, 2010.

Unforgiven

I n 1992, Clint Eastwood's *Unforgiven* opened to critical praise and audience amazement. A film of mesmerizing visual and narrative power, it
dared to tackle the complexities and ambiguities of American history. We
are, after all, a society born of violence, drenched in blood, and perpetuated by aggression that nonetheless struggles to fold into its body politic
democratic ideals of freedom, peacemaking, and tolerance. How do we
tackle such a conflicting and explosive heritage? We usually forget and
move on, continually recreating our national image according to the various templates provided by the rhetoric of our two main political parties.[1]
Even so foundational a transitional passage as the Civil War rarely has surfaced as a conceptual arena to explore the origins of our current problems
(e.g., gang activity, ethnic divisions, anti-immigrant sentiment, affirmative
action and its detractors, and so forth). We rarely visit our own racial history, except briefly at the fortieth anniversary of the death of Martin Luther King, Jr., and recently at the election of Barack Obama. How many
citizens know about the Trail of Tears or realize how many soldiers died as
a result of the Civil War and its aftermath? How many know the number of
men, women, and children sold into slavery or are aware of the brutal

---

1. And with the help of penny novels, tabloids, pulp fiction, movies, TV shows, and
other media that have sought to harness memory and create a semblance of a "national"
(and unified) history, as Benedict Anderson shows in *Imagined Communities: Reflections on
the Origin and Spread of Nationalism* (London: Verso, 1983).

abuse and murders of blacks that extended long after the signing of the Emancipation Proclamation?[2]

Unforgiven explores history and history's meaning. It both tells a story (Will Munny's return to gunfighting) and presents a story about stories (replays of the myth of strong and glorious heroes embodied in westerns). It simultaneously testifies to the vitality of the genre and mercilessly dissects it. As Kent Jones has written:

> With *Unforgiven*, Clint Eastwood's urge (or perhaps desire) to explore the reality of violence bloomed like a hearty desert flower, and it came as a genuine shock. *Unforgiven* took violence, broke it down, and patiently laid out the distinctions between intent, action, and aftermath, a rarity in American movies. Eastwood wasn't merely commenting on his own past, he was speaking to a country whose national profile had been tainted by the righteous postures of self-defense and hubristic bullying and whose commercial images were brimming over with violence.[3]

Eastwood is acutely aware not only of the particulars in the tradition, but also of the power of the myth to express the longings and the tensions of a people on the move. The film offers an ethical vision, not by any tidiness in its plot structure (e.g., an uncomplicated bloodbath or total conversion), but rather by the accumulation of images that convey the fragility of the human condition.[4]

Will Munny, the protagonist, is not drawn either as a blameless hero or as a seamless villain. He is a deeply conflicted person who struggles to carry over his religious convictions into his everyday worlds of work and family. At the movie's start, not only does he believe that he has been forgiven for robbery and murder, but he also realizes that he needs to continue to ask for forgiveness. His wife, Claudia, whose grave he appears to be digging on the far distant horizon imaged in the prologue, would have

2. See David W. Blight, *Race and Reunion: The Civil War in American Memory* (Cambridge, MA: Belknap Press of Harvard University Press, 2001).

3. Kent Jones, *Physical Evidence: Selected Film Criticism* (Middletown, CT: Wesleyan University Press, 2007), 182.

4. Matt Pacult, Northwestern University Eastwood class, Winter 2009, writes: "The formal and narrative qualities of the framing device reveal how Eastwood advocates for a more thorough engagement with the philosophical understanding of time, violence, American and film history, the societal constructions of myths, and the responsibilities one has for the next generation given the imperfect world in which people must live."

introduced him to the central Christian forgiveness narratives: the thief on the cross (Luke 23:39-43) and the woman taken in adultery (John 7:53–8:11). The movie's plot recounts the testing of that forgiveness, radical by any measure. Even if she had lived, though, Will could not be cordoned off from the violence that suffused American society in the postwar years or shielded from the corrosive effects of extreme poverty. By the movie's end, he rides off into a dark and merciless downpour, which simultaneously signals despair over his return to violence and a hope that he might once more reclaim new life.

Nonetheless, the film has drawn criticisms from theologians who are alert to the seductions and threats of myths of "redemptive violence" that are alive in American movies, for example, acute readers of the culture such as Robert Jewett and L. Gregory Jones. Jewett and John Shelton Lawrence have written extensively about "culturally endorsed stories of regeneration through violence," and Jones comments that in *Unforgiven,* "forgiveness is assumed to be impossible or, at most, ineffective. Habits of sin, and more specifically of violence, are inescapable; they cannot be unlearned."[5] Furthermore, Jewett notes, *Unforgiven,* despite its director's claim that it is an antiviolence movie, actually conforms to the plot of the American monomyth: yet another tale of heroic violence that restores community.[6]

Although such criticisms recognize the exploitation of fantasies of American dominance beloved by moviemakers and marketed through comic book figures, they completely ignore the actual cinematic text of *Unforgiven* itself. Viewers must ask: Does *this* film glorify killing? Does it crown a savior on a white horse or in a government-issue cop car who rides into town with guns blazing? The answer is a resounding "No." In fact, the reverse is true. Will Munny is neither the Man With No Name nor Dirty Harry Callahan, although Eastwood welcomed the script enthusiastically in part as "a vehicle to address his developed stance on violence."

5. L. Gregory Jones, *Embodying Forgiveness* (Grand Rapids: Eerdmans, 1995), 73. See also Richard Slotkin, *Gunfighter Nation* (Norman: University of Oklahoma Press, 1992).

6. John Shelton Lawrence and Robert Jewett, *The Myth of the American Superhero* (Grand Rapids: Eerdmans, 2002). The outline of the monomyth is given on p. 6, a co-opting of the biblical redemption story; see also pp. 159-62 for a description of *Unforgiven.* Note that the authors misspell Will Munny's name, calling him "Bill" in several places (160-62). See also the superficial dissection of the film in Clay Motley, "'It's a Hell of a Thing to Kill a Man': Western Manhood in Clint Eastwood's *Unforgiven,*" *Americana: The Journal of American Culture 1900-Present* 3, no. 1 (Spring 2004): http://www.americanpopularculture.com/journal/articles/spring_2004/motley.htm.

According to David Breskin, Eastwood commented: "[I]t could be that the guy has all these violent images portrayed on the screen, and here comes along a piece of material that allows him to do something he's never been able to do in the past — which is to show where it all leads to. To philosophize about what is the value of it all."[7]

First of all, a well-defined frame story encloses the turbulent, confusing, and tragic tale of William Munny's attempt to start afresh. Note, however, that the movie does not "start" with the sight of Will in the mud with the pigs. Its prologue sets the stage for all that follows: images, music, and scrolling text place the events to come through the eyes of a horrified mother whose daughter married a murderer and died young, not at his hands but from smallpox. Note that the text sets the stage for the spectator to believe that Will was actually a murderer, an allegation never proven in a court of law or demonstrated by evidence other than hearsay and Will's own "confessions." By the time the epilogue scrolls down the screen, the question has become *why* the daughter had married a man "known" as a thief and murderer, "a man of notoriously vicious and intemperate disposition." Note, too, that the text issues from the mother's perspective, not from a male voice-over (as in *Million Dollar Baby; Bob le Flambeur;* or *L.A. Confidential* — three famous examples of effective voice-overs) or an omniscient observer, also presumed male.

Most critically, the objective camera and the distancing effect of the framing device remove the inner workings of the plot from the viewer's emotional engagement. The filmgoer remains at a significant distance from the mythmaking that often (usually) spins westerns out of control with worship of violence and the "heroes" that dispense it. The opening frame engages two other perspectives: that of the audience and that of the filmmaker, who controls the order in which the viewer takes in information. In this case, the viewer engages with Will Munny himself, but only after being preprogrammed to dislike and fear him.

The final saloon sequence in the movie, while it does fit the structural expectations of the genre (a showdown between an admired hero and an assortment of villains), is heavily qualified by the cinematography of the scene and by nearly two hours of criticism of killing that has preceded it. The film insistently criticizes the violation or killing of another human be-

7. David Breskin, *Inner Views: Filmmakers in Conversation* (New York: De Capo, 1997), 385. Thanks to Caitlin Kunkel and Austin Presley, Northwestern University Eastwood class, Winter 2009, for this and other notes on the *Unforgiven* plan and script.

ing, and it does so via words, glances, editing strategies, and events, the quiet exchanges that mark Eastwood's careful and deeply human visual style. The conversation between Ned and Will as they ponder whether or not to take on the bounty assignment takes place in a darkened, cramped cabin room that is surrounded by the refreshing green bounty of the farm of Ned and his wife. The leisurely ride from Kansas toward Wyoming crosses lush golden fields; the men reveal the depth of their friendship not through harsh, so-called manly insults but rather through humorous exchanges (the masturbation sequence, for instance). When they finally arrive in Big Whiskey, sex again becomes funny, as Ned and the Kid barely escape death by jumping out a window with their drawers partly down. The campfire scene, discussed in detail below, explores the men's past as they ruminate on death for a good five minutes of screen time. This is hardly the snap-crackle punch of John Wayne in *The Searchers*, for example, which begins with the older man, Ethan, dismissing the younger, Martin, endangering his life, and ends with Ethan (not much of a sleeper) shooting the camp's invader in the back.

The majority of *Unforgiven's* narrative segments specifically call into question any legend that would glamorize or valorize violence. As with many of the scripts Eastwood has filmed, he made few changes to David Webb Peoples's original script of *Unforgiven;* but the ones he did make underscore his antiviolence message. The killing of Davey Boy, the younger cowboy marked for death, is filmed carefully to show in detail not only Ned's inability to kill a man in cold blood, but also his revulsion at the act once Will takes over from him. Davey is portrayed as a fool figure: somewhat slow of speech, he has a high-pitched voice and a sweet and open face. He doesn't die with the flash and explosion of a villain; his death takes long and painful onscreen minutes. The viewer witnesses it through the eyes of the killers themselves, the unwilling Ned and the notably ineffective Will. The ambiguity of the scene is underscored when Munny allows one of the other cowboys to bring the dying boy water.

Will delivers the fatal shot. With the next sequence comes another long meditation on the horrors of murdering — not "killing" — another human being. The Kid disintegrates in tears and remorse for his part in the "Cut Whore Killings" (as the film was originally entitled). Even the final sequence in Greeley's saloon, which many critics view as Will's return to his old ways in joy, not sorrow, is heavily weighted by image and narrative preparation to be interpreted as an aberration, not only for Will, who when sober wished to live in peace, but also for life on this good earth. The

A reborn Will Munny (Eastwood) is nurtured by Delilah the Angel (Anna Levine).

first and last frames of the film — golden tableaux visualizing the imagined beauty of the west — display the quiet corner of the earth where the former gunslinger had hoped to make his home.

We come to know Will Munny as the film progresses: who he is and where his life has taken him. He has come out of Missouri, as the legends announce, with its bloody history of extermination of native peoples and its history of slavery. Missouri was a national ideological battleground, the terrain out of which the Missouri Compromise was carved.[8] Guerrilla warfare raged among the civilian population before and during the Civil War, bloody events that propel the action in *The Outlaw Josey Wales*. The corrosive atmosphere spawned the "God-damn son-of-a-bitch cold-hearted killer," to quote one of the many phrases (always pronounced in stilted, quasi-literary tones) that various characters express about the Will Munny of western legend.

The Civil War is not mentioned in *Unforgiven*. But the uncontrolled violence that emerged from the prewar border wars between Missouri and Kansas and the Civil War itself are referred to repeatedly in this movie, as

8. On February 27, 1821, after a nearly two-year battle over the admission of Missouri to the Union, slavery was prohibited in the new territories north of the 36-degree latitude, but allowed in Missouri, which was admitted as a slave-labor state. Maine was admitted as a free state at the same time. Debate and then violence between slavery and antislavery forces broke out in earnest along the Kansas-Missouri border in 1854, when Kansas was opened up for settlement. By 1856, when the antislavery settlement of Lawrence, Kansas, was attacked by proslavery men from Missouri, the Bleeding Kansas/Missouri border wars were in full swing.

they are in *The Outlaw Josey Wales.* As Rosemary Ruether has observed, the Civil War developed out of centuries-long enslavement and exterminations of blacks and Indians.[9] Even apart from the war's backstory, survivors had been brutalized in battle or in the hideous prisons of Andersonville and Fort Douglas, had seen their friends murdered, and had lost their homes and their livelihood. They saw death all around them — not only death in the war but evidence of death by the millions of their tribesmen and their source of food, the buffalo. Eastwood aims to strip the veneer not only from war movies in general but also from memories of the Civil War itself, a theological and ethical strategy he would follow in 2006 with *Flags of Our Fathers* and *Letters from Iwo Jima,* in 2008 with *Gran Torino,* and in 2009 with *Invictus.*

Despite the destruction and economic dislocation all through the North and the South during the postwar decades, Will never excuses his alleged past actions by referring to the harsh environment of his childhood, though sad and brutalized childhoods comprise part of the genre's staple stories. Rather, he repeatedly admits (both when sober and when drunk) that he has committed at least some of the acts ascribed to him in legend. In the main portion of the film's narrative, he reflects on those acts in the context of religious belief and the law: they were wrong. Specifically, he implicitly refuses the label of "redeemer," "avenger," "judge," when he says of one of his past victims, "He didn't do anything to deserve [his death at my hands]." The notion of "deserving" death carries with it the implication that someone, perhaps the angel of death or the avenging angel, judges and then exacts punishment. But judgment and execution are found wanting. Ned, who at first believed that the cowboys "deserved" to die for cutting up a woman, decisively refuses to avenge that act.

When the Schofield Kid first appears at Will's farm nine minutes into the film, he delivers to Will a short lesson on the myth of the western hero, in case we have forgotten its details: murder without remorse; fearlessness;

---

9. "The treatment of Indians and blacks became the models for how America should deal with other 'inferior races'; they should be either exterminated or enslaved." Ruether further observes the "racial exclusivism" of the rhetoric of manifest destiny: the new nation was identified with white, Protestant Christianity. Unbelievably, this same rhetoric emerged repeatedly during the political campaign and party primaries that led up to the 2008 election, with Sarah Palin's references to the "real America" (i.e., white Americans) and "white voters," who would naturally vote, Palin assumed, for Hillary Clinton or herself, not for a black man. See Ruether, *America, Amerikkka: Elect Nation and Imperial Violence* (New York: Equinox, 2007), chap. 3, esp. 72-73.

the fracturing of social boundaries; the killing of innocent women and children. He recounts for Will the various *stories* he has heard from his uncle Pete about Will's exploits, stories that Will either does not remember or has chosen to forget: "Are you the same Will Munny who . . . ?" Will responds: "I ain't like that no more, kid. 'Twas whiskey done it, much as anything else. My wife, she — cured me of that. Cured me of drinkin' an' wickedness." This exchange provides us with *fabula* (story) details, except that many of the Kid's details may be exaggerated or wrong, storytellings that satisfy the needs of the myth and fit the tellers' fantasies.[10]

The Kid reflects those legends, serving up variations of old ones and introducing new ones with odd, artificial flourish, always contrasting Will's present behavior with what emotions or actions Will Munny, as a hero of a certain kind of myth, ought to display. The lines of the legend are these: Will is a cold-hearted, ruthless, fearless man who has killed without remorse or reason. "You was the meanest . . . on account of you're as cold as the snow. You don't have no weak nerve nor fear." The Kid himself tries to mold his own behavior according to these versions of the western myth.[11] "Gon' kill a coupla no-good cowboys," he announces as the purpose of his mission, as though killing is justified if the victims are known to be evil (defined as "bounty-hunters" or "mutilators of women"). Some fifteen years after the end of the Civil War, this young boy seeks a protector, a patron, a "big man" under whom he can learn the killing trade — a classic setup for a child soldier, as William Murphy points out.[12] The Kid's

10. English Bob's story, as relayed by his chronicler Beauchamp, thoroughly shows the ease with which legends are created, embellished, and perpetuated. English Bob, however, is thoroughly discredited by Little Bill's "witness," while Bill himself does seem to validate the litany of evil deeds that haunts Will: "[Are you] the same William Munny who blew up the train in sixty-nine, killing women and children?" Ned also corroborates a certain number of the stories, at least the ones that haunt Will the most: the drover and the man whose name he has taken.

11. The figure of the Kid suggests the infamous Billy the Kid (real name: William Bonney), a self-created screwball who murdered randomly until his death at twenty-one in 1881. He is one of the first media stars to capture the American public's imagination. Is this another "what if" situation? What if Billy the Kid had been sickened by killing after his first murder, as Edward Buscombe suggests in *Unforgiven* (London: BFI Modern Classics, 2004), 34? What if Munny had refused to accept the Kid as his apprentice in killing, exhorting him instead to refrain from murder, as Walt Kowalski pleads with Thao in *Gran Torino*?

12. William Murphy, professor of anthropology at Northwestern University, in an unpublished manuscript on child soldiers and language in Sierra Leone, which he has shared with the author.

stilted language reflects his schooling in brutality at the hands of a big man: like a catechism, it repeats certain key phrases.

But *Unforgiven* as a movie neither advertises nor promotes the murder of Delilah's two violators. It distinguishes visually between the principal culprit, Mike, and his simple partner, Davey. It does not applaud the violent purging activities of Little Bill and his deputies — the brutal beating of English Bob — which ironically takes place on July 4, Independence Day, before a horrified audience, including his own deputies. The merciless near-fatal beating of Will and the whipping death of Ned add to the picture of the sheriff as a sadist. When English Bob is beaten, the camera looks at Little Bill from the ground up, emphasizing the man's 6-foot-4-inch frame and his menacing features. Will is weak and feverish when Little Bill brutalizes him. And as Ned is being whipped, we glimpse not only the man's anguished face but also his killer's delight in the pain of his victim. Eastwood the director here represents violence as abhorrent, not manly or cleansing.

In the final saloon scene, for instance, the natural setting, low light, and prowling camera sniff out each man's fear of death and emphasize the senselessness of the bloodbath. Will Munny has not been endowed with superhuman qualities. He is given neither star-lighting nor image-boosting that would seduce viewers into wishing that he stain himself with these murders. Every step of the film deglamorizes such extreme acts. As Richard Locke has written, "The film's relentlessly dark style prevents it from glamorizing this sordid violence and the man who dispenses it."[13]

Will is not a slickly marketed hero who puts on or takes off his disguise and emerges from the darkness shouting that he is the savior of the world (or America, or the city of Gotham). The protagonist is a man much like everyone else, but a man who has tried to shake off his bloody past. He clearly announces his past actions as wrong and takes the consequences of his actions, even his final, murderous ones, upon himself. For Will has been changed radically by his love for Claudia. Eastwood has yet again reworked a long-standing plot device in the western: the transformation of a (bad) man through the love of a woman. He refuses to sentimentalize, trivialize, or romanticize the love of Will and Claudia, whose surname, Feathers, suggests either an Indian or a dancehall ancestry. For

---

13. Richard Locke, "Grand Horse Opera," *The American Scholar* (Summer 2008): 135. "There is nothing heroic about these murders; they will only lead to barbaric replication ad infinitum."

three years after Claudia's death, Will sustained his reformed life through narrative (the reciting of her virtues and her teachings, and what that love meant to him) and relationships (his children, the land, his animals). His constant refrain, "I ain't like that no more," establishes an ethical norm in the movie where "wrong" means "to kill other humans." Will is trying to develop a new identity with a new center, a restored "character" shaped by the "habit of practicing virtue," creating a new and converted life. As the movie reveals, that's a tough task when undertaken during severe economic hardships of settling land — and without the support of a surrounding community.

The fragile economy of the Kansas that Will and his children inhabit was destroyed by market forces. Some would say that they were cursed by living in a land that belonged to the indigenous tribes, now dead or displaced. Droughts and plagues of locusts descended on the state in the 1870s; the plague of 1874 nearly destroyed all crops. Starvation threatened the settlers, and it was also during those years that the state was flooded with cattlemen and their herds in the millions, who were looking for railway passage from Texas through Kansas and Missouri to markets in the East. The television series *Rawhide,* which gave Eastwood his first starring role, recounted those drives, as did the movie *Red River* (Howard Hawks, 1948). Will's pigs' sickness may well have come from those herds, which were later quarantined.

Set in historical context, then, the Kid's proposal would appeal to a man with a family to feed. Criticisms that Will is easily seduced or is charmed by the memory of his past ignore these historical facts and the misery of his life, which the visuals in the beginning of the film make painfully clear. Will is no longer a creation of legend or a conscious maker of legend, the stories we create to keep chaos at bay when faced with life's disorder. The film's images reinforce this. Since Eastwood shoots with natural light and on location and rarely uses stunt doubles, Will's spills in the mud and struggles with his horse feel natural, even personally painful. The pace of the editing reinforces this sense of weariness: it is rather slow, giving time for situations (falls, bungled target practice, missed mounts) to play out their sense of age and desperation.

The first scene in Greeley's saloon, about one-third of the way into the film, underscores the tired old man's fallibility. Will does not respond to taunts with guns blazing, as the genre demands, or because he is nobly self-restraining like Shane, or because he has sworn off fighting, as Will Kane did in *High Noon*. The reason he doesn't fight back is simply that he is ill, his gunpowder is wet, and he is still strongly under the influence of his dead wife.

Even without those qualifiers, Will is poorly suited to behave like a macho man who angers and strikes in the continuous present. He is struggling under posttraumatic stress disorder — the profound depression that sinks a person who cannot shake off nightmares and flashbacks of horrific events. The night before, as the three men huddled around their pitiful campfire, they questioned not only whether they did what others say they did, but *whether what they did was right,* making plain the connections between apocalyptic events and ethics. The horror of Will's memories — his confession to a receptive Ned and an uncomprehending Kid — gives rise to conscience. The killings were not only wrong but disgusting, defiling, and foul. Will reflects on killing and death in ways that depart from the formulaic rehearsals of his sins that he had displayed earlier for his children ("I seen the error of my ways . . . the sins of my youth") or even his confessions to Ned ("Claudia . . . cleared me o' drinkin' whiskey an' all. Just cause we're goin' on this killing, that don't mean I'm goin' to go back to being the way I was. I just need the money"). He meditates on the concrete effects of pulling a trigger.

Extreme close-ups of Ned's and Will's faces allow Will's deadened delivery to convey more power than his words, as he begins what will become a refrain of recollections on the brutal facts of death, memories of what happens when a bullet rips into a skull or a chest. Teeth fly out the back of the head, brains spill out — an image that recalls a passage in the *Iliad*:

> Then his teeth flew out; from two sides,
> Blood came to his eyes; the blood that from lips and nostrils
> He was spilling, open-mouthed; death enveloped him
>   in its black cloud.
>
> (Book XVI)[14]

Of the drover, to whom Will refers in his ravings: "He didn't do anything to deserve to get shot." Will has abandoned whatever superiority he enjoyed as hero of a legend; he is "just a fella now . . . no different than anyone else — no more."

Will has tried to live with the consequences of his acts, though he seems doomed to recall the acts themselves — endlessly, without relief —

14. Translated by Samuel Butler: http://classics.mit.edu/Homer/iliad.html.

The sun sets over Claudia's grave and Will's vengeance.

as do the protagonists of *Saving Private Ryan* (Steven Spielberg, 1998), *A Very Long Engagement* (Jean Jeunet, 2004), and *Flags of Our Fathers* (Eastwood, 2006). The narrated memories of violent deaths, deaths that he himself caused, echo the constant visual reminders of Will's own mortality, his trouble catching hogs and repeated difficulties mounting his horse. He blames both failures on his earlier mistreatment of animals, but his son's shrug and sober glance at his little sister tell the viewer that their father's powers are failing. He can no longer sleep on the ground without discomfort and illness; he is slow, tired, and sick during most of the film's scenes. Will, Ned, English Bob, and Little Bill are all of a "certain age," totally unlike themselves as figures in their legends.[15] Heroes do not age, and heroes of westerns do not reflect on the morality of their actions. Legends

15. The protagonist in the original script was 35-40, which would fit into the post–Civil War profile. Eastwood held onto the script for about ten years to be sure that he was old enough to fit the way he conceived of the role, as Richard Schickel reports (Richard Schickel, *Clint Eastwood: A Biography* [New York: Vintage Books, 1996], 453). He gathered around him men of around the same age: Morgan Freeman, Gene Hackman, and Richard Harris.

not only inflate deeds and conflate versions of stories, but they also stop time: they defeat aging and death itself, freezing the hero in the endless present.

Little Bill, unlike English Bob and the Kid, insists on telling the truth about both written accounts of western history and the human condition. All the men in this film (and also all the women) are violent. In another intensely theological film about evil, *Le Cercle Rouge* (*The Red Circle*, Jean-Pierre Melville, 1970), the police commissioner articulates this view of human nature:

"All men are guilty. They are born innocent, but it doesn't last."

"Even policemen?" asks his operative.

"All men," he responds.

If civilization is to progress in this wild country, Little Bill reasons, strong men must hold absolute power and must eliminate the weak. In Big Whiskey, he dispenses justice with complete abandon because he is technically within the law — his law. He enforces morality, a rejection of violence, by means of violence. In Little Bill's theology, human nature is as violent and as lawless as nature itself. Edward Buscombe notes: "Doggett is a man with a past who is trying to live it down, and no more than Munny can he lay his demons to rest. At least he has the law on his side, his brutality covered with the fig-leaf of legal authority."[16] "Reality," in this version of the west, is not simply what is shaped and told about the past or what is shaped and written, but also what the legends of the west itself reveal about human nature.

Despite the collapse of Little Bill's and Will's ethical universe, Eastwood satisfies the viewer's desire for engagement, puzzle, and hope for renewal: rebirth for the individual and reconstitution of the fragile social order in a new community. *Unforgiven* constructs a solid ethical structure where killing is presented as wrong, whether undertaken for vengeance, money, or justice; the sale of human beings (prostitution) is deglamorized; and we are reminded that slavery was abolished in theory less than twenty-five years before the story begins (1878). The ideal community, one that

16. Schickel, in *Clint Eastwood*, thinks that Eastwood had the beating of Rodney King and the image of Daryl Gates, police chief of the LAPD, in mind when he created this character. He also could have been referring to the debates inside the Christian church during and after the Civil War era. Churchmen endlessly quoted Romans 13:1-6 to defer to authorities, as English Bob pontificates: "Men must defer to the aura of royalty." Defenders of segregation during the Civil Rights years endlessly quoted Romans as well. But the appeal to "law and order" was countered by a higher conception of the Law, one based on Jesus' teachings.

Eastwood envisions, abhors violence and leans toward peace: Ned refuses to shoot Little Davey ("I can't, Will") and rides away from the death squad, and the Kid sobs with disgust and remorse after he has shot one of the "villains" at close range.

Two sequences balance death's horrors with life's regenerative power: the deathbed scene in the mountain cabin outside Big Whiskey and the morning when Will awakens from his own near-death. As he lies dying, Will "sees" the angel of death and "sees" his wife — not only on the plane of spiritual reality, as Ned thinks, but at the level of phenomenon (physical reality), that is, as her rotting corpse would appear if exhumed. The dying man's head is supported by his beloved friend as the Kid looks on, all three figures barely illuminated by a flickering fire. The tableau recalls paintings and sculptures of the Virgin Mary cradling the head of the dead Christ (such as, for example, Michelangelo's *Pietà*). Will lies at the point of death for three days, sustained by Ned's tender care and by the food and water of the prostitutes. The shack where he lies is situated "outside the camp," far removed from the so-called civilization of Big Whiskey, its outcasts hidden from the faces of the respectable. (But note that we see almost no one in Big Whiskey except Little Bill and his deputies: no children, no women except the prostitutes, no school, no church.)

Recall that Sergio Leone used the iconography of the resurrection at the end of *Fistful of Dollars,* when the Man With No Name comes back from death and appears in a cloud on the main street. As the man pulls aside his poncho to reveal his secret device (the iron plate that has protected his heart), he shifts from the mystical to the rational world. Eastwood removes Leone's clever debunking of mysticism in *Unforgiven.* The dying man is sustained and brought back to life not by magic but by the sustained care of the prostitutes and his friends. Only the ancient formula (three days in a tomb for our defeated hero) remains the same.

The sequence that depicts Will's near-death is the climax of the succession of shifting postures toward death in the film. "I seen the Angel of Death. . . . He got snake eyes. . . . I'm scared of dyin'. I seen Claudia, too. . . . Her face was all covered with worms. I'm scared. . . . Don't tell nobody. Don't tell my kids none of the things I done, hear me?" He means: Don't poison my children's memory with these tales, real or legendary.[17]

---

17. The symbolic resonance shines through, remembering Job 19:25-26: "For I know that my redeemer lives, and at last he will stand upon the earth; and after my skin has been thus destroyed, then from my flesh I shall see God. . ." (RSV): http://ebible.org/kjv/Job.htm.

In the cave-like enclosure of the mountain, Eastwood captures the inexpressible experience of being near death, which he re-creates fourteen years later in *Letters from Iwo Jima*. His films are full of campfire scenes of confession, where characters assess their lives and deal with guilt: *The Gauntlet, Pale Rider, A Perfect World. Gran Torino* includes two confessions, a false one and a real one. In *Unforgiven*, Will attempts to put words to the recurring nightmares that even his conversion was unable to quell. Will's feelings on committing his first murder have been transposed and put into the mouth of the Kid.

For death is "really" like Young Davey's, with blood and thirst and abandonment. It is the end of the life we know, and we should not glamorize it, as the Kid realizes when he actually kills a living, breathing human being. When men are drunk, they may kill heedlessly; when they become sober, they have to drink again to forget that they have "take[n] away all [a man's] got, and all he's ever gonna have": his breath, his earthiness (humanity, from *humus,* means "from the earth"), and his spiritual identity.

The prostitute Delilah, whose slashing had set the revenge plot in motion, visits Will's hideout. She is a fragile but lovely young woman whose inner loveliness has not been ravaged by her afflictions; rather, she is lit with angelic radiance.[18] As she gives the weakened man food and drink, the exchange unfolds slowly and delicately. Munny says, "You ain't ugly like me. It's just we've both got scars. You're a beautiful woman." The extreme close-up on Delilah's face conveys her pleasure in his compliment. Her gentleness, soft voice, delicate frame, simplicity, and admiration for his fidelity to his wife bespeak her inner goodness. In a two-shot, she is framed as his equal against a radiant blue sky. But hers is an angelic radiance. Her tenderness visually echoes Ned's motherly care for the dying Will, as he cradled his old friend's head on his lap.

A standard Hollywood film would have ended here, with Will healed, Delilah rescued from her sordid life and married to Will, and the two friends and Delilah riding back home safely for an emotional reunion with their families. Indeed, the original script for *Unforgiven* played with the romance angle.[19] The Kid would have had glasses made and gotten a job in a shoestore. Will's farm would grow sunflowers and soybeans, and his chil-

---

18. Eastwood uses women carefully: sometimes they are young, innocent, and fragile, like Laura Lee in *The Outlaw Josey Wales* or Delilah in *Unforgiven;* sometimes they are feisty catalysts for the action, like Strawberry Alice in *Unforgiven* or Sue in *Gran Torino*.

19. Caitlin Kunkel and Austin Presley, presentation in Northwestern University Eastwood class, Winter 2009.

dren would become lawyers. In the old westerns, the hero and heroine took off into the sunset to settle down on a farm or went to California to rear a family.

However, Eastwood imagines a much deeper and more profound agenda. Working backwards from the final frame, we hear a rumor that Will and the kids moved to California, where he became a successful capitalist. Ned is dead. The Kid disappears, shattered by the trauma of killing another human being at close range. Eastwood has caught the young man at the moment of his first murder. In Terrence Malick's *The Thin Red Line*, a nervous young soldier, Doll, about to leave Guadalcanal, boasts that "I killed a man and no one can touch me for it."[20] The Kid, by contrast, immediately feels the horror; he resolves to "never kill no one, ever again."

From the perspective of 1992, Eastwood, a student of war and war films, looked back and examined two world wars, Hiroshima and Nagasaki, the firebombing of the German cities and Tokyo, the cold war, and a string of wars America either plunged into or started. Moving to 2003, Eastwood said that he did not support the invasion of Iraq.[21] Seen in the broader context of devastating wars, the bloodbath sequence in the saloon makes sense. Via his camerawork and pacing, Eastwood comments on the endless cycle of violence that made its way into sophisticated weaponry. The poverty and diminished vision of Big Whiskey's men give yet another signal of the price humans pay to continue their battles.

The saloon sequence activates the film's suppressed genre elements: purification of a polluted space by searing violence. A lone gunman seeks personal revenge. But Eastwood handles the elements with care. Paradoxically, it is impelled by love of his friend that Will appears to emerge as the quintessential hero of the myth, the one who commits the unthinkable, killing unarmed men in the name of an enlarged conception of justice that transcends Little Bill's petty tyranny. Ned has "died for what we done," as

20. Cited in Michel Chion, *La Ligne Rouge* (first published in London by BFI in English in 2004), 74-75: "Nobody can touch me for it." To paraphrase: "It isn't simply a question of murder, it's that in wartime, no one recognizes killing as murder. You cannot be disturbed by committing murder or expect to be pardoned." The writer notes the similarity in that justification for murder and that of Cain in justifying of the murder of his brother.

21. Quoted online at Breitbart.com: The United States's goal of trying to impose democracy on Iraq was flawed, Eastwood said: "I wasn't for going in there. Only because democracy isn't something that you get overnight. I don't think America got democracy overnight. It's something we had to fight for and believe in": http://www.breitbart.com/article.php?id=070209031318.4mdxg006&show_article=1.

Will says, died *exactly*, not *symbolically* as his wife had, for Will's sins. He is the scapegoat Will seemed to need to purify his own tortured conscience.

The Will who enters Greeley's saloon the second time, gun barrel positioned approximately where it would be if the moviegoer were holding the gun, is a Will reborn not simply of whiskey and his own bloody past but also of Ned's sacrifice in the name of all that keeps human society from degenerating into a living embodiment of death, full of worms and snakes.

Conflicting versions of a savior theme are held in tension at the end: the redeemer as cleanser, like the rain (think of *Pulp Fiction*); the redeemer as an agent of transformation who steps into a social and religious void; the redeemer as the wish-fulfillment of a passive and misled viewing public. The killings can be seen as driven by the whiskey Will consumes, alluding to the American myth of purifying justice by violence, or the opposition to killing and torture performed in the name of civilization, where the viewer experiences the hideous death act as a personal violation of human dignity. Any one-dimensional glorification of violence, however, has been undercut by the film's rejection of violence, even as the film's dramatic structure appears to push the story to its explosive conclusion.

The writer Beauchamp is thrilled to witness a "real" savior at work. Note, though, that in the larger scheme of the movie, Beauchamp is portrayed repeatedly as a gullible and confused fool, and the adventures he seeks to immortalize, those of English Bob, are exposed as total frauds. Might his reaction to Will's killing, which could be taken on the surface as praise for violence, be discounted as one more proof of his idiocy, identical to the viewer's own thrill of delight as the guns start blazing?

Unforgiven dares to turn ideas about justice and community upside down. Its text asks again and again when, if ever, we need to kill; it insists that as flawed human beings we can and must be redeemed by love. Myths and legends of the old west perpetuate our violent heritage. But *Unforgiven* recognizes, dissects, and rejects this destructive code. As Richard Locke has written about *The Man Who Shot Liberty Valance* (1962), "the entire film is a dramatic analysis of the evolution and problematic value of heroic Western legends."[22]

Unforgiven's ending allows multiple interpretations, which can range from disgust about its gratuitous violence to violence appropriate to the context to complete rejection of violence. If you commit violence to right violence, then you are trapped. Might forgiveness offer a way out? The cut

22. Locke, "Grand Horse Opera," 133.

prostitute wants to forgive, but the community won't let her. Eastwood's way of treating violence is thoughtful and carefully reasoned, yet there's no resolution. Ambiguity — uncertainty about what this film "means" — remains long after the movie is finished, and so does its powerful mise en scène: the isolated cabin rimmed by distant mountains and lit in the golden sunset; the hotel, which represents the little that exists of family, communal meals, and human connection in this town; Little Bill's crooked house, a physical symbol of his desire to create a civilization with his own hands according to his own (crooked) code; and the near-death sequence in the hideout cabin. But ambiguity, as Mikhail Bakhtin has observed about Dostoevsky's novels, marks a great narrative.[23]

23. *Problems of Dostoevsky's Poetics*, ed. and trans. Caryl Emerson (Minneapolis: University of Minnesota Press, 1984), passim.

PART II

The Mysteries of Life

When *Mystic River* appeared in 2003, critics and Eastwood fans felt that something new had happened in his work. If they had seen *Bird* in 1988, *White Hunter, Black Heart* in 1990, or *Unforgiven* in 1992, however, neither the concepts nor the tone would have seemed so strange. Once the audiences had considered the range of subjects Eastwood had explored previously — multiple facets of the American experience, from out-of-control capitalism in *High Plains Drifter* to poverty, bust, and hope in *Honkytonk Man* — they would have perceived a slow yet marked shift from a concern with the workings of earthly justice (a legacy of Eastwood's favored film *The Ox-Bow Incident*) toward increasing attention to events in his characters' lives that exceeded their ability to understand or their strength to bear.

Mystic River brings into full focus the theological undertones of *The Outlaw Josey Wales*: the deaths of Josey's wife and little boy; the wrenching sorrow of the father, bowed like Job; and the inexplicable madness of war. Who or what allows or even causes human suffering? Has the universe slipped out of control? Does a benevolent deity inflict injury not only far in excess of perceived wrongdoing but also randomly on human creatures, even on little children, who know no guile and have done no wrong? Or does every violent act originate in human freedom and will?

In *Mystic River*, the moviegoer feels the weight of these questions: the viewer lives inside the head of an abused child and a grieving father, and experiences a despoiled American neighborhood in simultaneously observed moments of the plot as it slips toward an unsettled conclusion.

The group of the Eastwood's films I discussed in Part I, all westerns, probed the stumbling course of earthly justice, particularly as felt by people who live on the edges of American society: women, native Americans, blacks, criminals, the homeless, war veterans, children, the elderly, and, most of all, the poor. The social order shown in those films — not their "plot summaries" but their actual substance — shows not the triumph of the American dream but rather the fractured lives of its victims and the rippling effects of genocide and land theft. Richard Locke refers perceptively to the "moral, even moralistic," cast in *High Plains Drifter* and *Pale Rider,* the "two elegant, fluent, beautifully constructed" westerns. In *Unforgiven,* moreover, the disturbing elements of its rich plot — what happened, who's to blame, what can be done — take on a distinctively theological cast of innocence and guilt, blame, confession, exoneration, and forgiveness more troubling and yet more grave than the vengeance story itself. The arresting shot of Will Munny flailing in the mud with his sick pigs captures the sad fall of a man once reborn and now desperate, locked into an economic system imperiled by the postwar beef economy and cattle disease. Once (reportedly) a man of violence, he has tried to limit the amount of damage he now brings into the world by giving up the alcohol that fueled his destructive behavior and by building a home for his family. Bad luck, the death of his wife from smallpox, is followed by the sickness of his animals — diseases with possible human or social causes, but each touched nonetheless by unfathomable mystery. The last great western "never stoops to sentimentality or glamour (or reverse chic) and is never self-important or vain. It's an inexorable condemnation of the Western gunman as a psychotic monster."[1]

Two years before *Unforgiven* was released, *White Hunter, Black Heart* had appeared, a movie little seen or known even among Eastwood's biggest fans. A film about "American arrogance and power," Jonathan Rosenbaum has written, its main character, John Wilson (Eastwood, playing film director John Huston), penetrates deep into the Congo to film a movie *(The African Queen).* But he is obsessed with killing an elephant rather than intent on making a movie. That desire to kill a magnificent creature of nature leads to the death of an innocent man and the awakening of Wilson's conscience. While he revels in thinking early in the film that he would commit not only a "crime" but also a "sin," his friend and guide is killed instead. When Wilson returns from his disastrous elephant hunt to face the man's

---

1. Richard Locke, "Grand Horse Opera," *The American Scholar* (Summer 2008): 134.

grieving family and village, the force of "sin" strikes him. The universe itself weeps at the tragedy: the life of a good man, a tribal leader, has been destroyed because of the pride and presumption of a madman.

In the westerns in Part I, and in the deeply personal movies in Part II, crimes are more than mysteries for detectives to solve. They beg for tears. But most of all, they beg for answers: Why has this happened? Who is responsible?

The questions are not new, and the responses animate all great works of art: Rachel weeps because her children are no more (Jer. 31:15; Matt. 2:18); bombs are dropped on Dresden and throughout Europe, killing hundreds of thousands of German civilians and most of the pilots themselves; schools, hospitals, and prisons collapse in Haiti due to faulty construction and population density, killing a quarter of a million people; a driver loses control of his car and plows across a Little League field, killing or severely wounding all the team's seven-year-old children; a plane overshoots the runway, killing a six-year-old boy who is sitting in the car outside his house waiting for his father.

A baby dies at five days, or five minutes, or five years on the Trail of Tears, or in Hiroshima, or in an Afghan village, strafed by Israeli bombers or blown to bits by Palestinian missiles, swept away by a raging flood in New Orleans or shot in the arms of its mother on the streets of Los Angeles or Chicago. Or she peacefully expires in a state-of-the-art hospital nursery in a well-fed, affluent, highly developed city in the United States, or in her crib at home a few steps away from her sleeping parents.

How do we wrap our minds around such events? Yet we must. And I submit that Eastwood is one of the few American directors to think intentionally about the problem of evil as something other than a Technicolor or digitalized subject to divert audiences and feed their thirst for distanced retributive violence. In *Mystic River* and *Changeling,* the crimes involve frightful acts of violence — acts of violence against children — that may or may not be connected with human agents. Even the accident in *Million Dollar Baby* is caused indirectly by child neglect or abuse, as we see when the movie starkly details its heroine's abusive family and observes the corrosive surroundings from which Maggie was frantic to escape.

A Perfect World provides a transition from *Unforgiven* to Eastwood's current fertile period, not only in its searching title but also in its link between child abuse and a young adult's suffering. Red Garnett (Eastwood), the Texas Ranger, sends the young Butch Haynes (Kevin Costner) to prison to protect him from an abusive father who otherwise would have killed him. Yet Butch's suffering has no end: despite his attempt to reach Alaska, the "perfect world" where he dreamed his childhood might be restored, he will never get there. He only lays hold of an elusive and fleeting present.

A Perfect World was released in 1993, unheralded despite its stars (Eastwood, Kevin Costner, and Laura Dern). It would be ten more years before Eastwood, in *Mystic River,* would recapture the similarly intense rhythm of a theological quest woven into an apparently simple thriller. Who murdered Katie, the only child of the widower Jimmy Markum and Maria, his beloved wife who has died? The murder becomes entangled with another crime, the four-day sexual abuse of Jimmy's childhood friend, a troubling event that has haunted the entire neighborhood for twenty-five years. Nothing can ever bring back the boy's innocence and put his world to right.

Eastwood's mysteries have intensified with each year's stunning output. In *Million Dollar Baby,* why is Maggie poor? Why is the wise man Scrap condemned to live in a back room in the gym where he sweeps the floors and cleans the toilets? How can the rupture between father and daughter ever be mended? And what happened to Walter Collins, the abducted son of a loving single mother? *Changeling* sets out on a multilayered quest to wrest the answer from the universe itself.

The universal questions embedded in Eastwood's westerns (the search for justice in a puzzling and brutal world) are now set in vastly different surroundings: a poor Boston neighborhood; a seedy corner of Los Angeles; and a corrupt city that could be anywhere. They take on even greater urgency as the distance between four appealing stories, all of which also feature strong women, is brought close to our own time and the price of injustice made glaringly, heartbreakingly human. The viewer seeks answers but finds only layers of questions woven into the films' dense, poetic textures.

Mystic River

During their decades as teachers and coaches, my mother and father fed and sheltered thousands of boys and girls — farm kids and children of immigrants who sought refuge in factory towns throughout the Midwest, displaced by the gross political upheavals of World War II. Mother and Dad welcomed little boys and girls who had too little to eat on their hardscrabble farms or in crowded flats from Pittsburgh to northern Indiana to Chicago. By day they taught them the same skills — reading, writing, problem-solving, and critical thinking — that future generations of these children might later learn at private schools; by night they taught the parents how to find a job, shop, and survive in an alien land. Ever the historian, my father continually reminded us that not so long ago our own ancestors had emigrated from war-torn parts of Europe to make a new life in the "Promised Land," and just so, we should welcome our new neighbors and help them to find their own way.

In the world that Clint Eastwood portrays in *Mystic River*, rescue lines of the kind my parents offered do not exist for the three boys whose story the film follows, modern descendants of the Irish immigrants who landed in America as refugees from the massive potato famine of the mid-nineteenth century. Instead, the movie quickly and hellishly descends through vivid images of borderline poverty (crowded houses, concrete play spaces, gaunt cheeks, absent parents) on the sensory level, lowering into a grim narrative parable about the consequences of abandonment, of a neglected and abused child, a fragile neighborhood, and the lost sense of human decency. In dire circumstances, if you or your child is harmed, who's going to avenge you? Not the police, but your kin. And it will be revenge in blood sacrifice, a tribal response that still obtains in too many parts of our world today. Distant news images of Afghanistan, Bosnia, Rwanda, Congo, or Sudan come to mind. Yet here, even in this corrosive little corner of contemporary South Boston, only your kinship network (a false and exclusive "community") "has your back."

In Eastwood's 2003 movie, Dave Boyle (Tim Robbins, in an Oscar-winning performance), the child sufferer who escapes death at the hands of sexual predators, becomes a sacrificial victim to avenge another death in his own neighborhood, within his own family. How can we parse the sense of justice in a lifelong death sentence like his? As it engages the religiously freighted justice language of *Unforgiven* ("Deserve's got nothin' to do with it"), *Mystic River* reveals a part of the universe seemingly devoid of a spectrum along which innocence and guilt can be tracked and punishment meted out by an all-seeing and benevolent deity.

Mystic River upends the redemptive plot of *Hang 'Em High* or *The Outlaw Josey Wales,* where a person who survives rape, lynching, or assassination ultimately finds primal vengeance endlessly debilitating and turns toward love, forgiveness, and reconciliation. It lacks the strong redemptive narrative of Eastwood's other films, in part because it lacks the empathetic voice of a chorus figure to witness and interpret events and contrast them with a better way to live. The camera provides the commentary. It shows plainly the barren space where the three boys play, unprotected; the intense unreality of the lush park where Katie is murdered and her father's violent vengeance is unleashed; the uncomfortable close-ups of Dave's delusional nightmares and jumbled thoughts; and the poison spit out hesitatingly with Celeste's confession of Dave's "guilt" or Annabeth's seduction of her remorseful husband.

But it would be easy to lose this harrowing and deeply disturbing movie in abstract theorizing about tragedy, sacrifice, and evil when its genius lies in its palpable, gritty particulars — the rumbling Bach-like bass line as Dave rants about vampires and wolf-boys; the close-ups of a sorrowing face of a father who has been ravaged by the murder of the child of his bosom; and the film's deeply evocative opening, a telling sequence in which the director captures the confined and corroded atmosphere in which eleven-year-olds Jimmy Markum (Sean Penn, also Oscar-winning), Sean Devine (Kevin Bacon), and Dave seek to move out of childhood into adolescence.

The movie begins with a long God's-eye aerial pan across Boston Harbor that sweeps past the lattice of back-yard porches in South Boston's three-deckers, rickety havens that provide fathers with escape from the street out front where their boys play. We barely see or hear the men, who are cut out of our direct visual field. Theirs is a rudimentary culture of beer and baseball, with too little work to season the long summer days. These men, as a friend who resided in Boston has observed, are the "Southies" who threw rocks at buses in the early seventies (approximately the same time as the movie takes place), when the courts had ordered busing to desegregate schools.

It was their kids who retreated at the end of the day to tiny kitchens and cramped bedrooms, closed-in spaces that mirrored a social and familial world where nothing they ever did was right. Eastwood's camera captures the peeling paint and claustrophobic interiors as markers of ever-increasing economic decline. Today as I write, Boston's signature dwellings "are being foreclosed on at disproportional rates, left to decay and even razed," according to reporter Abby Goodnough. Whereas for generations the three-deckers provided "an affordable and reasonably spacious place to live" for late-nineteenth-century immigrants, today three-family homes "represent 14 percent of the housing stock but make up 21 percent of foreclosed property."[1] The "gentrification" of the world of *Mystic River* to which the adult Jimmy Markum obliquely refers appears nowhere today, nor does any real threat of urban renaissance touch the movie's dense, doomed sense of place.

Stepping outside, the camera turns to three boys passing the time playing street hockey and talking about their future. For hooligan Jimmy, a future crime boss, being grown up means driving a car, even if he has to "borrow" one to drive around the block. Stuck in the here and now, though, a sewer abruptly swallows their ball — and their lives with it. Idled now, they draw their names in fresh cement, providing an opening for two predators to invoke the image of the law against their transgression.

With a few cinematic strokes, a luxurious black car driven by a man with a badge, his passenger adorned with crosses at his neck and on his ring, drives up, and young Dave, whose single mother lives on another

1. Abby Goodnough, "Hard Times for New England's 3-Deckers," *The New York Times*, June 20, 2009, A1-3. Goodnough notes that Dennis Lehane, who wrote the novel *Mystic River*, on which the film is based, grew up in Dorchester, a "tough neighborhood in East Boston." He commented to Goodnough: "There's a sublime beauty about them. Anything that is a unique characteristic of a region, that really tells you where you are, is exciting; it gives flavor."

Jimmy (Sean Penn) is sacrificed to the rituals of violence.

street, disappears into the ominous cavern of the vehicle. This lovely child, large and ungainly, poor, fatherless, innocent-eyed — his "difference" marked in every frame — gets into the car. His plaintive gaze at his friends out the back window is captured by the camera in a steady shot, echoed at film's end when the adult Dave is similarly abducted by the men who will murder him.

After young Dave is kidnapped, the film tumbles toward chaos. In an interview on the *Mystic River* DVD commentary, Eastwood refers to child abuse as the "stealing of someone's life, someone's innocence," a subject he had explored ten years earlier in *A Perfect World*. The shots that follow Dave's abduction flash before us with scant context or connection to other events: a murky glimpse of the neighborhood dads scrambling for help; a shadowed shot of legs descending basement stairs, the two men's faces revealed only by a sliver of light; and the sight of a little boy lying on a rumpled bed crying, "Please, no more." A delirium of nighttime images tears at the screen as the child darts and flees through a forest as though pursued by demons.

This blackness will infect the visuals throughout the rest of the film, as the same lighting scheme appears whenever the narrative slides into nightmare. Years later, when Dave sits by his son's bed telling him about the wolves and vampires that haunt him, the sliver of light "exposes a portion of a face against a sea of darkness."[2] The pattern repeats itself when Dave tells Celeste of his dreams of vampires, "the undead," and again at the edge

2. Alex Schwarm, Northwestern University Eastwood course, Winter 2009.

of the river, as Dave recounts the murder of the pedophile and falsely confesses to Katie's murder.

The forest we see in the escape sequence becomes the abode of wolves, not picnickers resting from urban noise and concrete, just as the verdant park in the center of the neighborhood will harbor murderers, not playful forest sprites. Amplified sound and discordant music (drumbeats, slashes, howls) create a horror-film atmosphere that becomes part of the movie's sound design and signals its tragic trajectory. We feel the dull, sickening threat of something hideous hiding behind every corner, a driving, lurking force in the movie that is never resolved. (The alert listener will recall the discordant music and grotesque lighting that undercut the Stranger's and the Preacher's false-savior identities in *High Plains Drifter* and *Pale Rider*.) In *Mystic River*, the adult Dave's association with vampires and monsters erodes the viewer's sympathy for him as an easy victim, which is key to perceiving the ways in which Eastwood uncovers the viewers' fascination with and loathing of a sufferer.

Distanced by the camera and wrapped in an anonymous blanket, the child disappears into his shabby brownstone, with faceless neighbors watching, watching. The circular ascending and descending theme present from the beginning of the movie, CDBC/DEGEFD, assumes ritual resonance that echoes Krzysztof Kieślowski's magisterial film *Dekalog* (1989), in which neighbors gather silently in thick darkness to witness a child's body being pulled from the lake in their common front yard. Where is absolution and cleansing in the narrative configuration that follows Dave's escape? Eastwood elides scenes of reconciliation with mother or friends. Instead, we only hear a bystander pronounce that the child, seen at a distance from the back as he enters his house, "looks like damaged goods."

The upstairs bedroom shade is pulled down, which effectively closes off the child from his community. He has been defiled and must bear the burden of his stain. As Paul Ricoeur has written, "Defilement dwells in the half-light of a quasi-physical infection that points toward a quasi-moral unworthiness." That is, somehow the young boy "deserved" to be punished.[3] No communal rite of purification takes place, and the community is left feeling that it, too, might become contaminated. The child himself "must" be responsible for his own fate, a judgment that is often made on

---

3. Paul Ricoeur, *The Symbolism of Evil*, trans. Emerson Buchanan (New York: Harper and Row, 1967), 35.

women who are the victims of sexual violence. Little Dave is now impure, separated from any possibility of a chaste, innocent, idyllic childhood that is free from the knowledge of good and evil.

Further, despite repeated images in the movie of washing — Dave's bloody hands; his stained clothes, scrubbed hastily by a frightened wife, Celeste (Marcia Gay Harden); Jimmy intoning that the river is where he can be washed clean — the stain cannot be removed. In his beginning lies his end. His life prepares him to become the scapegoat twenty-five years later for the death of another child, Katie, daughter of the boyhood friend Jimmy, who will murder him.[4]

As the movie unfolds, the viewer experiences Dave's suffering and escape from captivity only through flashbacks mediated by his tortured memory, replays of the shots that immediately followed the kidnapping. We never learn whether the little boy received medical care or pastoral counseling for his injuries. Of the years between his ordeal and the present, we only hear of his athletic success in high school, nothing else. Eastwood chooses to leave certain bits of the story offscreen. We infer the rest from the verbal and visual exchanges that populate the second part of the movie: Dave's isolation and intensifying nightmares; his flashbacks; his wife's fears; and the neighborhood's quick leap to accuse him of Katie's murder.

Moments after we have been introduced to the grown-up Dave and his son, Michael, the lanky man rounds the corner onto his own street. Suddenly in terror, Dave sends his child into the house as he gazes at the cement sidewalk square where he and his friends had begun to write their names when the pedophiles drove up and their lives as children ended. The colors in the frame disappear from this film of greens, grays, and darkness: the crowded houses (familiar to us from the film's opening shots) bleach out, and a blinding light removes Dave from time and space as he glances around in confusion trying to reorient himself.[5] Indeed, white is the color of evil, the unknown, as we once learned in *Moby Dick*.

---

4. Whereas in older societies the defiled were carried outside the city walls to be tortured and killed, Dave endures a lifetime of suffering within the confines of the neighborhood and inside houses too small for his gangling body. For the stoning of Stephen, see James G. Williams, ed., *The Girard Reader* (New York: Crossroad, 1996), 169-71.

5. Yet another spot of visual shorthand occurs in the sequence. Dave's flashback dissolves from a close-up of the face of the main kidnapper to a return shot of Dave, who, we learn at the end of the movie, killed a pedophile the night of Katie's death and dreaded becoming one himself.

Each time we see Dave from now on, the film's opening musical theme reappears in a new and discordant form, leading us deeper and deeper into his madness and pushing the tragedy toward its horrifying conclusion, a lynching in every way as repulsive as the one that climaxes *The Ox-Bow Incident.*

Neither the law nor divine power punishes the child rapists for their crime, as if any adequate punishment, even death, could expunge the injury or the memory of four days of repeated rape. But then, Eastwood the director engages vengeance itself — profound, primal, animal fury at other human beings and the universe. It is as though even the exhaustive, piercing brilliance of *Unforgiven,* with its complex take on vengeance, did not fully explore the dark side of human nature. Eastwood observed of *Unforgiven, The Outlaw Josey Wales,* and *Pale Rider:* "The past is often associated with a trauma, with a drama that has been repressed but keeps coming to the surface. The past poisons the present."[6] But what then? Can past crimes be expiated in this one neighborhood? Although the central characters all seem to be related by blood or extended kinship bonds, the "blood" of kinship is replaced by raw, bloody violence. Primordial violence obliterates meaning.

To explore the annihilating path that vengeance can take, Eastwood had to violate one of the unwritten rules of cinematic narrative: never harm a child. Alfred Hitchcock reflected on his narrative error after he allowed a child in *Sabotage* to be blown up. His interviewer, François Truffaut, commented that "making a child die in a picture is a rather ticklish matter; it comes close to an abuse of cinematic power." Hitchcock responded, "I agree with that; it was a grave error on my part."[7] Conversely, in *Schindler's List,* Steven Spielberg used the deaths of children to his advantage without a marketing misstep by conveying an overall sense of horror (children *did* die in the Holocaust), mediated by a brief shot of the red coat worn by a little girl seen earlier in the film now lying on a truckload of victims' belongings. Further, the shock of young Ivan's murder in Russian director Andrei Tarkovsky's *My Name Is Ivan* (1962) is offset in part by the film's thorough grounding in the precise details of the older soldiers' res-

6. Michael Henry Wilson, *Clint Eastwood: Entretiens avec Michael Henry Wilson* (Paris: Cahiers du Cinéma, 2007), 161.

7. François Truffaut, *Hitchcock/Truffaut: The Definitive Study of Alfred Hitchcock* (New York: Simon and Schuster, 1985; first published in 1983 in France by Editions Ramsay, with the collaboration of Helen G. Scott), 109. For an odd take on harm to a child, see M. Night Shyamalan's *The Sixth Sense.*

Dave (Tim Robbins) is haunted by vampires and wolves.

cue, care, and sustaining love for the orphaned, war-soiled twelve-year-old child.[8]

In *Mystic River,* Eastwood maintains focus on the theological magnitude of the horror of the two events: the symbolic death of Dave and the real death of Katie, Jimmy's daughter. The two deaths are linked apocalyptic events that upend the neighborhood ethic with its illusions of protective kinship and encroaching gentrification. The film is full of illusory visions of escape: Dave from his captors; Katie (Emmy Rossum) and Brendan (Thomas Guiry), her sweetheart, from life in this decayed part of the city; Jimmy from prison into the role of respected businessman (and crime boss with control over the neighborhood); Sean from a poisonous past into a vocation as a police detective.

In one key sequence, a Christmas tree twinkles in the background, shorthand in Hollywood mainstream movies for the possibility of renewal (e.g., *It's A Wonderful Life, Miracle on 34th Street, Die Hard*). At the end of the movie, the neighborhood celebrates the nation's birthday with flags, a parade, and marching bands as though all were well. But sentimental religious symbolism and jingoistic patriotism are not going to save the day. The film's troubling narrative heart cannot be resolved by a sugary ending.

In all these cases, the vision clearly belies the reality. The young Dave

---

8. In Tarkovsky's movie, the soldiers try to protect Ivan from combat. Older men, as we have seen recently in war zones in Sierra Leone, often recruit orphaned children as child soldiers, using the men's power and favors to overwhelm the children's reluctance to murder. (Anthropologist Bill Murphy discusses his research on child soldiers in Sierra Leone and Liberia in his forthcoming book *Words and Deeds of Violence.*)

escapes physically but not psychologically. Katie is murdered, her broken body lying in an abandoned bear cage, her suppliant hand upturned. Brendan, an engaging character and overlooked moral touchstone of *Mystic River*, remains trapped in his murderous family. Even the few stolen moments of their happiness, when Brendan hides in Katie's car to surprise her (like Romeo and Juliet, they are children of two warring families), predict her tragic death and Dave's murder. Not too many hours after their meeting, she will be surprised again when her car is invaded, this time by her murderers. Katie's teasing words that her father would "shoot" Brendan and then "kill" him if he knew they were dating anticipate Jimmy's fatal judgment of the innocent Dave. The Christmas tree stands as stark, taunting backdrop to Dave's descent into madness, frightening his wife Celeste into betraying him to Jimmy, on a contract with death.

Furthermore, though Dave seems passive and gentle through most of the film, he is capable of erratic outbursts.[9] At his breaking point, he paces like an animal in a cage. His talk about vampires refers both to the forces of evil that increasingly suck life from him and to his own barely repressed murderous impulses.

Only Sean appears to have escaped the confines of the neighborhood. Not only is he a law-enforcement officer, but he also is paired in vocation and friendship with Whitey Powers (Laurence Fishburne), a black man whose color — in the distinctive Eastwood tradition — is never an issue. At times, when Sean talks about his neighborhood, we expect his partner to speak about his own childhood in a Boston ghetto of a different and possibly far worse kind — perhaps Roxbury. But neither race nor bitterness infects Whitey's performance as a detective, team player, and wise counselor for his sorrowful partner.

In their nontraditional pairing, Whitey and Sean transcend the grievously prevailing neighborhood norms. Furthermore, Whitey acts as a pastoral presence for Sean on two levels: breaking through Sean's fear of the old neighborhood by well-placed questions at the time of the murder, and urging him either to get on with his life or to move toward his wife in reconciliation by confessing his own wrongdoing.

Eastwood resists the temptation to structure this relationship as a replay of something from the *Dirty Harry* series, *Witness*, or *The Gauntlet*, where the hero's partners too often end up dead. Sean is not like Dirty Harry in any way other than his deep sadness and estrangement from his

9. Gabby Aiuto, in Northwestern University Eastwood class, Winter 2008.

wife. Failed romance frequently marks Eastwood characters (as in *True Crime, Blood Work,* and *Tightrope*); here, though, with Whitey's sensible and constant support, Sean becomes the center of a small forgiveness drama, an interpolated tale in the style of Dickens. Alienated from his wife and child (perhaps also the tortured legacy of the neighborhood trauma), Sean finds in the return to his roots the grace to move both his emotional and physical life away from the local cycle of destructive recrimination. The reconciliation of Sean and his wife offers one of the few sources of life and hope in the film.

All the other players in the film — Jimmy and Dave, their wives, and Dave's child — will be sucked into the sewer that devoured their childhood ball. The rituals of the Catholic Church, ironically imaged at film's beginning in a community confirmation service full of bright colors and inspiring music to symbolize a child's welcome into the family of faith, offer neither consolation for Jimmy nor a livable model for ways to face profound grief and sorrow. For a purely pastoral motif, the movie alternates tight, dark, cramped urban spaces with green spaces, but unlike the common poetic symbolism associated with pastoral landscapes, the greenery in this movie hides more misery, for example, the forest through which Dave escapes and the lush park where Katie dies.

Traditional means of spiritual relief and comfort are simply not available in this movie, apart from the friendship of Sean and Whitey and Sean's reconciliation with his wife. After Jimmy has purged his sense of wrong with the blood of his childhood friend Dave, he stands at his bedroom window looking out onto the street. The tattooed cross that covers his back is a symbol of continual suffering, not love, as though he has singled himself out as a sacrificial victim. We wonder: What caused him to take on such a ponderous symbol? Might it be the same sense of relentless fatalism that led him to configure past memories according to the inexorable logic of blood revenge? If he, instead of Dave, had gotten into the kidnappers' car when they were kids, he never would have had the "juice" to court Katie's mother, he tells Sean in an eerie confessional scene in the sterile green cafeteria of the police station. But if he had not married Katie's mother, Katie never would have been born — and thus she never would have been murdered. He feels "at fault" for her death somehow. Yet Jimmy never links his own vengeful murder of "Just Ray," the father of Katie's murderer, to Katie's death — a point that's obvious to the film's viewers but not to him, obsessed as he is with his own sense of injury.

In a stumbling attempt at confession, Jimmy tells his wife, Annabeth

(Laura Linney), that he has murdered the wrong man, that an innocent victim died to atone for the sins of others. He and the Savage brothers have exacted vigilante justice on an innocent person. Worse, rather than being horrified by this revelation, Jimmy's wife casts the murder in fairy-tale language. In this movie, she stands in for *Unforgiven*'s Little Bill by echoing, "Innocent? Innocent of what?" Guilt and innocence are irrelevant; power is all. In full Lady Macbeth mode, as she senses her uxorious prey slipping away from her toward guilt and repentance, Annabeth pronounces that a person is allowed any action if it is to protect his children, covering her husband's tattoo with her body as she croons those seductive words. Jimmy and Annabeth collapse onto the bed. While the sequence is not as stylized or explicit as a parallel scene in David Cronenberg's *A History of Violence* (2005), the link between sex, violence, and power is emphasized by the prowling, voyeuristic camera work and by the scene's drawn-out and uncomfortable length. Then the screen goes dark.

Every scene of *Mystic River* cuts to the core of the ethical and theological issues that haunt America's past and resound as well through its contemporary life: poverty, displacement, sexual abuse of children, and a barely submerged culture of vengeance that resurfaced after 9/11. Eastwood's direction moves artfully between the two dimensions of the human condition, the specific and the universal: the individual, caught in a web beyond her control, and the larger history within which each person lives out a personal sorrow. As an impersonal God's-eye camera sweeps over the harbor, the voice-over dialogue of the police dispatcher links the observer, Sean Devine, with the "old neighborhood" that draws him back into its ineluctably murderous social scheme. The convenience store that Jimmy owns (ironically named Cottage Market), viewed up and down its narrow aisles, speaks simultaneously of the man's ambition and of the neighborhood's shabbiness: poverty and abundant snacks all in the same visual moment.

The scene of the meal after Katie's funeral also portrays multiple, conflicting levels of sop and sorrow: a beer cooler in the corner of the living room; a confrontation between Jimmy and his father-in-law in the cramped kitchen; and the awkward exchanges between the grieving Jimmy and his twitching childhood friend, Dave. The old wrong done to young Dave has caused a cosmic imbalance that the neighborhood cannot confront — neither his two friends, Jimmy and Sean, nor the grown Dave himself — until there is a second violent act, Katie's murder. Inflamed by the madness of the sorrowing father's grief, the neighborhood (through

Annabeth (Laura Linney) baptizes Jimmy's crime.

Jimmy and the Savage brothers) finally rises to seek to right the balance in a horrifically wrong-headed and misdirected act of vengeful, "sacrificial" expiation.

Mystic River is "a masterpiece where compassion, suffering, and despair breathe through every image," wrote Noël Simsolo when the film first appeared in Paris.[10] Critic David Walsh, taking another view in an online review, refers instead to the "grim theology" of the film. Walsh argues that the abusers' "bestial, uncivilized impulse" comes from the same source as "grief, loyalty, and even love," and that Eastwood, far from operating out of a religious or spiritual center, holds a deeply pessimistic view of human nature that observes human tragedy without offering a plausible redemptive view of such horrors.[11] Critic Jonathan Rosenbaum might echo this assessment. He has suggested that *Mystic River* shows Eastwood's dim, "conservative" view of human nature — the inability of humans to change.[12]

Walsh objects to transcendent readings of *Mystic River* and ecstatic responses of critics such as A. O. Scott, largely because, he argues, the film and its critics seem to believe that human nature is evil and weak, this miserable "Southie" working-class community in particular. By contrast, Scott writes: "*Mystic River* is the rare American movie that aspires to — and achieves — the full weight and darkness of tragedy," echoing Simsolo's

10. Noël Simsolo, *Clint Eastwood: un passeur à Hollywood* (Paris: Editions Cahiers du Cinéma, 2006), 235 (my translation).

11. David Walsh (November 3, 2003): www.wsws.org/articles/2003/nov2003/mystn03.shtml.

12. Jonathan Rosenbaum, in a lecture at Northwestern University, February 19, 2009.

praise. "When Sean realizes he must tell his old friend Jimmy that his beloved daughter is dead, he wonders what he should say: 'God said you owed another marker, and he came to collect.'" This "grim theology," Scott continues, "is as close as anyone comes to faith."

> Mr. Eastwood's understanding of the universe, and of human nature, is if anything even more pessimistic. The evil of murderers and child molesters represents a fundamental imbalance in the order of things that neither the forces of law and order nor the impulse toward vengeance can rectify.[13]

Scott's observations are borne out in the discovery of Katie's body in the park, where a distant camera views her in a verdant pastoral embrace. It shows the viewer a no less richly and tragically compassionate aerial view of Jimmy, again shot from the wounded heavens, screaming and weeping to break through the police lines to touch his beloved daughter. He and the Savage brothers thrash around as though the movie's frames cannot hold them. What strength has official power against the grief and terror of a father whose child has died?

To his credit, Walsh notes a disturbing undercurrent in the film: the ways that external forces such as rampant capitalism have ravaged the lives of Jimmy, Dave, Sean, and their families and have ripped away at one corner of a great city, shredding its social fabric. It would be hard to argue with such an assessment. Walsh could have just as appropriately been describing Detroit, then crumbling under the burden of its own massively failed industry and disregard for human life, a portrait that Eastwood carefully observed in the same grim light in *Gran Torino*.

"Capitalism," however, is too broad and flat a target for a movie that also works hard to visualize positive, contemporary ritual in Katie's sister's confirmation, with all its verbal, sartorial, and musical frills. But the uplifting ceremony, complete with smiles, tears, and angelic faces, is jarringly intercut with contrapuntal shots of another young girl lying a mile away, her body broken within a ritual circle of death. In this depth of vision, the church is both all-powerful in infusing young men and women with an awareness of sin and guilt and poignantly powerless against predators (Dave's rapists) and murderers (Katie's murderers, two young boys with

---

13. A. O. Scott, "Dark Parable of Violence Avenged," *The New York Times*, October 3, 2003: http://movies.nytimes.com/movie/review?res=9904E2DA173CF930A35753C1A9659C8B63.

no sense of right or wrong). "Follow the money" can only get us a little way into the morality of this tortured tale.

From the beginning, the director's timing was uncanny. When he began to plan *Mystic River* in 2002, the extent of the child abuse problem within the Boston diocese had only begun to surface. Subsequently, other massive sex-abuse cases with priests were settled in June 2008, with more cases coming to light all the time, as *Doubt* (2008), directed by John Patrick Shanley, encourages us to remember. Child abuse is not limited to priests or to Boston. However, because of Boston's pride of place in the religious superstructure of the conservative American Catholic Church, child molestation and the church's long history of denial and cover-up seem the more astounding and indefensible for happening there.

Moreover, the intensity of the visuals and music in *Mystic River* seems expressly designed to underscore the disparity between the stated doctrine of the Christian church and the actions of corrupted individuals within it. At the heart of Jesus' ethical teaching lies this saying: "He who would harm a child, it would be better for him if a millstone were hung around his neck, and he were thrown into the sea" (Matt. 18:6; Mark 9:42; Luke 17:2). When children look to the church for rescue from the misery of their ordinary lives, the horror is so much greater when that trust is abused. Deeper and more expansive still is the sadness of knowing when children within a neighborhood are neither nurtured nor protected — when even their parish betrays them. Each of the boys in *Mystic River* has been abandoned: Dave, fatherless; Brendan and his brother, fatherless; Jimmy, who forms a family through crime; Sean, whose community becomes the police force, but who cannot himself sustain a mature relationship. Even the much-loved Katie is eager to escape the looming sense of damage and danger all around her.

Rather than simply prepare a bleak and abstract treatise on the darkness of human nature, though, Eastwood takes a historical and political problem — neglected and abused children — and brings its most appreciable human cost inside the sentient scope of the viewers' own experiences. Yet, in doing so, he never loses sight of the larger picture within which that abuse has arisen, the despoiling of a once-pristine part of the New World. He returns repeatedly to a God's-eye view of the city, the neighborhood, and the river at night, the larger experiential stage on which this small chamber drama is playing out — the "old neighborhood," as Sean succinctly describes the area to his partner, Whitey, while they stand on a bridge gazing across the river toward the south.

Eastwood dissects false images of America as the "City on a Hill" and the "New Jerusalem" with such mastery and passion because he believes in the beauty of our true images, such as life in community. This we can see in Josey Wales's ragtag family as they dance and sing after chores are done; we can see it in *Bronco Billy*'s Wild West troupe as it cavorts with the asylum inmates, and as their imprisoned friends stitch a big-top tent made of American flags, under which all, even prisoners, can enjoy the show. "Life in community" means caring for each other in the present and the future. Eastwood images a better world, a paradise, when Maggie and Frankie in *Million Dollar Baby* dream of a cabin they will share in physical and spiritual wholeness, and when, in *A Perfect World*, Butch dreams of Alaska, with its pristine wilderness and sparkling rivers. Still, for every promise of a stream of pure flowing water, Eastwood reveals the underlying river of blood.

And blood runs deep in *Mystic River*, a symbolic echo of the pollution of the South Flats' nearby river, which once — before the arrival of settlers and the upstream factories — ran pure and clean. The lives of these people were also once clean, despite the hierarchical theological climate of the church that settled here.

As the movie unfolds, the camera lurks around corners, flattening the image to crowd the actors against buildings; or it shoots inside a confined space in semidarkness to emphasize the constricted living rooms and kitchens. Alternating with the judging camera's close attention to physical space and to faces, it also repeatedly pans up to the heavens and then looks down. Most memorably, the initial views of the bridge and harbor (cinematic tourism) yield to the series of swinging shots of Katie's car, the nearby park, the dead body displayed in the bear cage, and the juxtaposition of Jimmy's howling body and the empty cage, the body now removed and only the sorrow left in.

The small boys who had talked about a brighter future (even if Jimmy's one big dream was to steal a car) have been stained and defiled, all three of them, by the sexual assault that one suffered. The past weighs heavily on the present and the future and cannot be reconciled. Like Eastwood's earlier nameless characters — the Man With No Name, the Stranger, and the Preacher — the boys are all forced to live in a twilight zone, neither dead nor alive. In Ricoeur's terms, Dave has been excluded from a sacred space, yet he must return to its midst, reliving the nightmare and suffering flashbacks "inside his head" that force him out to hunt pedophiles as an adult.

Can such stories as Jimmy's, Dave's, and Sean's only be told through mythic or fairy-tale distancing? Must such grotesquely intimate encounters as Dave's rape and Celeste's "confession" to Jimmy be turned into a neatly told tale, only to be quickly forgotten? Can we learn to escape the endless cycles of violence? Some of the haunting and detailed after-images of the movie's denouement strongly suggest that we have no such hope. In shocking contrast to the near-blackness of the river sequence where Dave is murdered, the moment of his death is marked by a blinding light and organ music that segues into the cheery brightness of a noisy parade that is proceeding along the neighborhood's main street. It is as though nothing had happened. The underlying darkness of vengeance is not overcome. Yet Dave is dead. His wife has betrayed him. His small, timid, sad-faced son rides quietly on his baseball team's float, and the world fails to notice. What will become of that little boy, abandoned and forgotten during the weeks and months after the revenge drama fades away? His life may repeat his father's if no one rescues him, and surely no potential rescuer has surfaced in the movie's plot.

Mystic River is no Hollywood melodrama with clearly marked villains and victims and a sugary, easy-access resolution. As in *Heartbreak Ridge* (1986), the too-bright patriotic parade at movie's end distances the painful events at its narrative heart: a phony war with painful human consequences in Eastwood's earlier drama; a wrenching, primitive tragedy spun out of control for the characters we come to pity and the neighborhood they inhabit in *Mystic River*.

Jimmy, Sean, and Dave live in a corner of a once-great city that has been forgotten by the onward rush of prosperity and bright hope. "Justice" asserts itself as an anarchic, ancient act akin to the lynchings that despoiled the settlements of the west and the long, dark night of slavery and Jim Crow. Eastwood does not forget the many victims. He witnesses, tells the tale, and exposes the individual stories — even Jimmy's — as deeply, richly human and worthy of our attention. Jimmy, Dave, and Sean are not heroes who reside in a romantic world of giants; they are ordinary guys caught in the backwash of history. Jimmy may cast himself as the avenger who will right the wrongs in his neighborhood and his life, but that role more accurately belongs to Eastwood the director, who mediates between flawed human beings and the justice that perpetually eludes them.

But tellingly — and typically — Eastwood turns the ending of his source novel from retribution toward possible forgiveness. In Dennis Lehane's book, Sean tells Jimmy that he will seek justice for Dave's death.

In the film, however, Sean merely points his finger in mock pistol at Jimmy (a quintessential move for Eastwood the actor, as we see in Josey Wales's clicking empty pistols and Walt Kowalski's threatening gestures in *Gran Torino*), as though he knows that vengeance must stop with the murderer's supposed remorse. Noël Simsolo comments on the similarity of Sean's action to childhood games of cops and robbers.[14] Sean's fragile but genuine reconciliation with his wife and baby tempers the subsequent daylight mood, trumping the false gaiety of the Fourth of July parade. Something deeper and more substantively abiding than public ritual is going on here.

Only love can resist the darkness of the human heart, the corruption of institutions, and the unnerving fragility of the social fabric that we absorb over the movie's 120 troubling minutes. Perhaps, as Eastwood suggests in this one fleeting moment of family redemption, some form of radical forgiveness does lie on the other side of overwhelming visual darkness. We cannot know. We can only experience this film's rich world as our own, and we long to redeem it.[15]

14. Simsolo, *Clint Eastwood,* 238.

15. A surprising number of students from my 2009 class thought Dave was better off dead. As one said, "His death might be interpreted as a relief, an escape from the vampires and werewolves who spent thirty years running around in his head." Others noted not only his personal suffering but also his disruptive effect on the neighborhood. Yet Dave is a living, suffering human being.

Million Dollar Baby

I n *Million Dollar Baby*, William Butler Yeats's poem "The Lake Isle of Innisfree" holds a central interpretive place. Not only does the poem offer a utopian image of natural beauty and peace — a sacred space far from the ravages of interstate highways, urban blight, and rural poverty — but it also sings with the rhythm of Irish bards celebrating the pulses of life even as death stalks outside the window.

> I will arise and go now, and go to Innisfree,
> And a small cabin build there, of clay and wattles made;
> Nine bean rows will I have there, a hive for the honey bee,
> And live alone in the bee-loud glade.
> And I shall have some peace there, for peace comes dropping slow,
> Dropping from the veils of the morning to where the cricket sings;
> There midnight's all a glimmer, and noon a purple glow,
> And evening full of the linnet's wings.
> I will arise and go now, for always night and day
> I hear lake water lapping with low sounds by the shore;
> While I stand on the roadway, or on the pavements gray,
> I hear it in the deep heart's core.[1]

1. http://www.bartelby.com/103/44.html. Taken from Louis Untermeyer, ed., *Modern British Poetry* (New York: Harcourt, Brace, and Howe, 1920). Marcia Gealy, in Northwestern University Eastwood class, July 2010, has noted the resonance of the opening line with the King James Bible translation of the parable of the Prodigal Son: "I will arise now and go to my father and say, 'I have sinned against heaven and against you . . .'" (Luke 15:18-21).

The poem softens the nightmare in which the main characters are trapped. Near the end of the movie, we capture Maggie Fitzgerald (Hilary Swank), a scrappy boxer out of Missouri, and her trainer, Frankie Dunn (Eastwood), in a moment where they must learn to cope with the way their world has been turned upside down. Maggie has been woefully injured and sits motionless opposite her companion, listening to the lilting rhythms of the verse as he reads aloud to her. Yeats's poem suspends time and space, creating a sacred corner shaped and colored only by their imaginations. For Maggie, newly introduced to poetry's power to transform the moment, the reading speaks of a real cabin where she could live with Frankie to return the love he has given her.

Maggie knows that such retreats exist, peopled by seekers and refugees from injury and violence; from the beginning of their friendship, Frankie had spoken of her need to protect herself, to buy a home where she would always be safe. They could not have known that her final home would be with him in a hospital room, that death and pain would claim her long before she could make peace with her history, her body, and her dreams. The "deep heart's core," Yeats's poetic summary of longing, contains all that the friends will ever know of a perfect world, an earthly paradise where love rules.

In *Million Dollar Baby,* Eastwood continues to ask the theological and ethical questions many of his other movies address: What is a life all about? Which lives are to be valued, and why? What can we say about suffering? How might we define "righteousness"? The tension between the desire for a perfect world and the wrenching imperfections of the world we actually live in appeared in Eastwood's earliest movies, *Play Misty for Me* and *High Plains Drifter,* and became more defined in *The Outlaw Josey Wales* and *The Gauntlet.* In *Pale Rider,* he forges the ethics of forgotten lives against the backdrop of apocalypse, both imagined and real: the threat of the end times figures in both the film's opening assault by faceless men on horseback and the violent death of the protagonist in his past life. *Unforgiven* contains one of the most provocative lines in all of Eastwood's work: "Deserve's got nothin' to do with it."

"Deserve" figures mightily in *Million Dollar Baby,* a film full of darkness and light. Critics such as Richard Corliss *(Time)* and Jonathan Rosenbaum *(Chicago Reader)* joined Roger Ebert in pronouncing it "a masterpiece, pure and simple," and the movie works on multiple emotional and theological levels simultaneously.[2] In *Million Dollar Baby,* East-

2. Roger Ebert, in a *Chicago Sun-Times* article online, January 5, 2005. Jonathan

wood defies stereotypes within the boxing genre and storytelling overall. We watch the story play out as "plucky heroine rises from trash" and as "small-time boxer makes good," but beneath this surface plot line East-wood offers a story infused with more tightly focused compassion, grief, and love than the movies before *Unforgiven* could muster. His deliberate pacing, unrushed exchanges between characters, and refusal to glamorize boxing highlight the intrinsic worth of each person.[3] We watch as a small family is slowly born: Frankie Dunn, a tough old manager; Scrap (Morgan Freeman), his former protégé turned janitor and friend; and Maggie, a Missouri refugee who seeks a better life through competitive boxing.

The movie's tight construction and Gothic look create an atmosphere that begs for theological debate and ethical argument — a "scorchingly real redemption story," as Chicago critic Robert Kennedy suggests. The film certainly continues to resonate with viewers; as of 2010, it had risen to number 143 in IMDb's top 250 movies (close to *Unforgiven*'s number 105). But it has its detractors. Anti-euthanasia and pro-life activists protested the movie's treatment of Maggie's death, and disability activists deplored its representation of a quadriplegic as a victim. Providing a peaceful death may be the most meaningful ethical act of the movie, if "ethical acts" are created out of moral choices arising from the wish to honor a loved one and relieve suffering.

The film's ethical sweep takes in far more territory than scrutinizing individual acts; it also includes social judgment through its aesthetic: the seedy interior of the gym and the poverty of its characters betray an environment where a young American woman of good will lacks the education, resources, or self-respect to carve out a meaningful life apart from offering herself to be beaten up as part of a public spectacle.[4] Most of the

---

Rosenbaum, "A Little Transcendence Goes a Long Way," *Chicago Reader*, December 27, 2004, online: http://www.jonathan rosenbaum.com/2p+5992; Richard Corliss, *Time*, August 1, 2008. Paul Haggis adapted the script from two stories in F. X. Toole, *Rope Burns: Stories from the Corner* (New York: HarperCollins, 2000), a collection of short stories based on the experiences of longtime fight manager and cutman Jerry Boyd (whose pseudonym is F. X. Toole).

3. See Martha Nussbaum's discussion of intrinsic worth and human vulnerability in *The Fragility of Goodness: Luck and Ethics in Greek Tragedy and Philosophy* (Cambridge: Cambridge University Press, 1986).

4. Or prostituting herself, e.g., *Pretty Woman, L.A. Confidential, Unforgiven*. When informed on Fox News (September 9, 2005) that some political conservatives believed that she and thousands of other black Americans should have gotten themselves the education and money to allow them to exit New Orleans ahead of Hurricane Katrina, a poised high school

work of the film is done through manipulation of light and shadow. Faces and figures are often etched against a black or intensely colored background, or the screen suddenly cuts to black. Robert Kennedy continues his commentary on the film's aesthetic: "It's a darkened, extremely spare film style that utilizes the dimly lit edges of people in shadows or standing in the corners, never really in the picture at all, always just barely there. Overall, the tone is sharp, tightly scripted, dimly lit, like in the shadows of what's real, exploring the edges of the frame."[5] The careful use of the narrative voice-over, heavy use of darkness and shadows, and stylized set pieces (the gym; the boxing rings; the visit to Missouri) give the entire movie a slightly unreal aura, a visual and sonic rhythm that continues throughout — as though the images existed only in a dream world.

The Epistle to the Hebrews (echoed in Augustine's *City of God*) reflects that: "In this world we have no lasting city." In *Million Dollar Baby,* the heavenly parallel to the earthly city (here Los Angeles, the "City of Angels") exists only in symbols: the church, its priest, and the whiff of a just-completed Mass as Frankie departs the Sunday service. We find little physical sign of transcendence in the deserted grimy streets or vacant buildings that lie just outside the Hit Pit gym, Frankie's domain. Little of welcome exists in the wasteland of shabby trailers and prefab housing we see in the Missouri where Maggie grew up. The cramped, low-lit interiors and shabbiness of the gym echo the desolate cabin where Will Munny and his children lived in *Unforgiven.* The confectionary treats of Disneyland, visited by Maggie's family, lie just beyond this corner of a vast and untended city center — a center filled with plastic images of the lasting city, the City of God to which Augustine refers.

Almost by definition, urban movies evoke unspoken images of a heavenly city, the way cities should be constructed if human values (love, companionship, and reciprocity) and human needs (Martha Nussbaum and Amartya Sen's ten capabilities) are to be nurtured.[6] The Dardenne brothers' *The Silence of Lorna* (2008), Alejandro Gonzáles Iñárritu's *Amores Perros* (2000), and Spike Lee's *Do the Right Thing* (1989), among other recent movies, train their cinematic eyes on the squalor and misery of the in-

---

student replied: "I didn't know it was a crime to be poor in America. And I didn't know the punishment was death" (transcription from a live broadcast).

5. Robert Kennedy, Chicago film critic, email to the author, May 27, 2007.

6. Martha Nussbaum and Amartya Sen, *The Quality of Life* (Oxford: The Clarendon Press, 1993).

Maggie's late night practice (Hilary Swank).

ner city, what can be seen, and on the unseen words of desire, the ideal human community. Alfonso Cuarón's *Children of Men* (2006) plays the contrast from another angle: the movie begins with an apocalyptic, infertile human-created wasteland. By the end (seen as a miracle, but without sentimentality), the mysterious birth of a baby ignites hope for the redemption of the destroyed world. The same palpable contrast is implicit in the voice-over narrations that open Curtis Hanson's *L.A. Confidential* and Peter Cattaneo's *The Full Monty* (both 1997): the falsity of promotional ads that trumpet the beauty and promise of a (commercially hyped) paradise where life can start anew. (However, Agnès Varda's *The Gleaners and I* observes the transformation of refuse into art.)[7] Clint Eastwood is as much a city filmmaker as a chronicler of the sickness or health of the vast terrain of the open prairie, or of the forests and deserts on the way to Texas, a strength that surfaces in *Million Dollar Baby* and again in *Changeling* and *Gran Torino.*

We don't see much of Los Angeles in *Million Dollar Baby*. The God's-eye aerial shots that repeatedly moved over Boston in *Mystic River* are lavished here on boxing rings. We see the confined interior of Frankie's house, where he squirrels away the letters his estranged daughter, Katie, returns to him, and where he witnesses the evidence of his defeat as a boxing coach: his star fighter's victorious championship fight under another manager.

7. Rachel Koontz suggests the poem "The Wreckage Entrepreneur" by Alice Fulton. Fulton shows us how we make our own beauty out of the garbage heap and how "it takes faith — this tripping through the mixed blessings/of debris with eyes peeled for the toxic/ toothpaste green of copper keystones."

We retreat with Frankie to the comfort of his gym office, where he reads poetry, teaches himself Gaelic, and chats with his longtime friend Scrap — a created island of dignity that soothes him in his losses.

Frankie creates spaces of solace for himself and a few others that are models for order against the chaos outside. More subtly than in *High Plains Drifter,* the chaos that threatens human happiness lies just behind the veil of artificial beauty. The tragedy of the hurricane that struck New Orleans in August 2005 ripped apart the Disneyworld/Disneyland version of American life portrayed in magazines, newspapers, television, and movies. Cities such as New Orleans, New York, Los Angeles, Chicago, and Detroit have always festered with poverty and underserved human needs, even without natural disasters; but in 2005 that reality was beamed around the world for all to see and cry, "Shame! Is this the American dream? Is this American democracy?"

The Hit Pit gym that Frankie and Scrap run provides a refuge for some of those who have been left behind in our country, the lowest of the low, for the "oddballs, those pushed to the edges of American society," as Eastwood comments in the movie's DVD extras. Maggie is only the latest of decades of American refugees from the failed promise of education and success, and the crotchety old team of Scrap and Frankie weave her into this small community. "She grew up knowing one thing," Scrap tells us in a voice-over. "She was trash." Eastwood takes an angle opposite that of *Rocky* and other boxing movies. This is not a typical American Horatio Alger rags-to-riches story. Rather, the movie forces us to ask: Why does such poverty exist in a rich country like ours?

Boxing may offer Maggie a chance to earn money and respect, both of which are woefully absent from her life — as we learn through flashbacks. Most of all, it provides her with purpose and meaning, a reason to keep on living.[8] Even Billy the "Blue Bear," Maggie's nemesis, was a prostitute before she became a boxer; it was one way for a poor young woman to survive. Hit Pit gym becomes Maggie's home, her family, and her community.

Frankie takes on Maggie and trains her as a boxer, despite his early loud refusals to do so and the males-only code of the sport. Gender is al-

---

8. Maggie's desperate repeated pitches to Frankie to train her echo the mantra of the protagonist in *Rosetta* (Dardenne brothers, 1999), who desired only the basics of a name, a job, and a place to live — markers of worth denied Maggie in the United States and Rosetta in Belgium. Both women lack money and status. *Rosetta's* representation of poverty in the midst of Belgium's wealth spurred lawmakers to enact a law that helps teenagers get jobs and lift themselves out of poverty.

ways prickly with Eastwood. Despite his own macho image and the dearth of female companions for his lonely male protagonists, the director portrays loneliness as a loss, not a warrior's badge. Harry Callahan suffers, as do Josey Wales and Will Munny, from appearances of their competent wives in dreams and visions. Even the Stranger and the Preacher, disembodied and gun-happy as they are, need — and pick — clear-sighted women as lovers; and in *The Bridges of Madison County,* the thoroughly physical Robert Kinkaid (Eastwood) coaxes a full-blown sexual partnership from Francesca Johnson (Meryl Streep) with his gentleness and kindness.

We may well wonder what drew Walt Kowalski's wife to him, but his deep and abiding love for her eventually allows him to welcome another woman, Sue, into his masculine world. More important than his heroes' particular shortcomings, Eastwood the director has consistently given roles of substance to women, culminating in *Changeling* (2008). But Maggie's character is one of the strongest: she fills the spots left empty by Frankie's wife and alienated daughter while carving out her own distinctive place in his heart.

Although Frankie has money and education, he does not discriminate against Maggie or his other fighters based on their wealth or race. We feel this instinctively. The gym's only real "outsider" is Danger, and even he — "simple of spirit," as Eastwood puts it — is protected by Frankie and Scrap. The relationship between coach and fighter builds slowly, beginning as Frankie admires Maggie's increasing mastery of boxing skills. The progress is visualized through tight shots as he moves her feet to an unheard rhythm, with the camera staying close to their faces and bodies as the dance grows in confidence and partnership.

We see the poetry of the evolving relationship play out onscreen. The rapid montage of Maggie's knockouts is played almost for comic effect and balances the more somber exchanges between coach and pupil, which are more horizontal, more grounded, and shot in near darkness against moody green backgrounds in at least five sequences. Eastwood told interviewer Michael Henry Wilson that he approached and shot the film "as if it were in black and white," a strategy he also followed in *Unforgiven* and the war movies.[9] The authenticity of the relationship is established in part by tactile closeness conveyed in close-ups, in part by the verbal exchanges that

9. Michael Henry Wilson, *Clint Eastwood: Entretiens avec Michael Henry Wilson* (Paris: Cahiers du Cinéma, 2007), 173.

**Frankie (Eastwood) reads Yeats's "The Lake Isle of Innisfree"
to an immobilized Maggie (Hilary Swank).**

show Maggie's total dependence on Frankie, and in part by the magnitude of Frankie's grief over his lost daughter.

Even before the unthinkable accident that overturns Maggie's life, she and Frankie bond through the blood sport that is their common calling. They bond both through and against the cheering crowd, through her opponents and against them — a refreshing change from the mostly male westerns. Long before Maggie lies wounded and helpless, she offers herself and is offered as a sacrifice to bloodthirsty crowds who feast on the spectacle of spilled blood, mashed noses, and bruised kidneys. The matches are filmed with an elegance that masks the ugliness of the sport. Maggie's early bouts border on the burlesque, with crowds as raunchy as dancehall customers in a painting by Toulouse-Lautrec or peasants in one of Pieter Brueghel's pieces.[10] The camera only catches bits of bodies, snatches of over-lit faces set against darkened spaces, faces like interchangeable masks hiding unknown desires. Maggie's body is on full display, that is, until the camera hustles her out of sight when she strikes the winning blow.

Lest we miss both her meteoric rise in the world of boxing and the shadiness of the sport, Scrap's voice-over intervenes as chorus and interpreter; the illusion of "reality" is broken. The camera pulls back to spot her

---

10. Henri de Toulouse-Lautrec (1864-1901) painted in Paris during the late nineteenth century; Pieter Brueghel (1525?-1569), a Flemish painter, worked in Antwerp and Brussels. Both of these painters, like Eastwood, crossed the thresholds of economics and social class, both slide slightly into the grotesque, and both use fool imagery.

before a fight: in a barely lit corner of the locker room, she is silent, and the view of her face and emotions is obscured by the distance.

But as Maggie's career advances (and as the amount of money at stake increases exponentially, the ever-present theme of "commerce" that haunts Eastwood's films), the camera registers ever more stylized crowds viewed at steep angles and long shots from above. To underscore the unreality that surrounds the matches, Eastwood begins to disjoin image and sound in an almost silent-movie display that the asynchronic sound design creates. As in any film, the tonality, rhythm, and volume of the music interweave with the other elements.

Here the boxing tableaux increasingly resembles Toulouse-Lautrec's dancehall girls encircled by distorted images of leering spectators, as the absence of "real" sound moves the spectacle from a ringside seat into the symbolic realm. The unnatural, highly stylized, and surreal lighting punctuates and interrupts any smooth, linear progression of the story line. It differs both from the glaring light of the Missouri trailer park and from the warmer darkness that embraces Frankie and Maggie in the locker room before her first fight, or in her apartment, when he counsels her to protect herself, or when they dine together at ringside. Darkness — along multiple emotional registers — extends from the shadows at the edges of the boxing ring to the embrace of light and darkness as they travel home from Missouri toward California to the nighttime that Frankie enters after ending Maggie's life.

Maggie's match with Billie the "Blue Bear" exposes the real-life world of competitive sports and its corruption, extreme violence, and disregard for human life. The film's narrative structure initially encourages us to concentrate on Maggie's string of successes, the creation of her new identity, and her pursuit of recognition. But as the movie progresses, it reveals that boxing resembles human sacrifice more than economic or spiritual redemption. In that gladiators' arena, human beings are put up for sale. This is not true of Frankie, who protects his fighters; rather, it is true of the underground managers who work in the shadows to cut deals and urge athletes to dope up and play dirty.

The possible parallel between boxing and religious ritual — with the crowd as a congregation gathered to witness an ancient rite — raises crucial issues for us as we question the legitimacy of the sport along with Eastwood. What values are articulated and symbolized in such a gathering? What dynamic emerges with the presence of boxing's "fans"? Is it instead "magic," as Scrap declares in an early voice-over? Do the steps, the fakes, the fades, and the elaborate rules parody religious rituals? Does this gathering support or mock community, as it is envisioned as a place of safety? Unlike the Hit Pit gym's office and club, which establish a protected space to nurture human interactions, the boxing ring in *Million Dollar Baby* is uncovered as a profane space, a contaminated space, a mockery where bodies are meticulously prepared for display before injury and possible death. The ring, shot with canted angles and a distanced camera, represents a perverted, carnival-like space that is similar to the open hallway where Katerina Ivanovna plays out her tubercular and desperate death scene in *Crime and Punishment,* a suffering human being who is battered but not quite crushed, playing to imagined fans even as the onlookers mock her.

Let us pause to read this film as echoing ritual movements between sacred and profane spaces: the Hit Pit gym and Maggie's hospital rooms, sites of luminous transformation, contrasted to the various boxing rings that were created to display and destroy life. Return to our first sight of Maggie and follow the ways that she prepares herself for the sacrifice of her body. We see her first in a darkened and confined hallway, her clothes, hair, and face shaded slightly green and marked by too little food, too much sorrow.[11] The obscuring shadows make her look old and tired, even slightly cadaverous. As the film continues, an overhead shot captures only a part of her face as she devours restaurant leftovers in dim light, only a part of her body visible. (In another instance of Eastwood's resonant metaphors, the one who devours will become the devoured.)

In the fifth chapter of the movie, the production design and cinematography shift into the mode that will be sustained up to the moment Maggie is injured: long shots of Maggie silhouetted sharply against the blue-green of the gym wall, punching the bag Scrap has loaned her. Such shots, held for long screen seconds, return with variations from three early scenes. The color bridges the prefight concentration, the locker room talks, and her apartment. The moments of preparation "aestheticize" her training, bringing the beauty of her inner life into the composition of the shots. The stylized, gorgeous shots of her training, and her exchanges with her two mentors, Frankie and Scrap, take place in various shades of darkness

---

11. These shots recall the framing and lighting of the vampire in F. W. Murnau's silent film *Nosferatu* (1922), from the novel by Bram Stoker. This visual reference raises a question posed by my students and other audiences to whom I've spoken: Is Maggie an angel or a devil?

that bring the "reality" of the shots into question. Fans of Robert Bresson's *Diary of a Country Priest* will recognize the meticulous rituals of a priest's preparation for Mass.

During the months of her training, the protected space of the old gym where Maggie trains becomes the home to which she returns after each venture out — whether to fight or to waitress — a place for companionship, counsel, and touch. She uses her earnings to buy a house, not for herself but for her family, a physical dwelling ripe as a site where she might reconcile with her past.

Frankie links Maggie's need to find a house of her own specifically with his other mantra: "Protect yourself." But Maggie uses her money, not to protect herself and her economic future, but to create a site where her family might remake itself into a loving community. Her gift is rejected. Harsh, uniform, filled white lighting (which could be interpreted as the untamed glare of the summer sun or as the director's severe judgment of what we are witnessing) evokes disgust. Maggie's family members pollute every space they enter. Nearly halfway through the movie, Frankie, the stand-in for viewers, witnesses the moral degradation of Maggie's mother and sister, and he suffers as Maggie is publicly humiliated: "People hear 'bout what you're doin' and they laugh," her mother says mercilessly. "They laugh at you." Many shots of Maggie at the gym and later on her deathbed are highly stylized rather than realistic. The sequences of Maggie's family also seem overheated in almost an operatic way, underscoring their ugliness and heavily judging the family's selfishness, ignorance, and cruelty.

While some viewers might think Eastwood has gone over the top with his portrayal of Maggie's family, each harshly lit sequence with them develops her more fully as her family's scapegoat — the one who bears the sickness of the family, the one who is abused even as she gives everything she has.[12] Sadly, the scapegoat motif parallels the sacrifice motif; we learn that Maggie gives her earnings to that same mother who neglects and humiliates her.[13] Those who consider Eastwood's cinematic prose in the family

12. David Walsh lambastes Eastwood's presentation of Maggie's family, "caricatures of 'poor white trash,'" as "slander against a healthy portion of the American population. . . ." He fails to notice the harsh lighting, elevated and exaggerated speech, and unrealistic settings that make these sequences more symbolic than representational; he also displays quite a bit of prejudice himself in making such a comprehensive statement about ("real"?) Americans. See www.wsws.org/articles/2005/mill-j22/shtml.

13. Eastwood is making no general statement about "white trash." But this may be the only film in which he presents any group of any color or class (except murderers and rapists)

scenes overly florid and unfair to poor whites should remember Dostoevsky's handling of the innocent Sonia's prostitution in *Crime and Punishment*. The parallels are nearly exact. Although the young woman sells all that she possesses — her body — to feed her family, her stepmother berates and even beats her in public. A tearful reconciliation between Maggie and her mother might have pushed more emotional buttons for moviegoers and sold more theater tickets, just as Eastwood could have altered his source material to have Maggie revive or to have Frankie reunite with his lost daughter. But Eastwood rejects sentimentality. He remains true to one sad dimension of human experience: some abandon and others rescue.[14]

Frankie's most successful rescue is himself, as he allows himself to love and be loved by Maggie — his surrogate daughter — in an affection conveyed through wondrously lit intimate conversations. During those luminous moments, and to the low accompaniment of a guitar, Maggie relates a story about her father and her pet dog in almost total darkness as the two refugees return to California from their disastrous trip to Missouri to see her family. (The story about Axel, a dearly loved pet put out of its misery by her much-cherished father, anticipates Maggie's own death.) The alternating shots are lit only by flashes from passing cars and shadows that pass across their faces as she declares, "I got nobody but you, Frankie," and he replies, "Well, you've got me." The scene overlaps past, future, and present, but it does more: it seems composed of equal parts joy and sorrow, happiness and tragedy. As viewers, we are lost in time and space, light and dark, and we are prepared and perhaps strengthened by the familial bond between Maggie and Frankie to bear the anguish that is to come.[15]

Light softens and diffuses as the camera peeks through the dirty windows of Ira's Roadside Diner, where the friends share homemade lemon

---

without compassion. Lucia Rijker, the actress/boxer who plays Billie the "Blue Bear" (and coached Hilary Swank in boxing during the filming), cries when she recounts her own story in the DVD of *Million Dollar Baby*, grounding the film in human experience. Like Maggie, she fought to buy decency for her family; like Maggie, her gifts were refused. Maggie's scapegoat status and her sacrifices to buy dignity for her family also recall D. H. Lawrence's short story "The Rocking Horse Winner," in which a little boy rides his magic rocking horse to supply his bankrupt parents with cash, yet it is never enough.

14. Professor Sofia in Krzysztof Kieślowski's *Dekalog*, Episode 8 (Polish TV series, 1988): "Some are born to rescue, others to be rescued."

15. Matt Mckenna, Northwestern University Eastwood class, Winter 2010.

Frankie's moral dilemma.

pie.[16] After a several-second shot of the diner lit against the pitch of the night, the camera observes Frankie and Maggie through a pane of glass before moving into a large, inviting space full of customers. The diner envelops Maggie and Frankie as father and daughter, each rescuing the other. Frankie's happy comment on the pie, "Now I can die and go to heaven," is greeted by Maggie's antiphonal response, "I used to come here with Daddy," a reference both to her relationship with Frankie and her return to moments in the past where she felt loved and secure. The sequence closes as the camera moves outside once more and the noodling of the guitar resolves.[17] Eastwood could have ended his movie with the tender scene in Ira's Diner: it replicates and defends the protected space of the Hit Pit gym already inscribed as a haven in the world of this film.

But the following sequence, halfway through the film, begins a new journey for Maggie, Frankie, and Scrap: a journey toward the title, a stunning climax to her boxing career, complete with bagpipers and near-

16. The old Missouri board-and-batten structure may date to post–Civil War days, when Missouri spawned ravaging gangs and gunslingers like Will Munny in *Unforgiven*. Board-and-batten siding was originally put over log cabins to provide warmth and protection against the wind. Its vertical lines contrasted with the horizontal lines of the logs. The joints between the boards were covered over with strips of wood, or batten.

17. "Blue Diner" was written by Kyle Eastwood. Earlier songs were written by Kyle and Michael Stevens, with David Potaux-Razel. "Blue Morgan," written by Clint Eastwood, plays under the end credits at first with single piano melody, then backed by a full orchestra score as if to underscore Frankie's move from a solitary life toward a love relationship. The movie lists "Music by Clint Eastwood" and "Orchestrated and Conducted by Lennie Niehaus" in the credits.

victory over a vicious fighter. Even before Maggie falls, the visuals become heavily stylized: a silent crowd of watchers recalls the crowd circling the lake of death in the first episode of Kieślowski's *Dekalog*. The scene is observed both in close-up and from an overhead shot of the ring where Maggie lies. The music, until now elegant and spare, is reduced to strings only. We see Frankie and the doctor from Maggie's point of view, and we hear sounds as she hears them, as if she were underwater, recalling the subjective anamorphic hospital shots at the beginning of Kieślowski's *Blue* and the frighteningly dreamlike sequences of Julian Schnabel's more recent *The Diving Bell and the Butterfly* (2007). The lights spin and the screen goes dark. Eastwood changes the camera's role from an invisible observer to an expressive and involved agent that aims to transport the viewer into another world.

The sequences that follow her horrific accident unfold the deepening love between Maggie and Frankie, as he strokes her head, feeds her, bathes her, and masterminds her care, their figures suffused in "pools of light amidst the somber gloom," as Matt Mckenna has written. They model a perfect healing relationship: she is helpless; he is ever-present, not condescending, never blaming her. He never reveals his overwhelming despair to her; on that, he opens his heart only to his priest and to Scrap. The gulf of class and economics between Maggie and Frankie has been crossed; he is teaching her Gaelic. He reads "The Lake Isle of Innisfree" to her, which captures a shared dream of absolute beauty and peace, a place (in reality or in a dream) where her broken body and his aching loneliness can be made whole.

Everything that follows in *Million Dollar Baby* should be viewed through the lens of that healing segment. The sequences now tumble one after the other in ever-descending panic: the cruelty of Maggie's rapacious family; her disintegrating body; her sores and the loss of her leg; her passionate request to be released from pain; her suicide attempt; Frankie's struggle with the teachings of the church (and his refusal of the priest's request that he "leave her to God"); and his love. Frankie wants to keep her with him, yet at the same time honor her wish to die. The bright, unforgiving light and static shots that exposed the greed of Maggie's family now yield to a restless camera and close-ups of her face as she asks for the favor that would prove his love: to be released from this life.

Although Eastwood's score plays underneath this scene, it does not direct the viewer's response. Nor does Scrap's voice-over, which, with its comforting and objective tone, guides us toward the film's conclusion. The suffering, Michael Henry Wilson writes, "creates a spiritual community among the three principal persons, a kind of trinity of suffering where Maggie is the Christ figure."[18]

What kind of conclusion can we accept from the critical social and religious questions this film raises? Is boxing a displaced form of human sacrifice? Is Maggie a scapegoat in an uncaring social order, yet the willing victim of the sport of boxing? After all, the only way she can escape poverty and crushing emotional abuse is to offer up her body for the fight. She discovers by chance the loving community of Frankie and Scrap and their little band of outcasts. What weight can we give those weeks and months in the balance of her life, now destroyed because of the very sport she loves?

In an intimate and yet unsatisfying confession to his longtime spiritual sparring partner, the parish priest, Frankie sets both religion (especially its rituals and practice) and ethics (which centers more around action) into dialogue with theology. What does Frankie's love for Maggie mean, and in what ways do his beliefs as a Catholic influence the expression of his love for her? Does Eastwood, the director of this primal drama, support the actions he shows? We have to step back from the emotion of the moment to reflect more carefully on the movie's actual words and visuals.

In this sequence, the church's teachings clash with the dictates of love and conscience. Frankie cries quietly and bitterly, wanting comfort and wishing to tell someone of the depth of his love for Maggie. But the priest only chides him for the vague guilt he imagines Frankie feels concerning his lost daughter and the peril Frankie will face if he helps Maggie die. (The counseling that is actually effective, words that clarify Frankie's dilemma and identify with his sorrow, comes from Scrap.) The theological question that hovers over this sequence is not "How can Frankie save himself from damnation?" but rather "Why does Maggie have to suffer?"

However, Frankie's decision to free Maggie from suffering does not belong entirely to theology, ethics, or religion. It cannot be explored within those categories alone. In the end it is achingly existential and yet intensely spiritual, so perfectly does Eastwood convey the texture of love through Frankie's actions. Eastwood the director makes no religious claims either here or in the sequence of Maggie's death, even though in that sequence Maggie is bathed in pure white light, like the dead mother, Inger, in the fi-

---

18. Wilson, *Clint Eastwood*, 172. Marcia Gealy, Northwestern University, has observed: "There are times when we must sin to realize the grace of God." Conversation with the author, July 2010.

nal sequence of Carl-Theo. Dreyer's classic film *Ordet* (*The Word*, 1955). But as the representations of protected space multiply, Eastwood seems to suggest a life beyond this one, at least in the human imagination. Since life must be lived in the here and now, whether or not protected space imitates a divine realm — a timeless, borderless kingdom — we honor Scrap's presence as witness, interpreter, and manager of Hit Pit gym and its welcoming community.

Critics who deplore Frankie's removal of Maggie's breathing tube should note that Eastwood, as director, is adapting a short story that, in turn, may or may not represent real actions taken by the author of that story.[19] Too often written about in movie reviews as though he were "really" Dirty Harry or the Man With No Name, Eastwood exists at least three removes from the event presented onscreen: he is Eastwood the man; Eastwood the director, who has adapted several short stories; and Eastwood as Frankie Dunn, who exists within this movie.

Million Dollar Baby's use of voice-over provides further distancing. What we hear and see onscreen visualizes Scrap's *interpretation* of the events he describes. To claim that what we see is "real" — a real director creating a real model for an action that he wants imitated — distorts the fundamental mechanism of narrative, written or filmed. Narrative always reflects the shaping and filtering — the reflective act — of creation.

Furthermore, the film never glorifies Frankie's action. He acts in "fear and trembling," as Kierkegaard put it. To help Maggie die comes from his tears and is motivated by a love both selfish and selfless. When we examine the sequence of her death closely, we see that he enters the hospital corridor quietly and reverently, knowing that he is entering the presence of unimaginable and undeserved suffering. He emerges from darkness, his lithe movements contrasted with her nearly comatose body, which is laid out against a white pillow. He explains (as he had promised) the meaning of the name he had given her, *mo cuishle* ("my darling, my blood"), sealing their love with a tender kiss close to her lips.[20] Apart from the emotion of

19. Michael Medved and Rush Limbaugh are chief among those who sought to spoil *Million Dollar Baby*'s Oscar chances by giving away its ending, which Frank Rich discusses in *The New York Times*, February 12, 2005. Rich writes: "What really makes these critics hate *Million Dollar Baby* is not its supposedly radical politics — which are nonexistent — but its lack of sentimentality."

20. To address a person, the speaker should use "A," unlike Frankie's "Mo chuisle." Eithne Ní Ghallchobhair, a scholar from Cambridge University, explains further: "Irish has a vocative case which always begins, A . . . it lenites the following noun and also slenderises the

the moment, when he confesses that she is blood of his blood, heart of his heart, Eastwood the actor never allows the scene to dissolve into hysterics, his or hers. Frankie exits the room, but the camera lets him slip out of the frame, pulling a black screen across our line of vision to shroud our access to the rest of his life.

The curtain pulls back to reveal our interpreter, Scrap, his watchful face etched against the edge of the frame, half in darkness and half in light, mirroring Frankie's face. Scrap, critic Wilson notes, is "not situated topographically," and Eastwood comments: "It's a deliberately abstract space."[21] Yet here, visually, as in their long friendship, Scrap, Frankie's rock and the movie's Greek chorus, offers no judgment — only tender and sorrowful observation. My students, while they acknowledge that Scrap may not actually be present in the same space as Frankie, always want to believe that he witnesses the final act of love.

The final montage of nine quick sequences pulls the film away from tragedy and back toward affirmation. The gym still runs as a welcoming community, even without Frankie. Scrap's letter to Frankie's daughter, the motor for all the film's images and sounds, may exist ultimately as *her* narrative using Scrap's voice, or Scrap's recasting of his memories, now half-seen with his one remaining good eye. Indeed, by the end of the movie, we wonder who controls the visuals. Darkness is appropriate to the things that Scrap half-sees, both with this blind eye and from the distance of memory. Still, we the viewers have been party to some scenes where Scrap was not present (the locker room, the hospital rooms, and the Missouri visit). We are left to wonder what consciousness gives us the information that the camera presents.

And finally, as the camera crawls in toward the grimy window of Ira's Diner, we think we see Frankie sitting at the counter savoring his memories of Maggie as he eats his lemon meringue pie and imagines paradise, his "perfect world," where everything that is broken will be made whole. Eastwood said this to an interviewer: "I decided to use the little restaurant because it resembled a wooden cabin, something like the one Maggie and Frankie envisage living in together. But I muddied the windows so that no

last consonant, if and when possible. Therefore, *cuisle* ('vein') becomes *a chuisle*, meaning 'my darling, or my life's blood' . . . along those lines. The A is the particle associated with the vocative case. *Mo* means 'my.' It's a possessive pronoun and lenites the following noun" (email to the author, March 8, 2008). So *Mo chuisle* would mean "my darling" also, but if he were speaking about her, not to her.

21. Wilson, *Clint Eastwood*, 173-74.

one could see who is sitting at the counter."[22] As voyeurs, we scramble to reconstruct the whole of his body and this place. We also desire what we cannot see and cannot have: the physical and spiritual healing imagined by Yeats's poetic "Innisfree." In blackness or near-blackness, our clear vision obscured, we reach beyond the realm of the senses toward the unknown. Memory, imagination, and hope coalesce.

Most mainstream Hollywood films do not grant ethical issues the serious focus they deserve: most often everything is sanitized and, more critically — and unforgivably, as Frank Rich observed — sentimentalized. "Eastwood's film," Rich continues, "has the temerity to suggest that fights can have consequences, that some crises do not have black-and-white solutions and that even the pure of heart are not guaranteed a Hollywood ending."[23] Like a Greek tragedy, the movie offers no answers, only greater wisdom — a "stunningly drawn map of the human heart disguised as a boxing yarn."[24] Once again, Eastwood wisely avoided Technicolor to bypass the appearance of crisply photographed reality and the temptation toward sentimentality.

The movie may not quite offer a catharsis, as traditional tragedy often does. Frankie's act is muted, and then he disappears. The last words and images belong to the gym and to Scrap, who concludes the memoir. Or perhaps the last image belongs to the dimly lit café, where dream gives shape to our longings. As Jonathan Rosenbaum wrote at the time of the movie's release, "In a bleak world, where neither family nor religious faith offers any lasting respite, *Million Dollar Baby* offers redemption that derives from the informal and nameless loving relationships people create on their own rather than inherit from family, church, or society."[25] Rejecting sentimentality (i.e., false sentiment), Eastwood has created an ethical vision of searing beauty, an image of a "modest paradise in the here and now."[26]

---

22. Wilson, *Clint Eastwood*, 174.

23. *The New York Times*, February 13, 2005, p. 4 of the arts section. "Black-and-white solutions" refer generally to a vision of the world incorrectly called "Manichean," where good does battle interminably with evil.

24. From a review by Peter Travers, *Rolling Stone,* posted December 20, 2004: http://www.rollingstone.com/reviews/movie/6223305/review/6660737/million_dollar_baby.

25. www.chicagoreader.com/movies/archives/2004/1204/041224.html.

26. Robert Jewett, email correspondence with the author, July 2010.

Changeling

Changeling touched my heart. After watching the movie for the first time, I sat for an hour in the bar attached to the cinema scarcely able to breathe, the sorrow for my lost children released at last. The little baby who disappeared under the ground — would I ever see him again? Am I like the mother, Christine Collins (Angelina Jolie) — holding on, holding back the tears, waiting until my child runs into my arms in another time beyond this world, the hereafter, a perfect world where children do not die young? My dear son, whose little hand once fit in mine so perfectly, companion of my lonely hours and days, would he fold his strong arms around me again and comfort me in my old age as I comforted him over the early years whenever his little heart was broken? As I absorbed Christine's bond with her son, Walter, I could feel my own grown son's hands in mine, a clever healer's hands. I nearly wondered aloud, "When will I see you again?" When can I find my own life again and whole-heartedly, trustingly throw myself into the embrace of my sons' and daughters' unconditional and life-giving love?

Christine and Walter are seen together for only a precious few screen minutes, but the viewer immediately senses the pure love between mother and child, wrapped up in their daily rituals during the few hours they spend with each other, heart close to heart. Christine is all Walter has; he is also all her world. The ensuing loss of her son evokes a sense of cosmic rupture that is nearly divine in its fearful potency, a cinematic *pietà*, the grieving of Mary at the foot of the cross.

Changeling, one of the most theologically probing and most astute of

Eastwood's films, marks yet another Eastwood exploration of the uneasy earthly face of justice, where the universe seems off-balance and imperfect humans struggle to right it. On the surface, the movie exhibits rudimentary elements of a crime drama (suspected murder, manhunt, innocent man or woman wrongly accused, a constant Eastwood theme since *Hang 'Em High*), with corrupt cops, a clever detective, and an attempted rescue. But its rich visual texture, with ominous rain-soaked exteriors and low-lit interiors, will not allow the plot's apparent contradictions to be superficially dismissed. The story's philosophical and theological undertow is too strong and relentless to shrug off. We are forced to look, listen, and feel the rhythms of the bond between Christine and Walter Collins, mother and son — their daily life together, her little personal triumphs despite her husband's desertion, and her richly depicted but limited means.

The period look, from its understated sepia-toned opening to its picture-perfect costuming, enhances the pre-Depression era feel. As I watched the movie, I felt as though I had walked into my mother's life at the end of the 1920s, with the Depression hovering just around the corner: the family had barely enough to eat, and they endured long hours of tedious, mindless work. Twenty years later, during the postwar years, she was still working six days a week, teaching days, and tutoring "DPs" (displaced people) by night. She still struggled to can food for the long Indiana winters, to help my dad pay on our little house, and to see that my brother and I had music lessons. In our household, the music that soaked into our ears came from the old Victrola or the little black radio, songs from the 1890s that her mother had sung to her, or tunes from happier days in the 1920s, when she first met my father.

The look, sound, and feel of *Changeling*'s opening segments capture the same lyrical intensity of devotion between parent and child that I remember from the brief time that I spent with my mother every day. The grounded reality — the restless camera, fresh from an aerial sweep of Los Angeles streets, zooming in on a modest bungalow — draws the viewer into the mother's daily routine. Waking in dim predawn light, a slight woman stirs her child and welcomes him into the new day with breakfast. A similar scene appears in *A Perfect World,* but the mother, a member of the Jehovah's Witnesses, is much less serene, and the kitchen atmosphere is distanced and tense. The son in *A Perfect World* is also snatched by a kidnapper; ironically, though, that boy's life only really *begins* when he leaves his constricted home environment.

In *Changeling,* the mother rises in a restful darkness, and her smiles, looks, and movements reflect the ease and pleasure she draws from her son's presence. She carefully measures his growth: the marks on the wall signal the years he has spent in this home under her watchful gaze. Even his response to his mother when she goes off to work on a Saturday — "I'm not afraid of anything" — speaks not at all of fear at being left alone, but rather of self-assurance sustained by a stable and loving maternal presence in his life. The brown, grey-green, and gold tones of the early scenes belong to the earth, calm and permanent, even as the characters themselves, Christine and Walter, evoke a larger dimension of Madonna and child. The slow, easy musical pacing that graces the central sections of *A Perfect World* and *Bridges of Madison County* works its magic here as well, as the viewer settles comfortably into Christine and Walter's sweet routine: breakfast, streetcar ride, off to school, and off to work. The backstories for mother and child, filled in on the way home from school, sketch out the father's desertion and the origins of the mother's fragile strength.

But beneath and beyond the seemingly steady earth seethe unsteady passions, the primitive composition of an unknown and unknowable universe where demons lie and madmen seize their unfortunate victims every day. The movie's title, *Changeling,* hints of such worlds, impervious to human love and desires, worlds where babies do indeed disappear. In ancient lore, a fairy or demon child would be substituted in the crib for the beloved human baby while its mother sleeps. The mother awakens to gaze on the dear one's sweet smiles, but stares instead into the eyes of a creature that is not her own, and she shrieks to the heavens to remove this unutterably strange, foul presence. But the heavens are silent, and the mother goes to her grave bereft, her own child surely dead.

Eastwood's juxtaposition of real-life tragedy and fairy-tale allusions increases the existential sorrow in the one, and the unbounded horror in the other; for in the space of one short Saturday, Christine's Walter disappears and the police, after weeks of maddening delays, replace him with a boy she knows is not hers. The identical mystery of uncertainty and almost certain loss are attached visually to *Flags of Our Fathers,* where images of lost and murdered boys abound. The first day Christine lives with the changeling child in her house, she carries him out of a darkened room into a lighted hall in a shot that echoes the opening of *Flags,* where Doc Bradley (still looking for his missing foxhole mate after fifty years) stumbles his way through a room of coffins into a lighted area. Doc and Christine pass into a world of horror that exists neither on this earth nor beyond it. The shots in each movie play with the indistinct features, the light at the end of

Christine (Angelina Jolie) searches for her missing son.

the hallway, and the feeling that at any moment Doc — and Christine — will tumble down the rabbit hole into a realm of fantasy and fright.

The multiple plots that critics such as Nick Davis think spoil the movie's unity — lost child, detective story, thriller, protest film — instead mirror the multiple facets of a woman's experience.[1] In a world entirely controlled by men, hostile to her desires, and apparently deserted by God, Christine pleads for a woman's rights as a mother under the law. If a man's child had been kidnapped — and if he was not a former CIA operative, as Liam Neeson plays in *Taken* (2008) — would the police department in Los Angeles, or anywhere else, have ignored his story, tried to palm off another child as his, and locked him up in a psychiatric hospital? Probably not — unless he was black or Hispanic. Carol (Amy Ryan), Christine's only friend in the Los Angeles psychiatric hospital where she is imprisoned, warns her to beware: "Would you believe some crazy woman, or a police officer?" As a woman, it is understood, you will have no defense against unjust accusations by dominant male forces that control the world.[2]

1. Nick Davis: "It passes from being a medium-build period drama to a medium-build *policier* to a medium-build nuthouse exploitation flick to a slightly dwarfish crowds-with-picket-signs domestic epic." And on the subject of Tom Stern's cinematography, which mirrors his work in *Mystic River* in so many places, Davis sees "Angelina Jolie as Olivia de Havilland, in the slammer with the kooks. Or better, Angelina Jolie as Winona Ryder, and Amy Ryan as Angelina Jolie, while cinematographer Tom Stern keeps thwacking all the actors with his customary planks of absolute darkness and with harsh, contracted spots of limestone white." http//www.nicksflickpicks.com/changeling.html.

2. The factual history behind the hospital episode in the movie supports Eastwood's interpretation — and Collins's. Women were routinely imprisoned in the mental hospital and

The deep and engaging mixture of genres and modes that enriches *Changeling* characterizes many of Eastwood's best movies. *Unforgiven,* for instance, moves seamlessly among realistic, mythic, and ironic modes, particularly in its final scenes. *Gran Torino* begins like a bad *Dirty Harry* knockoff, moves into a generation-crossing screwball comedy, morphs into an urban wasteland drama, and ends with Bergman-style confession, self-sacrifice, and redemption. *A Perfect World, Bridges of Madison County,* and *Million Dollar Baby* similarly blend genre elements: prison escape to road movie to confessional; confessional to love story to parable of sorrow; and boxing flick to confessional to love story to tragedy. The flexibility of the film form suits Eastwood because he constantly crosses boundaries of ethnicity, gender, nationality, and traditional definitions of good and bad, right and wrong. Across the range of human experience, Eastwood prizes the weak of this earth, and his camera focuses on lonely women like Christine or, similarly, on Butch Haynes (Kevin Costner) in *A Perfect World,* who sums up his sorry and sorrowful life this way: "I ain't a good man. But I ain't the worst, neither."

Changeling, which Eastwood took over from director-producer Ron Howard due to scheduling problems, may lack the "nuanced" and "ambiguous" spin of other Eastwood movies, as Kent Jones has suggested in an online roundtable discussion.[3] But whether or not Eastwood was involved in its genesis, he dared to make a movie that centers on a woman's life, a mother's anguish, without a hint of sentimentality or melodrama. Few directors have ever presented the other side of an American military conflict as he did in *Letters from Iwo Jima,* and few male directors have so thoroughly and honestly captured a woman's innermost anguish.

Despite the presence of two high-octane stars, Jolie and John Malkovich, and an enthusiastic reception of the film at Cannes, where it opened the festival, *Changeling* received little attention in the United States. It played in limited release in theaters in this country and soon vanished from public consciousness. While it was called a "magnificent" film in France, *Gran Torino* quickly overshadowed its reception, partly because the producers shaped *Gran Torino*'s trailer toward violence and the restitution meted out by the "one-man" heroic formula that has been so dangerously common in American movies, especially so during the Bush-

---

sometimes subjected to the cruelty of electroshock treatment for supposedly resisting police actions. As a result of Christine Collins's case, the practice was halted.

    3. http://alsolikelife.com/shooting/?p=935.

Cheney-Rumsfeld era.[4] For example, *National Review* readers needed only to look at the trailer and the opening of the actual movie and — based on that one quick glance — glibly put it on the list of the magazine's top twenty-five conservative-friendly films.[5]

But *Changeling* enters a realm of reason and emotion different from that of *Gran Torino*, indeed, different from most movies about the American experience. Christine is a victim of oppression and perhaps of fate (Eastwood does not take sides), but she does not fall into the prostitute/ sacrificial victim trap of *Broken Blossoms* (D. W. Griffith, 1922), *Pandora's Box* (Georg Wilhelm Pabst, 1929), *Jezebel* (William Wyler, 1938), or the contrasting women of *Sunrise* (F. W. Murnau, 1927). *Changeling* is not a preset female genre formula. The film is based on a much-publicized real-life incident that was soon forgotten.[6] Christine's story, rather than being dismissed as a tawdry tabloid news item of the time, was spiritually foundational to Eastwood. He and screenwriter Michael Straczynski believe her: she is not a hysteric, as the police lieutenant says and the psychiatric ward doctor concludes; nor is she a commodity to be marketed, as we suspect when the newspapers get hold of her story. Eastwood gets inside her skin, living her terrible loss and sorrow, dwelling with her as she lives with a changeling in her household, eating at her child's spot at the table, sleeping in her little boy's bed. The viewer enters her perspective as she skates her way at work through the lines of women, other telephone operators. As she fidgets at closing time, eager to get home to Walter before dark, the viewer's fears rise, stoked by the unknown.

Eastwood could have made an entire movie simply about American life during the years after World War I, the years between Charlie Chaplin's *The Circus* (1928) and Frank Capra's *It Happened One Night* (1934), which marked the end of the silent era and the beginning of film sound. The post–World War I boom created monstrous wealth for a few and left the rest a few steps behind its burgeoning technological advances, much as Christine runs a few tragic steps behind the bus that would take her home to Walter after a long day's work. Her life will soon become entan-

4. Interview with Eastwood in Pascal Merigeau, "Dans l'atelier d'Eastwood" ("In Eastwood's Studio"), *Le Nouvel* (6-12 novembre 2008): 63-64.

5. http://www.google.com/search?rls=gm&sourceid=gmail&hl=en&source=hp&q =national+review+top+conservative+movies&aq=2&oq=national+review+top+&aqi=g3.

6. The screenwriter, J. Michael Straczynski, played with a number of structures as he crafted the script from over 6,000 pages of documents from the period. Eastwood liked his original script and made few changes to it.

Christine (Angelina Jolie) is interrogated by the hospital psychiatrist.

gled, without her knowledge, in a world she previously had no idea existed: the great city, its little hell holes, prison/asylums, the countryside outside the city where murderers prey on people, news sensationalism, the church, the court system, and systemic corruption at the very heart of the law. Once the protected circle of her fragile family of two is broken, she is thrust into the widening, enveloping circles of a dark social order — unfolding layers of abuse. She becomes the victim of a corrupt and uncaring police force, which is backed up by doctors and a psychiatric hospital. She also becomes the unwitting darling of the moment for a grandstanding preacher, Gustav Briegleb (Malkovich), and the masses that turn out to see her and her supposed son.

Later in the film, the crowds who follow the preacher also come out to see Christine vindicated in the courts of law. The world does eventually become involved in her story. Yet Eastwood the director continues to focus on the mother's loss. By movie's end, what remained with me was not the wild-eyed face of the serial killer, the weird resonance of Malkovich's crusading preacher (like the ones Eastwood remembered from his childhood), or the satisfying sight of corrupt Los Angeles cops sentenced for their malfeasance.[7] Curtis Hanson's *L.A. Confidential* (1997) had already cornered the market on bad California cops.

Neither do the mechanisms of the modern world — recent tragedies such as a runaway car or a faulty ski lift or a badly executed war that kills children — take her son from her. Disembodied creatures or machines do

7. Merigeau, "Dans l'atelier d'Eastwood," 64.

not steal the child in a dull blur of customary movie-style sensation or horror, though *Changeling*'s screenwriter and Eastwood could have turned the script to focus on the murders. The movie doesn't punctuate the death so tidily. Eastwood's vision horrifies us with the underlying knowledge that only a short car ride from Los Angeles's clanging streetcars and humming phone lines, a madman murders children with an axe and his own hands. The film's idyllic opening remains in all its tangible details of lived life. I cannot forget Christine's uneasy mixture of disbelief, grief, and sympathy as she sits on the bedside of the boy who claims to be her lost son (a shot lit almost exactly like one in *Mystic River,* where Dave sits on his son's bed and begins to ramble on about vampires).[8] The aerial shot of a cold, frightened, and deserted Christine, small and lost, also remains with me, as she lies on a slab in the psychiatric hospital awaiting her possible death the next day. A similar aerial shot pulls together a sympathetic Detective Ybarra and the young boy, who has led him to Walter Collins's probable burial spot. Most of all, I cannot shake the questions that hover over the movie: What kind of society have we created where the innocent are persecuted? What kind of universe gives birth to and harbors a child murderer?

For forty years as a director, Eastwood has seized on the permeability allowed by screen artifice to suggest by image (seven bullet holes in the back; a cloud of mist; a radiant sunset over a single grave; a shadow seen through a dusky windowpane) and sound (howls and wails; a simple guitar or piano line) what mortal dangers might lie behind the everyday veil of reality. Again and again he has imaged profound loss, as — again and again, courageously and confidently — he has violated the unofficial movie commandment "Never harm a child."

Josey Wales drags the burlap shroud of his son across the ground and sobs and moans over the fresh grave.[9] In *Mystic River,* Jimmy howls when he hears of the murder of his cherished daughter, Katie, as I heard the father of a seven-year-old boy crushed by a runaway car howl at the heavens when his child was lowered into the ground. Furthermore, *Mystic River* is driven not only by the search for Katie's killer but also by nightmares that Dave, a grown version of a Walter Collins who might have escaped, en-

8. Thanks to Alex Schwarm, from the Northwestern University Eastwood class, Winter 2010.

9. The opening shots of *Unforgiven* visually echo the burial segment in *Josey Wales.* Will Munny, his shadowed figure etched against a sunset sky, digs a hole in which to place his beloved wife, who restored his soul. But the little boys' bodies in *Changeling* lie untended, unmourned, forgotten.

Christine (Angelina Jolie) and Walter (Gattlin Griffith)
on their way home from school.

dures.[10] In *Million Dollar Baby,* Frankie kisses the face of young Maggie, his own heart's love, as he eases the woman-child into the unknown.

Doc Bradley, in *Flags of Our Fathers,* cries out for his hapless buddy, Iggy, a simple boy dragged out into the fog of war, a boy who vanished in the darkness and was sucked into emptiness. Try as the political machine may to paint the bright face of cheerfulness and patriotism on World War II, *Flags* exposes the execution of the war as a crime against children. As a monstrous entity, war resembles the hideous schemes of the serial killer who stalks the plot in *Changeling.* As on a battlefield, we see mind-numbing numbers of boys whose bodies are mutilated, parts of their leg bones still left in their shoes, their chests ripped open and their blood soaked into the barren ground. The operation that sends 100,000 soldiers (U.S.) or 22,000 (Japan) to take or defend Iwo Jima — a barren rock in the middle of the ocean — discounts their individual lives. It forces the young and unseasoned men to murder close at hand or from a detached distance, by proxy, crazed by sorrow and terror, unhinged by vengeance, unmanned, and stripped of all that makes them human. The flags displayed so brazenly in the twinned movies (American in *Flags of Our Fathers* and Japanese in *Letters from Iwo Jima*) ultimately cover coffins, masking the mutilated remains of schoolboys in the bright public colors of heroic fantasy. *Changeling* indexes the earlier movies, steeped in horrors too unimaginable to be named.

10. I owe the visual and thematic connections between *Mystic River* and *Changeling* to filmmaker Alex Schwarm, Northwestern University Eastwood class, Winter 2009.

In the "perfect world" Eastwood imagines repeatedly in his most iconic movies — the green and fertile farm of Ned and Sally in *Unforgiven,* the peace pact between Josey and Ten Bears in *The Outlaw Josey Wales,* the little cabin that Maggie and Frankie dream about in *Million Dollar Baby,* or the warm, well-lighted spaces in flashbacks in *Letters from Iwo Jima* — no child would suffer abuse, be abandoned, or die young. No man or woman would be disdained for poverty, gender identity, ethnicity, race, or lack of power. No human being would ever endure loss or loneliness. Each person would flourish, and all stories would be told and heard. *Changeling* adds to the long list of Eastwood films that give us a glimpse of perfection, if only to give us a sense of how far our world has fallen from a state of grace. Yet it is precisely in the portrayal of everyday acts of brave and moral heroism that Eastwood honors the ones who are overlooked and forgotten in their time and passed by the sweep of history. He fashions an intimation of a perfect world, a paradise in our daily life, from loving moments among the everyday human beings his movies depict.

But ours is not a perfect world. "In a perfect world," Sally Gerber (Laura Dern) observes in the movie *A Perfect World,* "such things wouldn't happen," referring to the tragic waste of the childhood abuse, prison stint, and senseless death of Butch Haynes (Kevin Costner). Eastwood tells tales that bubble up from this imperfect world — tales that rarely surface in a power- and money-driven social order. He sets stories of the forgotten ones in dialogue with the evanescent thoughts and images of a perfect world, a place of welcome, comfort, and healing toward which all humans might yearn, a place where traditional equations of power are overturned and the weak and powerless are finally known by name.

Changeling lacks a Hollywood happy ending, even if the character of Christine Collins lives in hope. The film, a litany of questions, moves from the chronicle of a real-life story into the realm of transcendent meditation that affects the way we live together as citizens and members of the human community. The "perfect world" (if it existed) cannot be cordoned off from the real world as an oasis that belongs to only a few. Neither should those who suffer in our contemporary world wait for the next world, the hereafter. Peace and justice belong to the world in which all creatures make their home. Eastwood has told a tale of one woman's suffering and loss and has extended it to the vulnerability of all the world's mothers who have been subjected to rape, abuse, and the loss of their dearly beloved children.

Bird

Although Eastwood made *Bird* in 1988, in many ways it belongs to the great later phase of his artistry that surfaces in *Unforgiven* and has flowered with ever-increasing urgency since 2003's *Mystic River*. Its nonlinear narrative anticipates the Vermeer-like (and jazzlike) structure — flashbacks within flashbacks — that troubles and deepens viewers' comprehension of war memories in *Flags of Our Fathers* and *Letters from Iwo Jima*. Its tale, the meteoric rise and tragic fall of jazz great Charlie Parker (Forest Whitaker), called "Bird" by his fellow musicians and jazz aficionados, is shot in the dark and claustrophobic interiors of nightclubs and sad living spaces more akin to those of *Mystic River* than to *Big* (Penny Marshall, 1988). Warm darkness and too-bright light, judicious use of sound and silence, rain-slicked alleys and frighteningly deserted streets — Eastwood fans have seen all this before in Leone's Spaghetti Westerns, in *High Plains Drifter* and *The Outlaw Josey Wales,* and in *Million Dollar Baby* and *Changeling.*

Despite its searing beauty and a magnificent jazz soundtrack, *Bird* bombed at the U.S. box office. Why? At least partly because it also deals with the ultimate social, moral, and political injustice in America: entrenched racism. That is, *Bird* confronts the greatest "mystery of life" of all: the systemic exclusion of one entire segment of a population by their own kind. If Eastwood has paid attention throughout his career to the socially marginalized, *Bird* presents marginalization in its most extreme form. The "black Irish" made it to the inside, even to the pinnacle of Chicago politics; the "sloppy Scots-Irish" (to quote a history book from the mid-nineteenth century) cleaned up their act; the German-Americans and Japanese-Americans survived wartime hysteria. Hispanic Americans still struggle, as Eastwood's movie *Blood Work* (2002) suggests. But blacks remain "the other."

However, anyone who expected from *Bird* a polemical Oliver Stone–type movie, a scathing exposé of racism either by implication or sermon, would be disappointed. The critical undertow is present, but the movie principally honors jazz lover Clint Eastwood's lifelong hero, the legendary Parker, a young man who surmounted racism, soaked up the religious and artistic fervor that sustained black communities after slavery, and transformed the ways music was grasped, captured, and released to the world. His music brought a vision of paradise to his listeners and still exists for listeners in the "hereafter."

There are so many stunningly shot scenes in *Bird* that the viewer comes away dumbfounded with the film's virtuosity. For starters, the opening chapters establish the themes, visuals, relationships, and musical devices that appear throughout the film. As the opening credits roll, we meet a young boy, presumed to be Charlie Parker, as he plays the flute while he rides on a pony. This scene anticipates the young musician Parker, now called Bird, riding on a white horse through the streets of Manhattan to "rescue" his beloved Chan (Diane Venora, in an award-winning performance) from her upscale white background. Significantly, the opening shot of the Warner Brothers logo appears on screen in black and white, signaling that *Bird*, like the later films *Mystic River* and *Letters from Iwo Jima*, has been shot in color as though it were a black-and-white movie. The opening fragment of this sequence is shot in brown tones, as is *Beguiled* (Don Siegel, assisted by Eastwood, 1971), then cuts to a black screen before the title *Bird* flashes onscreen. We see one word alone, as if to anticipate the loneliness of Charlie Parker the man, musical genius and addict, whose life we are about to witness.

The young Charlie Parker continues to play under the actors' names in the credits until the fragment segues into an adolescent Charlie practicing "O Christmas Tree" on a saxophone. The camera pans along a long wooden porch where men are smoking marijuana, inert in contrast to the boy's constant motion, almost invisible against the peeling clapboard of the house. The sound fades into music from a nightclub and more credits. The moment we hear Parker play, the credit entry "Music by Lennie Niehaus" flashes across the screen.

The camera circles around Bird as a spotlight beams like a star on a man so dark that only the front of his face and the back of his suit are illuminated. As he plays, the restless camera moves around him to focus on his fingers and face, though we still can barely see them. Cuts begin to accelerate, viewing the charismatic player from multiple angles as he uses call-and-response with his clapping audience, who are spellbound in ritual admiration, murmuring like birds. Dizzy Gillespie (Samuel E. Wright), who appears in the film as a counterpoint character, applauds and cheers him on. Other than the smoky darkness of the sequence, we could be watching a documentary such as *Jazz on a Summer's Day* (Aran Avakian and Bert Stern, 1960).

The virtuoso performance fades out with Bird's face in the left corner of the shot, displaced by a flying cymbal that cuts across a blue surface the color of his suit. Before any story line can be laid down, the viewer has glimpsed Parker's childhood home, observed the male role models who surrounded him, gotten a scent of his life-shaping humiliation — not from whites but rather from men he admired — and witnessed his awesome career in full bloom, triumphant years slashed like the cymbal across the screen's blue background (which seems to symbolize the fabric of his life).

The third sequence of the film establishes further background for the genesis and development of Bird's music. We witness the tortured relationship between Charlie and Chan; the recent death of their child; Bird's return to drug use; and his suicide attempt, which we will learn later in the movie is not his first. Underneath some of the shots we hear Bird's music again, dipping and soaring. Sequences four through eleven spin various levels of backstory through shifting time periods. We learn from the doctor who admits him to hospital that Parker has few contracts (his self-destructive nature arises in part from the recent decline of his career, the pompous doctor intones); his drug use has escalated; and his lack of professional confidence somehow relates to a thrown cymbal.

As if to mark yet another difference between *Bird* and any other biopic or film biography, Eastwood now shifts the movie's focus from Parker to Chan, his wife. Her sassy, no-nonsense sparring with Bird and the doctor who wants to lock him in an institution reminds us of Strawberry Alice in *Unforgiven* or Sue in *Gran Torino* or even the prostitute Gus Malley in *The Gauntlet,* women who have no illusions about life and are every bit men's equals. As the sequence opens, Chan has just called the dismissive doctor's bluff. Positioned in his office, standing over the seated wife, he intones magisterially: "If your husband were my brother, believe me, I'd commit him." Chan, in control, snaps back: "Oh really? What's your brother's name?" In response, the doctor has to admit, "I don't have a brother," defusing the potential confrontation between a man used to dispensing orders and a woman who is as strong as he is. The scene prepares us to absorb the unfolding drama of years of fruitful collaboration between husband and wife that sours but never ends.

After the doctor leaves his office, the camera moves in on Chan's face, the screen darkens, and a lap dissolve carries us back in time to a younger Chan, who is emerging from her New York brownstone with a light step and a big smile. The jazz score dialogues with shots of neon club signs, period cars gaudy in their boxy pretension, and streets full of dapper young men and beautiful women. Once Chan has disappeared into the 18 Club, the all-seeing camera pans from right to left to follow the hawking doorman around cars, past clubs, through the crowds along jazz-hopping 52nd Street, and finally back to the 18 Club, where he meets Buster Franklin (Keith David). Then cut, cut, cut as Buster attempts to explode the myth of the "new man on the scene," Charlie Parker. A reprise of Bird's early failure feeds into the near-present of the new jazzman's wild success and Chan's rapturous love. Suspense and progression build, as in a musical composition.

Emerging from the double flashback into the uncertain present of the narrative, Chan refuses to have Bird committed or subjected to electroshock therapy, a treatment certain to extinguish his creativity. Eastwood would later transfer Chan's spirited defense of an innocent to *Changeling*, where an illegally incarcerated Christine Collins is strapped to the shock table with only the crusading preacher John Malkovich to rescue her. As with everything else in his career, the director nibbles on the same themes repeatedly, building on one as he tackles the subject — perhaps justice or confession — from a new perspective.

Any rescue in *Bird*, however, will not play out within the crazily non-linear narrative line. Time flips back to the courtship, then to a magnificent early Parker performance; to the winter of 1946, with the sinister apparition of a drug dealer on the street; to a rapturous performance with Dizzy Gillespie as "bebop invades the West"; and to the first of Bird's encounters with other white women and more false rescues and returns along the way. After the film's dizzying trips through time and space, the image of a drunken Bird staggering behind a garbage-crowded building fades into the beginnings of Birdland and Parker's acclaim in Paris, one of the narrative's most graceful moments.

It's slightly more than halfway through the movie, and Bird's band has yet to move through the South; the talented trumpeter Red Rodney is not yet hooked on drugs; Bird and Chan have not moved into their new apartment; viewers have not experienced the death of their little girl; and the couple has not yet moved to the countryside to seek peace — a retreat to a Dickensian paradise that cannot shield the tormented man from his demons.

Bird takes care to suggest that the demons come from within and from without. The viewer will think back to 1964, when blacks had few protectors, particularly in the South. Even earlier — in the late forties and early fifties, when Parker rose to prominence as a jazz artist and leader who shaped the bebop sound — racially mixed marriages were still illegal in more than half the states. Miscegenation laws dated back to at least 1661; they were struck down federally in 1947, but many Southern states were very slow to change their seventeenth-century statutes. However, that was the least of the worries that consumed the daytimes and nighttimes of black Americans. They had to worry about getting and holding a job, any job; obtaining a loan and buying a home; and getting an education. In bad economic times, blacks suffered disproportionately to whites — and still do. And come voting time in Southern states in 1964, black citizens were subjected to unfair tests to "verify" their eligibility to vote. But survival came first.

The miserable state of race relations — especially job and education opportunities denied America's own citizens — could have consumed Eastwood's entire movie on the life and music of Charlie Parker. But as a director, a lifelong jazz lover, and an accomplished pianist, he had had the good fortune (and perhaps the personal grace) to develop his own artistic gifts in the racially open atmosphere around Oakland and Los Angeles. He shaped the movie *Bird* with Charlie Parker the artist, the man, and his music at its center. Around that center, Eastwood was free to create a movie astonishing in its formal inventiveness, acting style, and emotional resonance. With its exploration of Parker's lifelong drug addiction, however, the movie ran afoul of some of the latter's supporters, who remembered the music but also the man's infectious and generous laugh.

Unfortunately, Parker's excessive drug use cannot be written out. At a personal level, drugs fueled Bird's wild self-destructiveness and derailed his career. From his high in the late 1940s and early '50s, he succumbed with greater frequency to the demons that had pursued him since his teenage years. The sight of a young man dead from an overdose remains in Bird's nightmares. Two flashbacks show us the young Charlie staring at the warehoused body of an addict, produced by a doctor friend who predicts

Red Rodney (Michael Zelniker) and Bird (Forest Whitaker): a class act.

the young musician's early death if he doesn't kick the habit. The ghoulish scenes are mirrored when Bird severely exhorts his trumpet player, Red Rodney, to kick it before it's too late, advice that the protégé throws back in his face.

The jazzlike structure of the film (theme, variation, riff, spin-off, spin-off the riff until the theme returns) doesn't allow for tidy analysis. Each sequence vibrates with its own musicality, repeating not only the cautionary side of drug use but also the threat of early death, as ineffective a measure as using the death penalty to deter crime. The threat of incarceration has its incarnation in the spectral white cop who trails Bird for ten years and later sends Red, not Bird, to prison. The threat of the loss of his livelihood — or worse, his gifts — is still not able to stop the genius's downward spiral into destitution. He loses his license, the clubs on 52nd Street turn into brothels, and he seems to play little after his daughter's death and the family's eviction from their Central Street apartment. Worse, as his daughter lies dying, then lies in her casket, he sits immobilized in another city with his mistress, able only to write endless telegrams to his wife but never able to board a plane home.[1]

1. James Mangold's biopic *Walk the Line* (2005) offers a thoughtfully crafted but mainstream look at country-music star Johnny Cash. Cash, too, was harrowed by addiction but overcame it with the help of the woman who became his wife, June Carter. Jonathan

But what a deliriously rich film, with its set pieces in sound and offscreen, its hundred shades of darkness, its quirky dialogue, and the sense of life on the streets during the great days of jazz. What did aspiring jazz players such as Parker and his friends do? They played clubs if they were lucky, but if not, they played Jewish weddings. Then they would take a jazz tour through the South, skirting racial madness by billing the white Red Rodney as "Albino Red." Red runs into stores to fetch the groceries, then hops into the band's getaway car and zips down the road, leaving the store owners furious. (A version of this scene, the denial of food, will be reprised in *A Perfect World* a few years later.) In his albino disguise, Red sees firsthand the roach-infested motel beds where blacks are consigned when on road trips.

Since Eastwood has created neither a hagiography (saint's life) nor a traditional biopic in Bird, what do we have? We have music — Charlie Parker's own playing (though digitally enhanced), which was isolated from his wife's old recordings — infusing almost every scene until the last half hour of the movie. It takes a second viewing, or listening, to realize how distinctive that sound is. It is better to hear Bird's performances — isolated, cleaned, and accompanied by new instrumentalists — than to listen to almost any other jazz musician, and far better than to keep those old recordings locked up in a closet.

How far Eastwood the director has come since Dee Barton's score for *High Plains Drifter*, with the eerie whistles and guitars in the style of Ennio Morricone, the composer for the Spaghetti Westerns. The wind and horror orchestration spook the viewer, who fears retribution for sins not yet committed. How far he has come from Jerry Fielding's lush country-and-western-flavored score for the wide-open spaces of *The Outlaw Josey Wales*, with its inset of "The Rose of Alabamy," a southern adaptation with roots in minstrelsy. Only three years before *Bird*, Lennie Niehaus, the jazz artist with whom Eastwood has worked for decades, had written original music for *Pale Rider*.

And providing a precedent for Bird's nonstop jazz, *The Gauntlet* (1977) opens and closes with the jazz-inflected gospel hymn "Just a Closer Walk with Thee," a song woven into the fabric of Jerry Fielding's score. (Curi-

---

Rosenbaum has pronounced *Bird* "the most serious, conscientious, and accomplished jazz biopic ever made, and almost certainly Eastwood's best picture as well" (*Chicago Reader*, October 28, 1988). *Bird* has been compared favorably to *Round Midnight* (Bertrand Tavernier, 1986), but *Bird* seems more inventive and more in tune with the spirit of jazz.

ously, *The Gauntlet,* but not *Bird,* was featured in the Museum of Modern Art's movie festival in Spring 2008, where it was honored for its jazz score.)[2] The opening of *The Gauntlet* juxtaposes the rich riffs of a jazz score against a barren urban concrete cityscape (the movie is mostly set in Phoenix). Electronic music or rap might have seemed better suited to accompany any part of the opening of *The Gauntlet,* from the hazy polluted sunrise to the shady nightclub from which the hero emerges to the broken asphalt and sterile geometry of the city's empty buildings. That film, a tale of police corruption and personal redemption, is set in the post-Eden, post–Gold Rush, post-Depression Southwest with its massive governmental attempts at social restitution.

Jazz creeps in and around the cultural markers of *The Gauntlet* (wasted lives and deserted buildings) like trailing roses, blooming when you least expect them to. Jazz soaks up suppressed passions, absorbs and transforms pain, erases race and class and gender, and paves the way for a love story. Only the power of the film's opening jazz score and its haunting, hopeful lyrics could sustain an assault on two lovers, Ben (Eastwood) and Gus (Sondra Locke), as they try to make it to the courthouse to testify at a trial. Eight hundred armored policemen with assault rifles line the road to the courthouse as their bullet-ridden bus drives right to the front door.

Bird and *The Gauntlet* are not alone in the world of jazz-infused films. Henry Mancini scored *A Touch of Evil* (Orson Welles, 1958) and *Days of Wine and Roses* (1963); Miles Davis provided a lush score for Louis Malle's *Elevator to the Gallows* (1958), with a young Jeanne Moreau; and Jean-Pierre Melville used jazz scores almost exclusively in the mid-1950s to early '60s, as in *Bob le Flambeur* (*Bob the Gambler,* 1956) and *Le Samouraï* (1967). Film music functions in differing ways, however, depending on the director's and the creative team's envisioned interaction between sound design and the other elements of a film: image, dialogue, narrative progression, and "meaning," to name a few. Music can elevate, as in *Chariots of Fire* (Hugh Hudson, 1981) and *Star Wars* (George Lucas, 1977); evoke a past moment of bliss or trigger a memory, as in *Casablanca* (Michael Curtiz, 1942); or drown us in emotion, as in *Brokeback Mountain* (Ang Lee, 2005).

Eastwood has increasingly composed more of his own material, in

---

2. Sandy Mandelberger, "Jazz Beats at MOMA Film Program," *The New York Times,* April 13, 2008, AR 20. *The Gauntlet* was also featured at the British Film Institute's retrospective of Eastwood's early works at London's National Theatre that summer.

marked contrast to composers for Hollywood films in the Golden Age, when he was growing up. Max Steiner, for example, head of the RKO music department and the principal film composer of his time, wrote the music for sixty films between 1935 and 1940.[3] But Eastwood takes his time writing music for his films. Although he scouts locations, sets up, and shoots in record time, the music — at least for *Mystic River,* for example — can take as long as four months to compose. And while his music, when it appears, interlaces closely with the events onscreen, his overall approach seems to be the one he established with *Bird:* the music is a character, an equal player; it is not a throwaway score that is mass-produced to lull the audience into complacency.

Music historian Peter Larsen notes that, with the 1950s and the advent of film noir, the film-going public wanted a different kind of movie from the old large-scale ones with lavish scores. Leonard Bernstein's music for *On the Waterfront* (Elia Kazan, 1954) and Leonard Rosenman's music for *East of Eden* (Elia Kazan, 1955) and *Rebel without a Cause* (Nicholas Ray, 1955) were "inspired by earlier atonal experiments" and the twelve-tone music of Schoenberg. But the traditional symphonic approach largely continued. Bernard Herrmann did provide "alternatives to the Golden Age model" with his music for Hitchcock's *Vertigo* (1958), *North by Northwest* (1959), and *Psycho* (1960).[4]

Herrmann's "distinctive sound universe" applies to *Bird.* Parker's bebop jazz is played diegetically, when he is seen onstage, and nondiegetically as mood or statement. Bird soars like his song when he plays, and at the funeral at the end of the film, "Kansas City" reminds the audience not only of the opening sequence of Parker's childhood but also of his dazzling stage performances. With *Bird,* the faster the sequences move as they flip in and out of time and space, the higher the viewer's spirit soars with the music as she or he becomes part of the jazz performance.

If Bird is neither an adoring biopic nor a "soupy Hollywood good black musician" putdown, what is it apart from its dizzying structure and sad ending? Is it "an expressionistic labyrinth, a circular and elliptical journey into a tortured musician's soul," where narrative is "discarded" and phenomenology is king?[5] Laurence Knapp comes close to capturing the almost

3. Peter Larsen, *Film Music* (London: Reaktion Books, 2005); trans. John Irons (2007), 87ff., esp. 92-97.

4. Larsen, *Film Music,* 125-27.

5. Laurence Knapp, *Directed by Clint Eastwood: Eighteen Films Analyzed* (Jefferson, ND: McFarland and Company, 1996), 133-37.

avant-garde approach of *Bird* by noting its call for the viewer to participate in what we see and hear, where "backlighting and intimate framing, subterranean lighting and transmutable montage" create a "nocturnal, underground film." The film, filled with "arc pans and camera tracks" to emphasize Parker's flight (like a bird, Knapp writes), is unusual for Eastwood.

Film critic Jonathan Rosenbaum objects to the film's too-easy treatment of interracial romance, preferring the raw, in-your-face emotions of John Cassavetes' *Shadows* (1959), which is also structured like a jazz composition.[6] But Eastwood is a different kind of filmmaker from the edgy Cassavetes: he is always treading carefully between the worlds of popular cinema and its audience's demands and the more arty, more philosophically inflected films he prefers to make (*Josey Wales* and *Bird;* in recent years, eight "personal" movies in a row). *Shadows* is a towering achievement, shot on the streets of New York City rather than in studios, spun out with a great deal of improvisation rather than a script — with fragments, extreme close-ups, and terrible betrayal and desertion as impossible to watch as it is to experience.

Eastwood had something different in mind when he made *Bird* — nearly thirty years after *Shadows* appeared. He offered a film that would add another register to Cassavetes' jazz-image-improvisation combination. The mythical ennobles the terrible reality we see on screen. If the relationship between Charlie Parker and Chan seems too quirky, too close, too loving to be real, that is entirely in keeping with Eastwood's habit of removing the polemic from "race."

Few American movies show black-and-white relationships at all. Here Eastwood considers the couple's attraction as one person to another — as opposed to a black person to a white person — and their problems as broadly human, not bizarre. Chan's white daughter calls Parker "Daddy" quite naturally. "Race" does not motivate the doctor who wants to commit him to the state asylum; he is simply practicing bad medicine, as Chan pointedly comments (though electroshock therapy was the preferred therapy not only in the late 1920s, when *Changeling*'s Christine Collins was incarcerated, but also in the 1940s, and still in the early 1960s, when I reluctantly assisted in such "treatment" at the hospital where I interned). Chan is a part of the club scene, and the audiences Eastwood shows in the post-

---

6. Shot with 16mm camera on the streets of New York, according to IMDb.com. Rosenbaum also prefers the eighty-three-minute documentary *Killer of Sheep*, shot on location by Charles Burnett (1977).

war jazz boom years are largely black, but mixed with white and black Navy men and white women.[7] Red Rodney (Michael Zelniker) is accepted into Bird's ensemble because of his talent, not because of or in spite of his color.

Eastwood, passionately opposed to racial prejudice, makes his points about injustice and intolerance in other ways. After Bird comes to fetch his love, Chan, at her apartment in New York, the couple goes to a club and dances to the tune of "Moonlight Becomes You." A crane shot establishes the club's clientele and the couple's position in the space. Whites at three different tables turn their censorious faces toward the dance floor, obviously scandalized by the presence of an interracial couple. An ugly scene could have broken out, with Bird and Chan thrown out of the club; instead, Eastwood turns the camera toward one of the band members, who cries out, "Look! It's Charlie Parker!" which effectively defuses a potential spectacle by emphasizing Bird's name, not his color.

More famously, though, in some of the funniest scenes in the movie, Parker and his band have to devise ways to survive during their tour in the South. In rapid succession, they market Red Rodney as an albino and their star; they send him for groceries and sneak him into motels. Bird's troubles with the law come from his drug use, not from his color (though the courtroom scene takes place in New York, not the deep South, where he never would have been allowed to plead his case). Throughout the sequences in the South, comedy leavens the approaching tragedy to relieve tension and expose the subject of racial discrimination without trivializing it.

Before the last half hour of the film begins, the sights and sounds of Parker in performance in real time (the Jewish wedding and the club in the South) or in memory (his various club appearances shown in the movie) begin to fade. Bird walks down a rain-slicked street in the dark with no music to sustain him. More brief shots of his life will follow before movie's end, but the music has disappeared onscreen and as background, only to resurface in the oddly distanced funeral, with the camera fixing its roving "bird's-eye" on Bird's lifeless body.

The final sequence begins with the cymbal's final fall, its circular shape mirrored in the dozens of umbrella tops we see from the camera's high perch above Adam Clayton Powell's church in Harlem. "Come with me if

---

7. Harry Truman began efforts to desegregate the armed forces in 1945. Only the high casualties in the Korean War forced the issue, and the three branches were almost fully integrated by the end of 1951.

you wanna go to Kansas City," croons the soundtrack ("Parker's Mood," re-corded in 1947), as the funeral attendees pack a partly visible coffin into the hearse and slowly process into the distance. It is 1955, a time when most white people would not even have considered this man's story worth tell-ing. The shell of Charlie Parker's devastated thirty-four-year-old body moves away from the viewer, leaving only his still-soaring spirit among us.

When Eastwood told the tale of Bird in 1988, one of his musical heroes, few recognized the movie as one of the greatest American tragedies — and one of the greatest poems about human creativity in the face of the mys-teries of human life.

PART III

Eternal War or the Dawn of Peace?

We've been fighting to-day on the old camp ground,
Many are lying near;
Some are dead, and some are dying,
Many are in tears.
Many are the hearts that are weary to-night,
Wishing for the war to cease,
Many are the hearts looking for the right,
To see the dawn of peace.
Dying to-night, dying to-night,
Dying on the old camp ground.[1]

"Tenting on the Old Camp Ground" (1864)

I n 2006, Clint Eastwood — a household name since his 1960s telenovella western series *Rawhide* — startled those who loved his hotheaded and simple Rowdy Yates character, his reckless and depressed Dirty Harry character, and his flashy but cool Man With No Name. He deserted the western terrain, both wild and urban, and abandoned the iconic screen persona (at least until *Gran Torino* in 2008) that had made him world-famous whether he was clothed in a dirty poncho, a drover's dusty jeans, a policeman's polyester slacks, or the open-shirted casuals of the itinerant

---

1. http://www.contemplator.com/america/tenting.html.

photographic journalist. He made two war movies in one year, and starred in neither one despite his successful acting turn in *Million Dollar Baby* not long before. In fact, one of the films, *Letters from Iwo Jima,* was shot in Japan with Japanese actors speaking Japanese, subtitled in English. But, more than setting his own persona aside, with *Letters* and its companion piece, *Flags of Our Fathers,* Eastwood dared to challenge a good many myths about the "Greatest Generation" and traditional American perspectives on the politics and history of World War II.

Over the course of the twenty-nine previous films Eastwood had directed and the more than sixty he had acted in, it always has been difficult to separate the plot of a given piece from its famous driving force — the actor, director, producer himself — surely one of the reasons that many confused spectators have misunderstood and underestimated him. So powerful and pervasive is the Eastwood presence onscreen or offscreen that the subtlety of his performances, the precision of his directing, and the profundity of his thematic engagements have been frequently overshadowed by the man's perceived dark double, the beautiful but deadly gunslinger who is condemned to haunt the noirish corridors of peace-loving consciences until the last days. In any theology of perpetual or "endless" war, the dark knight stalks the forces of evil. In this purview, war is inevitable, if not passionately desired.

The publicly consumed icon of the early Eastwood presents an actor without essential nuance, a mainstream vision of a hero who rises above a blasted landscape like a monolith or featureless mountain. But are humans by definition and history locked into endless war, perpetually in thrall to animalistic, cultic, and cosmic schemes of vengeance? Must they despair with Walter Benjamin's "Angel of History," seeing all of human history as "one single catastrophe which keeps piling wreckage upon wreckage and hurl[ing] it at his feet?"[2] Or can they see peace dawning somewhere beyond the battlefields? Does the admittedly more cinematic apocalypse text of Revelation 20 irresistibly lure even war-weary men and women to annihilate the enemy or themselves until time itself dissolves? Or can humans "transform the persistent violence of this world into a semblance of the promised kingdom of order and peace"?[3]

2. Walter Benjamin, a German philosopher, was for a time a member of the Frankfurt School of philosophy; his musings on nineteenth-century culture have influenced philosophy, history, literature, and the arts since his mysterious death in 1940, while he was fleeing the Nazis.

3. Kenneth Vaux, *Ethics and the Gulf War: Religion, Rhetoric, and Righteousness* (Boulder, CO: Westview Press, 1992), 99.

Benjamin's angel "would like to stay, awaken the dead, and make whole what has been smashed. But a storm is blowing from Paradise; it has gotten caught in his wings with such violence that the angel can no longer close them. This storm irresistibly propels him into the future, to which his back is turned, while the pile of debris before him grows skyward. This storm is what we call progress."[4]

Eastwood the director questions the idea of progress as an abstract, but he continues to make movies that counter the Samuel Beckett–like "pile of debris" with a living and breathing human connection and hope for the approximation of "a perfect world" in the hereafter — or at least a better one, a "paradise" of wholeness in the midst of the suffering of history.

"Never before have I seen such a waste of lives," quips the Man With No Name in *The Good, the Bad and the Ugly.* The look on his face as he gazes across fields of torn blue- and gray-uniformed bodies is not one of a detached observer. It is a look of profound sadness and disgust, a moral statement placed in words and sight within one of the great antiwar movies. Eastwood the director, taking his lessons from Sergio Leone's irreverent attitude toward blind, brutal war, tackles the conflicts between the Revelation 20 text and the Micah and Jesus reconciliation messages throughout his long career: "Get even" versus "beat your swords into plowshares, and [your] spears into pruning hooks; nation shall not lift up sword against nation, neither shall they learn war any more" (Micah 4:3).[5]

High Plains Drifter, though structured like a revenge tragedy with a ready-made savior, explicitly raises the "postwar reconciliation," the *jus post bellum* question. *The Outlaw Josey Wales* begins with peace, dissolves into seemingly endless blood revenge, and drowns out that life-denying narrative with a fresh vision of a reconciled community. Somewhat less successfully, *Pale Rider* also confronts the clash between personal revenge and social regeneration. *Unforgiven* escalates the disparity between mindless violence and reconciliation: spiraling violence as a legacy of the American Civil War, and harmony and compromise as spiritually informed social possibilities.

---

4. W. G. Sebald refers to the angel of history as he ponders survivors' lack of voice: though their cities lay in ruins after the fire bombings of 1944, the sweep of history left them dumb. Benjamin, "Theses on the Philosophy of History," in *Illuminations,* ed. Hannah Arendt (New York: Schocken Books, 1968), 257-58.

5. See also Micah 4:4; 1 Kings 4:25; 2 Kings 18:31; Isa. 36:16; Zech. 3:10. Joel 3:10 turns the peace text upside down, interpreting allegorically what may have been a historical plague of locusts to refer to Israel's enemies, who must be defeated.

Forty years after the Spaghetti Westerns, Eastwood seized the chance to portray a waste of lives that resembled America's Civil War, this time on a faraway Pacific island, again with boys too young to leave their mothers and wives. The Japanese soldiers on Iwo Jima were as young as sixteen, and many American soldiers were no older than nineteen; they were too poor to buy a pass out of the mass slaughter. Eastwood turns away from the telescopic despair of the death angel, turning instead toward the watchful bard who, in the lyric of the Civil War song, "looks for the right/To see the dawn of peace." He leaves the *Pale Rider* and Revelation 20's dark seductions behind.

To accomplish a reorienting of heart and vision, Eastwood shows both sides of the Iwo Jima battle, and in doing so he uses paired films, one from each perspective, rather than straining to weave each perspective into one film, as was done in the more classically structured *All Quiet on the Western Front* (Lewis Milestone, 1930), *The Battle of Algiers* (Gillo Pontecorvo, 1966), or even *The Thin Red Line* (Terrence Malick, 1998). Oddly, a number of my friends (of assorted ages) loved *Flags of Our Fathers* and compared it favorably to the book on which it was based; at the same time, they refused to see *Letters from Iwo Jima*, claiming that Eastwood had glorified the Japanese and had forgotten Japan's atrocities in China. On the other side, several of my students thought that Eastwood had Americanized the Japanese in *Letters from Iwo Jima* and thus discounted his insights about the "enemy outsider." As we shall see, however, Eastwood draws heavily on Milestone's *All Quiet on the Western Front,* which he considers one of the few propaganda-free movies set in wartime.

The filmmaker pities young men caught in brutally mismanaged battles and reveals the ugly side of the generals and politicians who support wars for their own gain. Through radically different narrative means, Eastwood creates two apparently discrete worlds that intersect with each other at the most basic human level.

Flags and *Letters* interlace as twinned panels of a religious diptych, a term recently used by French critic Michael Henry Wilson. Eastwood completed the series with *Gran Torino* and its coda, *Invictus*. Like the ancient two- and three-part art forms (diptychs and triptychs), the three images of war that Eastwood places before us hinge on each other to create a new work, a multilayered consciousness of the home front alongside the frontline of battle. *Gran Torino* concerns other battlegrounds — Korea and contemporary America — but its conclusion frames and illuminates the movie as a companion panel, the third panel in a triptych, an individual's gesture toward redeeming the moment and the community in which he finds himself. (*Invictus,* in which Nelson Mandela uses the Rugby World Cup as a means of reconciling the bitter warring factions within South Africa, resumes the war cycle after the conflict.) At the heart of *Flags* and *Letters,* though, we perceive two movies that attempt to capture in words and images the glimpse of light that makes art (and the desire for redemption) possible in the darkest moments of human life. Each film strengthens the light and suffuses the other. The films function as icons, providing the audience with a shorthand for perceiving "reality."

Film, with the performative power and immediacy of the image, can grasp at some measure of those truths that are too profound for speech. James Bradley's source book for *Flags of Our Fathers* and the collection of epistles that inspired *Letters from Iwo Jima* hardly approach the resounding depth or mordant eloquence of Wilfred Owen's dark poem "Dulce et Decorum Est," written from the trenches in 1917: "Bent double, like old beggars under sacks/Knock-kneed, coughing like hags, we cursed through sludge. . . ."[6]

But even here, in the most "haunting images" of this powerful poem — from the "misty panes and thick green light" to the "blood . . . gargling from the froth-corrupted lungs" of dying soldiers — mere words cannot convey the sickening reality conveyed by seeing its images in moving sequence and hearing the sounds of battle that create witnesses of, rather than eavesdroppers of, the harshness and violence. While poetry has a passionate relationship to the emotional truth of human experience, it is film that, as Robert Bresson once said, "makes visible what, without you, might never have been seen."

Director Sam Fuller says: "There's no way you can portray war realistically, not in a movie nor in a book. You can only capture a very, very small aspect of it. For moviegoers to get the idea of real combat, you'd have to shoot at them every so often from either side of the screen."[7]

Even in deathly darkness, Clint Eastwood seeks light on the screen and within the heart, wishing to bring it to bear on both sides of the common human equation. He does not limit his exploration of the gloom of war to one panel; he fills out the triptych, letting each film stand as a complete work in itself, while allowing the presentations that unfold to reveal a more gripping, penetrating concept of war and its effects on our humanity.

6. The full Owen poem can be found in Appendix A.

7. Samuel Fuller, with Christina Lang Fuller and Jerome Henry Rudes, *A Third Face: My Writing, Fighting, and Filmmaking* (New York: Knopf, 2002).

The nightmares of Doc Bradley in *Flags,* the hallucinations of Will Munny in *Unforgiven,* the venomous outbursts of Walt Kowalski in *Gran Torino* — these men, once boys, attempt to put words to their recurring nightmares. They long for confession to release their demons; but they cannot pronounce their own dispensation. As Kathleen O'Connor has written of the book of Jeremiah, "Violence destroys speech. To set the ruins into a poetic world [as Jeremiah does] creates distance."[8]

We can be thankful for the rare artist, like Eastwood, and recently for Katherine Bigelow in *The Hurt Locker* (2008), Paul Greengrass in *The Green Zone* (2009), and Ken Loach in *Route Irish* (2010), who dare to witness soldiers' suffering, hear their confessions, and absorb their narratives.

8. Kathleen O'Connor, "Building Hope upon the Ruins in Jeremiah," in *The Bible and the American Future,* ed. Robert Jewett (Eugene, OR: Cascade Books, 2009), 149.

Flags of Our Fathers

*F*lags of Our Fathers begins with the stunning immediacy of a chaotic battle that cannot be won. At the time of the movie's release, critic Scott Foundas wrote: "To an extent, *Flags of Our Fathers* is to the WWII movie what Eastwood's *Unforgiven* was to the western — a stripping-away of mythology until only a harsher, uncomfortable reality remains." Foundas continues:

> With *Flags,* Eastwood has made one of his best films — a searching, morally complex deconstruction of the Greatest Generation that is nevertheless rich in the sensitivity to human frailty that has become his signature as a filmmaker.[1]

Indeed, the movie systematically exposes in the machinery of war the layers of willful misunderstanding and calculated cruelty that fuel, then exploit, young men's agony.

Yet, in ironic counterpoint, as the film opens, we hear the gentle lyrics of "I'll Walk Alone," so huskily sung that the vocalist could be Eastwood himself, conjuring images of an abandoned wife and children at home. We imagine that we see a uniformed boy scarcely out of knickers pausing on a railroad platform with his knapsack slung over his shoulder, or a sweetheart with her ear to the wireless, hungry for news from the front.

---

1. Scott Foundas, "Print the Legend," *Village Voice,* 2006: http://www.villagevoice .com/2006-10-10/film/print-the-legend/.

News of the individual rarely comes in wartime — only officers with black-banded letters or unit mates bearing tales of a son bravely fallen, an aura of saintly sacrifice surrounding the telling.[2] Arms ripped from their still-warm bodies, guts spilled on the ground, eyes gouged out of screaming faces — the horrors evoked by war literature from Homer to Wilfred Owen, from hellish images of Goya and Picasso — who can capture it? Isaac Bashevis Singer has written:

> Where did all the years go to? Who will remember them after we're gone? The writers will write, but they'll get everything topsy-turvy. There must be a place somewhere where everything is preserved, inscribed down to the smallest detail.[3]

Who sees, who tells?

Until, suddenly, mud splatters the screen, and Eastwood begins to immerse the viewer in the horrors of war. A young soldier is running through green volcanic terrain. He hears voices with no meaning — friends or killers? Does it matter? No one can see his target. He's lost and wants to cry.[4] The camera draws closer to him until his fresh skin dissolves into the worn lines of an old white-haired man's face, sobbing in a darkened house. Then a voice-over intrudes, its words announcing the powerlessness of words: "Most guys I knew would never talk about what went on over there; they're still trying to forget."

As twinned motion pictures, *Flags of Our Fathers* and *Letters from Iwo Jima* resemble two panels of a twenty-first-century version of the painted diptychs and triptychs that once adorned cathedrals all over the world. The bold displays depicted incidents in the life of Christ or the saints, often accompanied by representations of the natural world and its human inhabitants presented as mirrors of the spiritual world. The images in a single panel represented one stage in life's journey toward salvation or damnation and prepared the worshiper to receive the other panel(s). Each panel tells only part of a story, and the viewer must view all the panels to comprehend the full sweep of the work of art and its message.

2. *The Messenger* (Oren Moverman, 2009) visualizes the delivery of the dreaded letter and its aftermath.

3. Isaac Bashevis Singer, *Shosha* (New York: Farrar, Straus and Giroux, 1978), 277.

4. I am reminded of the opening of *Three Kings* (1999), directed by David O. Russell (which was set during the first Gulf War), where Mark Wahlberg's character tries desperately to find out whether he's to shoot or not, and whether the figures he sees are friends or enemies.

Likewise, the moviegoer must see both *Flags* and *Letters* to fully absorb each. The familiar Eastwood film tropes surface: concern for the vulnerable, the problem of evil, the idiocy of war, themes that are all deepened further in *Gran Torino,* the third panel of the triptych, and *Invictus,* which we might consider the coda — the necessary and lived resolution — for all three.

Cinema, as André Bazin noted a half century ago, animates paintings in continual dialogue between "expressions of spiritual reality" and "duplication of the world outside."[5] Images can channel the transcendent, as they do so consistently in Eastwood's films. *Flags of Our Fathers* and *Letters from Iwo Jima* each echoes the essential truth of the other. It is hard to imagine that one might exist alone, so resonant are the echoing cross-references of the sinister links between war and commerce. In every sequence of the war films, Eastwood reaches for transcendence in Bazin's sense, the rhyming moments of epiphany in the work of art that exceed mere visual presentation and provide its intertwining spiritual connection with the world beyond.

In *Flags,* Eastwood takes the filmgoer deep into the lived experience of its principal characters, Doc Bradley (Ryan Phillippe), Ira Hayes (Adam Beach), and René Gagnon (Jesse Bradford) — young American soldiers trained to kill, then ordered to stage and thus relive the crime as public theater. By using identical battle settings and shots in *Letters from Iwo Jima,* he plays against glorifying the American side while keeping the focus on the common American and Japanese boys' basic longing for peace.[6]

The outside frame story of *Flags* presents us with the illness and approaching death of Doc Bradley, a funeral director, and his son James's discovery of a trunk full of war mementos (including a war medal still in its envelope) that his father never showed anyone. Eastwood repeats the "secrets" device in *Gran Torino,* though the later film shifts the meaning of the trunk's contents (and repeats its discovery) to achieve its own startling ending. In *Gran Torino,* Walt's trunk, found by his grandchildren, holds his medal of honor and photos of his squadron during the Korean War company (all of whom were killed except Walt, we find out later). Doc Bradley's trunk holds both his medal and a newspaper copy of the famous Iwo Jima photograph that every schoolchild has seen. The marketing of

5. André Bazin, *What Is Cinema? Essays Selected and Translated by Hugh Gray,* vol. 1 (Berkeley: University of California Press, 1967), 9-16.
6. Thanks to Alex Schwarm for his attention to Eastwood's use of duplicate shots.

The ice cream runs with rivers of blood.

that photo as a fantasized icon of American heroism and victory haunts the movie's earlier sequences and the veterans' nightmares.

Flags differs from *Gran Torino* in the ways in which it uses that revelation. In the latter, the discovery of Walt's trunk's contents by his irreverent grandchildren occurs early in the movie. It almost seems placed there as an amusing throwaway detail (something like Frankie and Scrap's discussion of socks in *Million Dollar Baby*): just one more example of the family's disrespect for convention and for Walt himself. Walt's grandkids send text messages during their grandmother's funeral, wear inappropriate clothes, and plan what they'll get when their grandfather dies. Their marks of nonchalance might seem over the top if their behavior did not ring so true. (The audience in the theater where I first saw the movie laughed along but rather nervously.) By the time the bitter widower makes his way through his ice chest of beer, a pile of Hmong food, several encounters with destructive adolescents, and the violation of Sue, his new friend, the medal has finally acquired a metaphorical — almost a metaphysical — significance: physical evidence as an amulet or tool to teach love and sacrifice over vengeance (to Thao, his protégé), and a symbol of nearly sixty years of hollowness that is about to be transformed.

In *Flags of Our Fathers,* the discovery of the medal does not come until near the end of the movie, almost as a surprise coda to the film's dizzying barrage of real and false combat. By the time we witness the discovery, we've also experienced the film's cold gray-and-black, "photo-realistic" exteriors illuminated only by exploding bombs and mysterious points of light, with jarring interruptions of the dark beauty of the shots by the elliptical narrative intrusions in the mode of Steven Spielberg's sentimental frame stories in *Schindler's List* and *Saving Private Ryan*. From the movie's eerie white letters reversed out of a black screen and the volcanic, "charred, moon-like" terrain that swirls around a young, isolated, and disoriented soldier, to its final aerial shot of newly arrived recruits romping in the ocean, Eastwood uses every image to trigger the next image concealed behind the visual curtain — the one that might reveal the truth that lies beyond mystery.[7] The film unscrolls like one of Doc's nightmares: it is "fragmented, uncertain as to time and place, dark or foggy grey."[8] We see inside the sick man's head and awaken from our morphine-induced daze only to hear the inane, disjunctive droning of the irritating postcombat frame characters.

If Eastwood's critique of mindless war was ever in doubt, consider the strong resemblance of *Flags of Our Fathers* to *All Quiet on the Western Front* and *The Thin Red Line* in its rhythmic combination of gritty, uncompromising realism and philosophical reflection. In *Flags,* we are immediately drawn into the film's terrible symphony of deafening noise, bright explosions, and hurtling debris and mud: mass killings legitimated under fire and flags, with hollow and futile attempts long after the war to rationalize both the physical and the spiritual losses.[9] By the end of the gruesome opening sequences, particularly after the film begins to expose the government's coldly manipulative marketing of its soldiers' suffering, neither the characters nor the viewers can bear such gross clichés, gloss, and hype.

In Milestone's still-jarring 1930 classic *All Quiet on the Western Front,* the main character, Paul (whom the young Doc Bradley uncannily resem-

7. Jens Notstad notes that, when the camera moves in on the soldier's face, it loses focus, which adds "complexity and uncertainty" to his character (2009). Eastwood leaves the complexity in place. Doc Bradley's feelings are exposed only through his face in reaction to events: when he murders a Japanese soldier at close range; as he tends to his dying friends; as the boys are co-opted into campaigning to sell war bonds; as he rescues Ira from a Chicago bar that has rejected him; and as he refuses to take annual phone calls from Washington. Only the false frame story purports to express his inner feelings, and they are not the ones we have been led throughout the film to expect: "I was only looking for you, my son. I wish I had been a better father to you."

8. Scott Foundas, "Print the Legend," *Village Voice,* 2006: http://www.villagevoice.com/2006-10-10/film/print-the-legend/.

9. Eastwood discussed the filming of the battle scenes in Michael Henry Wilson, *Clint Eastwood* (Paris: Editions Cahiers du Cinéma, 2007), 183-84. He placed dozens of hidden digital cameras inside the actors' equipment to capture the chaotic action.

bles), escapes the horrors of the front and an ill-conceived, ill-managed, and increasingly disastrous war by taking home leave. Once home, he seeks peace and forgiveness for the murders he has committed and witnessed. Alas, what once seemed "real" to him — his family, food, familiar houses, and his old classics teacher — has been irretrievably altered in the perspective of eternity that he experienced on the front.

> Once the experience of war makes visible the possibility of death that lies locked up in each moment, our thoughts cannot travel from one day to the next without meeting death's face. Thus war effaces all conceptions of purpose or goal, including even its own "war aims."[10]

As Paul stares into death's face, linear time disappears.

Like Walt Kowalski in *Gran Torino* and the survivors of Iwo Jima, Paul can no longer repeat the "old lie" about how "sweet and fitting" it is to die for your country. It is "dirty and painful," Paul reflects. "Better not to die at all. Millions out there are dying for their country. And what good is it?" As if to mirror the endless patriotic speeches that quote Horace's famous ode, Paul's classics teacher's passionate lecture on the glories of dying for the fatherland, and Paul's existential deconstruction of such poisonous ideas, one of the narrators of *Flags of Our Fathers* intones: "I told their folks they died for their country. I'm not sure that was it." Here the narrator speaks in darkened shadow against lighted curtains, with the poster of Iwo Jima above his head. "What we see and do in war, the cruelty, is unbelievable. But somehow we gotta make some sense of it. To do that, we've gotta have an easy way to understand truth. And damn few words."

In *All Quiet on the Western Front,* the "few words" completely vaporize in the final battle scene in the movie, with a shattered Paul silently reaching through sandbags piled around the soldiers' trenches to cradle a butterfly in his hand. Similarly, the ending of *The Thin Red Line* finds its resolution in silence as it returns to the film's opening frame: Private Witt, the innocent protagonist, alive once more, swims with the island children in the ocean that surrounds an idyllic prewar Guadalcanal.

The French-Algerian *Days of Glory* (Rachid Bouchareb, 2006) also ends in silence, as the sole survivor of a North African unit that fought to the death to liberate France visits the graves of his friends who were killed

---

10. Simone Weil and Rachel Bespaloff, *War and the Iliad,* intro. by Christopher Benfey (New York: New York Review Books, 2005), 22-23.

**"Heroes" Doc Bradley (Ryan Phillippe) and René Gagnon (Jesse Bradford)
are sick at heart.**

fifty years before. In silence, too, he returns to his miserable flat on the out-
skirts of Paris. Because North African veterans were denied their war pen-
sions to punish them for their country's rebellion (1952-1964), most spent
their subsequent lives in poverty despite their early sacrifice to save France
from the Nazis.

Flags engages the implied question "If not words, then what?" by following the inchoate narrator in its very next dramatic sequence: a soon-to-
be-famous and enormously profitable picture of six faceless young men
lifting a flag into place atop a mountain begins to clarify in its tray of photographic solution. Who needs words to tell that tale? The rest is marketing.

What truths about human nature and the meaning of life will the narrative of *Flags of Our Fathers* reveal? Will tragedy and loss be magically redeemed by manly valor and sacrifice? Does a classic nineteenth-century
sense of virtue still obtain — that the best vocation for an ambitious and
hopeful young man is to go to war? Has death become so unknowable and
the universe so hostile to human spirit and aspirations that soldiers are left
to bayonet or shoot each other at close range, with no hope of reconciliation or forgiveness? If all wartime heroism is shown to be artifice, are the
real men involved condemned to mere brutality?

Eastwood addresses these questions in *Flags*. The visuals far outstrip
anything the narrators could ever say. Eastwood's camera pauses on Doc's
face immediately after he has stabbed a young Japanese soldier. In silence,
Doc registers neither triumph nor shock. As French director Jean-Pierre
Melville, an underground operative in World War II, once commented to

an interviewer, "Wars do not spare the virtue of anyone, even if they have been undertaken for a good cause."[11] Doc's virtue (built around the moral stipulation of "Thou shalt not kill") has been tested and broken.

The all-seeing camera also pauses at the death scene with an American soldier whom Doc tried and failed to save. When Doc leaves the shot, the camera rests briefly on the kid's intestines spilling onto the ground, then for a moment on a bayoneted enemy soldier as, with his profiled features etched in light, he expires. To underscore Eastwood's desire to humanize the enemy, this shot is echoed in *Gran Torino* as Walt lies on the ground, dead.

Later in *Flags*, when Ira bayonets a soldier, the camera registers moral disgust, not Doc's stoic impassivity. It shows Ira's horrified face and then backs away and moves out to a long shot as if to remove itself from the murderous act. Similar camera actions appear in *Mystic River*, as the camera pulls back from Katie's body lying in the bear pit, and in *Changeling*, as the camera pulls away from the buried bodies of the little boys as if the sight of murdered children cannot be borne.

If the camera and Eastwood frankly face the horrors of war and soldiers' guilt, the men (until recently in American history, only men) who manage the war are exposed as soulless, racist, and cruel. The good soldier, Ira, eager to succeed via military service in an American culture that is closed to him, is called "Chief," not by his name, Ira Hayes; the murder that so unsettled him (and may have earned him a medal) occasions casually cruel remarks about tomahawks and his reservation. Yet in the most stinging insult of all, the idealistic young marine — American and Puma Indian — was sent to the front lines to fight imperial Japan and was chosen as a *Spieler* for the war effort, and yet could not get a drink in a downtown Chicago tavern not far from where I sit today as I write.

Author James Bradley, the real-life son of Doc Bradley, writes in the source book for the film that Ira Hayes had joined the marines in order to move more freely across the United States and among white society than was allowed him in Arizona. To add to the multiple ironies of Ira's marginalized place in American society, the first time we see him on an American highway, he has paused from picking produce to pose for a photo with a white family who, unlike him, can travel wherever they wish. Later (or perhaps earlier, because we are never entirely sure where we are

11. Donitz Bantchera, *Jean-Pierre Melville: L'Oeuvre et L'Homme* (Paris: Editions du Revif, 2007; 1st ed., 1996).

in time), he walks 1,300 miles from Washington, D. C., to Texas to reveal the truth about the flag-raising to the father of his dead buddy, Harlon Block. It was Harlon who helped raise the iconic flag. Yet the American government, which had taken Harlon and sent him to a barren island to die, had withheld the consoling truth from his family — just one of the scandals the film exposes.

The military brass and the wealthy élite disparage Ira's emotional embrace of the mother of Mike Strank, "the best damn marine I ever knew." In a curious shift from the source book, the cinematic narrative implies that Ira wants to return to his combat unit, where his loyalty lies. However, James Bradley writes in the book that the "loyalty" story was circulated to remove Ira from the flag-raisers' promotional tour because his raging alcoholism might distract from the hero image the government wanted to convey.[12]

World War II promoters also betrayed René Gagnon. Gagnon was cast as the soldier who joined for the pretty uniform, but the postwar jobs offered to "the hero of Iwo Jima" by gung ho glad-handers never materialize. In the movie, René's cut of screen time swirls around socializing, willingly dragged around for photo ops with his glory-hungry fiancée. After the war, we glimpse him in cramped apartments and hallways as he joins the ranks of returned soldiers who never escaped the drudgery of low-paying jobs. He remained a janitor all his life, disappointed and miserably sad.

The book *Flags of Our Fathers* underscores in words what the movie conveys emotionally through images, music, and rhythm. Ira was not the only returning veteran to suffer posttraumatic stress disorder, to weep over "the things I saw, the things I did," and finally to kill himself (we assume so, because he is found dead). James Bradley repeatedly mentions not only the ages of boys in those battles — seventeen — but also emphasizes the trauma of boys who had to kill other boys at close range. "The combat-weary boys dealt in various ways with the memories of what they'd seen and done," he admits. His own father, Doc, wept in the night for at least four years after he returned from Iwo Jima, slept with a knife close by, and regularly hallucinated. "The totality of it was simply too painful for words."

Critic Kent Jones writes that *The Big Red One* (Samuel Fuller, 1980; reissued in 2004) "gives us a sense of why men like my father, fifty years after the Good War came to an end, still breaks down in tears when the

---

12. James Bradley and Ron Powers, *Flags of Our Fathers* (New York: Bantam Books, 2000), 441-42.

memory of what they went through comes rushing back to the surface."[13] Unacknowledged grief and posttraumatic stress disorder, long
ignored and untreated, have accompanied recent discussions of the after-
effects of the seemingly unending wars in Iraq and Afghanistan (nine
years and counting for a nation still suffering from Vietnam, Korea, and
the Civil War).

Seeing *Flags of Our Fathers* and *Letters from Iwo Jima* side by side introduces yet another question: Was the battle of Iwo Jima managed on the
American side with the same careful planning that General Kuribayashi
(Ken Watanabe) gave to the defense of the island and his own soldiers? The
dark suggestions of the contemporary resonance of Bradley's interviews
and the movie's acid revelations are too painful for words. The inexcusable
mismanagement of the Iraq War and the bloody bungling of an operation
like Fallujah (an entire city leveled), for instance, display a jaw-dropping
arrogance of power that the world sees but that our own country still does
not acknowledge, deprived as we have been of real-time images of the carnage — even under a new administration. To this American, our government's callous and cavalier dishonesty in war seems only to get slicker and
smoother over time.

Set in places where killing "is what we're here for," what is the proper
response to murder? Different war movies elicit differing reactions: "I
killed a man and no one can call me on it" *(The Thin Red Line).* "Forgive
me; we could have been brothers" *(All Quiet on the Western Front).* "You
don't want that [killing] on your conscience all your life" *(Gran Torino).*
Or René Gagnon's memory of "looking down a barrel into someone's eyes
and having to kill him. There's no glory in it."[14] Humans swept up in the
inexorable, devouring forces of history — Iwo Jima's long month of
bombs and blood — cannot even hope to voice what has happened.

As for us, the viewers, we witness through the Kid in *Unforgiven*
what it feels like to kill a man at close range, what Doc Bradley never
could express and Walt reveals only after a sullen lifetime of bitter regret.
Jean-Pierre Melville, a member of the French Resistance during this
same conflict, opens his own war movie, *Army of Shadows,* with a long,
painful sequence of murder — not of a Nazi, but rather of a fellow Resistance fighter. The executioners quibble and weep: it is their first time to

13. Kent Jones, *Physical Evidence* (Middletown, CT: Wesleyan University Press, 2007),
194.

14. Bradley and Powers, *Flags of Our Fathers,* 292-93, 299, 367, 394.

kill, and they are devastated. So should we all be, as we pay to witness the worst in us all.

As in *Unforgiven, Mystic River,* and *Million Dollar Baby,* Eastwood refuses in *Flags of Our Fathers* to offer a definitive answer to the many urgent and eternal questions that the diptych poses. He only offers tragic wisdom, a "meditation on the inevitable place of conflict in moral life."[15]

15. Paul Ricoeur, *Oneself as Another,* trans. Kathleen Blamey (Chicago: University of Chicago Press, 1992), 247.

Letters from Iwo Jima

L *etters from Iwo Jima,* which emerged at the end of 2006, not long after the release of *Flags of Our Fathers* and the rerelease of *Army of Shadows,* further developed Eastwood's lifelong wish to get inside the skin of the enemy outsider, a dream that culminated in his peace movie *Invictus* (2009). With an elemental visual stroke of equalizing his protagonists in conflict, Eastwood shot his twinned war movies in desaturated color film. The rather rambling, sorrowful, and pain-filled plot of *Flags* is transformed with *Letters* into a tightly structured narrative with almost silent opening and closing contemporary frames, enriched in the central tale by a subtle exploration of "memory." The film's restless camera lives and dies with its doomed subjects, young Japanese soldiers, as it roams through the labyrinthine passageways of the island's deadly thermal caves, or nests, staying with the boys as they huddle to write letters home, dodge debris, or meditate on their approaching deaths.

As *Letters* opens, a modern-day archaeological team treads on a blasted beach dotted by rusted artillery that testifies to earlier, unhappy times: a futile battle suppressed in the Japanese collective memory and absent from its record books, a postapocalypse terrain reminiscent of that in Andrei Tarkovsky's *Stalker* (1979) or Cuáron's *Children of Men* (2006). Probing a mysterious labyrinth of caves and tunnels, the investigators uncover a buried trove of letters that we are dying to read (think of the trunk full of secrets in *Bridges of Madison County* and *Gran Torino*). Just as the letters to a farm wife from her lover (in *Bridges of Madison County*) find visual expression within the movie's heart, these dusty letters, barely glimpsed, suddenly wipe into the sepia of soldiers' uniforms and the dust from the ash they are excavating.

The "detective" frame (who wrote the letters? what secrets do they hide?) embraces an inner plot marked by highly controlled temporal and spatial displacement. From the beginning of the movie, until the return of the contemporary frame two hours later, the unyielding volcanic rock of Iwo Jima is punctured by multiple intrusions. The soldiers construct elaborate subterranean hiding places, as the illusory tight world of the island is penetrated repeatedly by entries from an unseen outside: Tadamichi Kuribayashi (Ken Watanabe), the battle's general; Baron Nishi (Tsuyoshi Ihara), an Olympian equestrian with his horse; plus an assortment of officers. Furthermore, the inner plot's forward movement is repeatedly interrupted by differently toned flashbacks that disturb the monochromatic image of an island of graves.

Spurts of color come and go, abstract artistry that plays in antiphonal rhythm against the film's unfolding human stories. The Japanese flag, for example, obscurely positioned, could easily be mistaken for an American flag. Fires and explosions have been treated on film to "bring them into the foreground acutely, their bright orange hue cutting across the black and grey landscape and lending them a surreal quality."[1] One interpolated tale, warmly colored and underscored with chamber music, simultaneously marks Kuribayashi's happy sojourn in the United States and reveals an inner split between West and East, not only in the general himself, but also in the complex presentation of the film. And most shocking of all, after nearly an hour's immersion in the caves' dark and silty hues with young soldiers the viewer has come to love, Saigo, the viewer's surrogate, spots the massive American fleet, massed offshore on the profoundly blue sea to begin a battle that will kill or unalterably scar everyone it touches. Yet, after this storm of exits and entrances, deaths, confessions, and redemption scenes, the final shot of the movie's interior plot rests calmly on a still image of the setting sun.

The movie's concept sprang from Eastwood's chance discovery of a book of letters and drawings belonging to Kuribayashi, *Picture Letters from Commander in Chief,* collected and translated into English by Tsuyuko Yoshida.[2] Though viewers are never allowed access to the collection, its

---

1. Ben Rudofsky, in the Northwestern University Eastwood class, Winter 2010.

2. Kumiko Kakehashi, *Letters from Iwo Jima*, trans. Giles Murray (London: Phoenix, 2007), a collection of eyewitness stories about Iwo Jima that includes Kuribayashi's letters.

Saigo (Kazunari Ninomiya) and Hanako (Nae): Must we be parted?

central conceit, letters written long ago by a father to his daughter from great physical and cultural distance, picks up on Eastwood's persistent theme of the rupture of parent and child as part of the movie's particularly complex engagement with memory. In *Flags of Our Fathers,* a son reconstructs his father's anguished wartime experiences from shards of artifacts: a newspaper article, a photo, a medal, a few interviews, a bit of historical research, and an ample imagination. The script for *Letters from Iwo Jima* was written — or rather, absorbed, filtered, and recast — by a Japanese-American writer, Iris Yamashita (along with Eastwood's valued earlier scripter, Paul Haggis). It was designed to place the viewer at once inside the Japanese boys' anguished experience within their island prison and to make the viewer acutely aware of the imperial madness that was to consume them.

 Letters from Iwo Jima was a daring artistic and commercial move for Eastwood. Raised on war films and rejecting most of them as "classic propaganda," Eastwood decided, in the process of shooting *Flags,* to "show the two sides of a battle," portraying the effects of war on both sides, a feat never attempted by any other filmmaker (as he told NPR interviewer Terry Gross in 2007) except perhaps Lewis Milestone in *All Quiet on the Western Front.* However, what the latter film *suggests* about the "other" side, *Letters* quite openly and viscerally screams.

 Flags of Our Fathers, Eastwood has declared several times, is "a film *about* propaganda," while *Letters* is clearly and plainly constructed to *counter* propaganda by daring to enter into the world of an enemy. *Letters* envisions life through the eyes of those who had been sent to Iwo Jima to die.

Eastwood immediately sets up the audience's identification with some of the young soldiers as he focuses on their individual stories and their unfolding relationships. The inner plot begins with the voice-over of the young conscript Saigo (Kazunari Ninomiya), a narrative device that immediately draws the viewer into his thoughts. His criticisms of the war are unprecedented in Japanese war films, as Eastwood observed to interviewer Michael Henry Wilson when the movie was released. They certainly violate a consistent cultural representation of Japan, positive or negative (as I believed Eastwood aimed to do): that is, the men within the plot are allowed to exhibit a human rather than a monolithic range of attitudes toward their country, their predicament, and their fellow soldiers. While a critic might well say that Eastwood westernizes his characters, he neither sentimentalizes nor glorifies them. The movie, after all, does not aim for complete historical realism. It reaches for something larger: to cross borders into another's being and absorb his suffering as your own.

The tour de force that Eastwood constructs builds on the fierce antimilitarism of *Flags of Our Fathers,* even as he visually creates an underground prison that houses child soldiers ripped from their human attachments and sent to die in the name of a national religion. The characters we follow and love in *Letters* — not only Saigo but also Kuribayashi, Nozaki, and Shimizu — could be Jamie and Josey, survivors of a futile and endlessly perpetuated war in earlier America, or Doc and René and Ira at Iwo Jima, young kids whose suffering was sold as propaganda to fuel an ongoing war in the European theater of this world war. Further, as in so many of Eastwood's movies, "patriotism" is taken to a deeper level in *Letters* (like Sergeant Highway's shepherding of the vulnerable kids under his wing in *Heartbreak Ridge*). The grizzled old soldier gives far greater service to his country by caring for his boys and their families than if he had touted the ill-conceived and mismanaged military effort (Grenada) that put those boys in danger. For his part, Kuribayashi loves his country no less in trying to hold off his soldiers' inevitable deaths as long as possible and forbidding "honorable" suicide.

Eastwood uses the blasted, apocalyptic terrain in *Flags* and *Letters* to test the American and the Japanese soldiers' humanity and to contrast the young men's suffering with the arrogance of their distant leaders. Apart from the devotion and brilliant strategic devices of Kuribayashi, who is the film's moral center along with the conscript Saigo, did anyone care about the 22,000 young Japanese men ripped out of their homes, social networks, villages, and vocations to be locked inside searing hot caves that

General Kuribayashi (Ken Watanabe) is dragged to the hilltop to die.

would become their thermal coffins? Eastwood intercuts the claustrophobic caves with flashbacks to Saigo's warm home space and loving wife, giving texture to the young man's backstory to underscore the wartime loss of everything that sustains human life. Even deprived of their means of survival, their bakery, the young couple lives for the future — their unborn child.

In his dying moments, the noble general recalls a world of reason and hospitality, his own and that of his American hosts, where peace allows chamber music, wine, and laughter, and the thought of war disappears into the abstract. Peace could have been forged during the months when East met West. But, whereas peace needs engagement, reconciliation, and connection to flourish (as in *Invictus*), *Letters* shows the collapse of communications. Soldiers fire on their own; commanders fail to relay battle orders, and hundreds are accidentally killed (the botched battle operations at the beginning of World War II); and the manic American commanders scramble to fix on a plan for Iwo Jima.

The "letters" in the title mostly go unsent. Even though we see soldiers writing their families and we glimpse Saigo taking yet another letter addressed to his wife to the island dispatcher to be mailed — even though we hear the texts of letters home recited in voice-over by Saigo and Kuribayashi — neither the letters nor the men can leave. The distant men who wished for the symbolic battle send their own general contradictory and unrealistic orders. Kuribayashi's fellow officers feud with him and with each other. He discovers, to his alarm, that the army and navy do not share information. His orders are either disobeyed or never reach their intended audience.

The few phone and radio connections, telegrams, letters, and messengers from the distant emperor only intensify the sense of absence and abandonment. Inside the island compound, with the war nearly lost, the piercing tones of schoolchildren singing about the "imperial land" crackle over the barely audible radio waves to underscore the empire's mindless recruitment of child soldiers. As a further and more painful irony, the schoolchildren come from Nagano, Kuribayashi's own hometown. The brittle transmission taunts the few survivors who gather to hear the bitter reminder of an outside world they will never see again and cannot save.

Letters, bereft of missives within its own central story world, nonetheless presents to us, the viewers, one long letter home that is full of redemption tales. One episode uncomfortably reminds us of the massacres of civilians in My Lai during the Vietnam War and the recent allegations of willful murder of Iraqi prisoners of war by U.S. soldiers. It is a tale about the end of Shimizu, to whom we have become endeared during his confession scene with Saigo. A former *Kempeitai* (élite military corps) recruit, Shimizu was initially isolated from the other soldiers as a possible spy. When confronted by Saigo, he unburdens himself in a series of Eastwoodian confessional shots. He had been sentenced to death because he showed mercy toward a mother and children when he refused to kill their pet dog, their only comfort. Now resolved to surrender to regain his own humanity, Shimizu and his friend give themselves up to the supposedly merciful American soldiers, anticipating a new life. After months of eating worms and drinking brackish water, he will have a meal. Unexpectedly and irrationally, the American guards casually murder the redeemed soldier and his friend. Kuribayashi and the other surviving Japanese soldiers, who arrive at the murder scene the next morning, gaze at their friends' dead bodies in disbelief.

Soon afterwards, Baron Nishi orders a gravely injured American soldier to be brought into his own barren command center. Another case study in mercy begins, foreshadowed in Shimizu's flashback.

"Shall I finish him off?" Nishi is asked.

"No. Treat him," Nishi instructs. "You would expect the same, wouldn't you?"

Light and shadows play across the men's bodies. Nishi takes off his uniform jacket and crosses over to Sam, his blindingly white shirt reflecting the light that breaks through from the cave's opening, the gateway to the forbidden outside world. He speaks with Sam gently as the latter lies dying, reassuring him that he is now in the hands of a man who knew

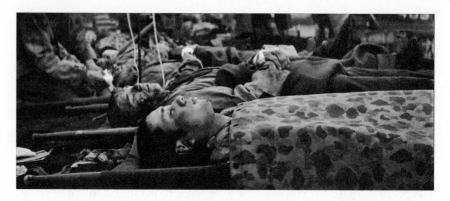

The wounded Japanese and American boys cannot be told apart.

Mary Pickford and Douglas Fairbanks (a unifying symbol appropriate to Nishi, who himself is quite a media idol).

In this sequence, Eastwood pulls together allusions from the overarching theme of marginalization that he has developed in earlier movies. The boy comes from Oklahoma, grandchild perhaps of the "Sooners," who rushed into the former lands of the Five Nations when the government opened up the area to America's land-hungry and economically depressed whites in 1885 and 1889. Now, just like the poor boys hounded out of the corners of a Japan impoverished by its leaders' imperial designs, Sam finds himself, not in the post-1930s dust bowl back home, but in a grayer and dustier grave — a deadlier dead end. (This sequence brings to mind the fourteen-year-old Witt [played by Kyle Eastwood] in *Honkytonk Man,* who fell heir to his grandfather's failed dreams of 1893 and the madcap ideals of his uncle Red.)

The key to the sequence is revealed after the boy dies, despite the humanizing touches of Nishi's conversation with him. Nishi reads the letter Sam carries with him, a talisman as dear as the Japanese soldiers' handmade belts and family photos. It's a letter from Sam's mother, which narrates the everyday incidents of a neighborhood and a country struggling to get along without its male children. At the sound of the words — an echo of all the voiced letters we've heard from Kuribayashi and Saigo throughout the movie — the soldiers sitting around the deathbed rise to their feet. "With each line, another soldier is drawn into the stranger's world, an alien place that is frighteningly similar to their own daily lives," writes Hayley Schilling. The letter concludes with the mother's counsel to Sam to "always do what is right because it is right." The line resonates not with cheap sentiment but rather with the power of a moral code to make sense of a world outside a prison where human beings are anchored to friends, lovers, a spiritual consciousness, and a sense of justice greater than themselves. "Mercy," Schilling reflects, provides the "unexpected means for the soldiers to reconnect with their humanity."[3]

"This scene is about as full of death imagery and religious symbolism as any in cinema; the density is palpable, enhanced by Eastwood's continued use of a washed-out, sepia color profile," Jesse Anderson-Lehman writes. The music begins with the movie's signature piano theme but fades out unnoticed into silence. The sequence, as Anderson-Lehman notes further, is a "microcosm of the entire movie. It contains a role reversal in the form of an American's death, and his living on in the form of a letter is a direct corollary to the very conceit which drives the film, that archaeologists have found Saigo's bag of letters."[4]

With the first voice-over of reluctant soldier Saigo, viewers have been drawn into the human tragedy seen from the soldiers' side: suffering that is both abstract, as the young men serve as sacrificial offerings to the god of war, and deeply individual, with the flashbacks to clean, well-lighted places. Through Saigo's eyes we witness an entire platoon's grenade suicides — bright bursts of orange against the caves' dank grey — the deaths of young men we have come to know and pity as they find themselves cruelly outnumbered. Eastwood's bold direction allows us to witness not only this remote corner of the war from the inside of a cosmic heart — that is, God's children needlessly massacred — but also to feel the firebombing of Tokyo (detailed on p. 175 in the *Letters* collection) and the on-the-ground horror of the atomic bombs dropped on Hiroshima and Nagasaki not long after the Battle of Iwo Jima ended.

Pointedly, considering our own wartime era, interviewer Terry Gross asked the director about the timing of his war movies.

"It is difficult not to think of Iraq [a war that Eastwood opposed] upon seeing the two films," he said. "Each war calls up comparisons," he had responded in 1976 when he was asked about the resonance of *The Outlaw Josey Wales* with the Vietnam War, a conflict that had been thoroughly discredited by then.

---

3. Hayley Schilling, in a paper in Northwestern University Eastwood class, Winter 2010.

4. Jesse Anderson-Lehman, in a paper in Northwestern University Eastwood class, Winter 2010.

The soldiers' cave.

"Most of the films on war," Eastwood has observed, "convey propaganda. I prefer those which try to avoid it." Eastwood mentions *Battleground* (*Bastogne*, William Wellman, 1949) and *The Steel Helmet* (Samuel Fuller, 1951) as war films that tell a clearer truth, films that have "aged well because they are based upon what the characters have lived."[5] Likewise, the letters home from Iwo Jima were genuinely lived.

In *Letters*, Eastwood probes justice, reconciliation, and the kingdom of heaven through a unifying poetic prism of images, words, and music. It is a daring artistic choice with which to defuse centuries of American demonizing of Japan. The Japanese soldiers, young and powerless and driven to madness or suicide, find their human counterparts in the American boys of *Flags of Our Fathers*, young men drafted out of poor homes like Harlon Block's in Texas, or those of Ira Hayes, René Gagnon, and the

5. Michael Henry Wilson, *Clint Eastwood* (Paris: Editions Cahiers du Cinéma, 2007), 183.

other soldiers, all from families that had not yet recovered from the devastations of the Great Depression or racism or the assaults of nature.

While *Letters* unmistakably functions as the second panel of the war diptych, a reflective twin to *Flags*, it deepens the latter film's fierce antiwar visual rhetoric and intermingles and somewhat confuses (or enriches, depending on the viewer's perspective) presentations of loyalty, patriotism, individuality, national religion, and the concept of war itself as a "good."

The muted color palette of *Letters* recalls the black, gray, and green wash of Jean-Pierre Melville's *Army of Shadows* (1969), one of the most searching works of film art to deal with the European battlefront in the shadows of France, and a perfect counterbalance to Eastwood's theological exploration of the Pacific front. The oppressive look of both films, the half-light given neither to sun showers nor to restful dark, suggests both a prison and a graveyard. *Letters* begins with the voice-over of Saigo, as he asks his absent wife, "Are we digging our own graves?" The film's ending — showing thousands of corpses and wounded stretched along the island's beaches — not only echoes the death-strewn hillside in *The Good, the Bad and the Ugly*, but also exposes the difficulty of telling one wounded man from another. The wounded Americans and Saigo, the Japanese prisoner, could be brothers, even twins, to echo a phrase from *All Quiet on the Western Front*.

The correspondences between *Army of Shadows* and *Letters from Iwo Jima* seem less obvious than those between *Flags* and *All Quiet*, for no shots or sequences are reworked or adjusted to fit the conditions of a barren battle zone. Yet Eastwood and Melville interweave in at least two ways: as explorations of the moral life and as war movies with no visible enemy. Melville removes almost all representatives of the German war machine from sight, as Robert Bresson had done in 1959 with *A Man Escaped*. The sense of oppression, of watchers, murderers, and torturers, lingers just offscreen in *Army of Shadows* and *A Man Escaped;* only sound in Bresson and the theatrics of concealment in Melville create presence out of absence. Similarly, Eastwood's characters, American and Japanese, rarely see each other except in the close-up throes of death. They contend with the void more than with mortal enemies. "Enemy," as Hayley Schilling has suggested, "is more of a conceptual than a human presence," as *Letters* underscores when Baron Nishi and his remaining men attempt to save the life of Sam, an "enemy" suddenly become a blood brother in suffering.[6]

6. Hayley Schilling, in a paper in Northwestern University Eastwood class, Winter 2010.

For Melville, the main characters — their "virtue" (classical *and* Christian) redefined daily if they are to survive — oscillate between bold action and furtive concealment, between escape and rescue. The second sequence in *Army of Shadows* begins with a murder, not distanced with bombs or a long-range rifle, but rather undertaken in fear and trembling, by hand and among friends, a slow, excruciating strangulation seen in close-up and accompanied by tears and remorse. The film also ends with a murder, not of a hated German operative, but of the Resistance team's own beloved mastermind, Mathilde, without whom they cannot and will not live, yet who in the calculus of wartime — kill one to save many — must die.

W. G. Sebald, writing about the absence of writing or discussion within families of what had happened during the fire bombings of the German cities, lamented the "inability to gauge the depths of trauma suffered" because history itself seemed to be struck dumb.[7] The 600,000 civilians killed during those pointless raids (proportionately, almost as deadly to the Allied pilots as they were to those on the ground) finally found their voice with Sebald, as Kurt Vonnegut had recounted decades earlier (in *Slaughterhouse Five*) an American soldier's anguished inability to escape the "haunting strength of memory" of those same firebombings — temporally distant, yet ever inside him.

As the Greek and Trojan dead found their voice with Homer, the thousands fleeing European villages and universities, churches and synagogues, gypsy camps, and salons found theirs in Simone Weil and Rachel Bespaloff, who channeled Homer for war-torn Europe. For poetry "repossesses beauty from death and wrests from it the secret of justice that history cannot fathom. To the darkened world poetry alone restores pride, eclipsed by the arrogance of the victors and the silence of the vanquished."[8]

Eastwood invokes such poetry in showing us a fully human Japanese perspective on a parallel war as it takes place on the other side of the world. He urges the necessity of retaining empathy and a moral compass: Always do what is right because it is right, to quote both the highly educated and philosophical General Kuribayashi and an American mother from Oklahoma, who exhorts her faraway son to remain human in the midst of madness.

7. W. G. Sebald, *On the Natural History of Destruction,* trans. Anthea Bell (New York: Random House, 2003), 3-4, 79-93 (a version of this book was originally published in German in 1999).

8. Simone Weil and Rachel Bespaloff, *War and the Iliad,* trans. Mary McCarthy (New York: New York Review Books, 2005), 49.

Friends have asked me whether *Letters* might have earned its high praise from garish and vengeful battle scenes that attract the American appetite for bloody action. I respond that audiences need only watch the film's opening frame, listen to its haunting piano melody, and give themselves to the unfolding stories of Saigo, Kuribayashi, and their friends. They will never see "the enemy" in the same way again. And they will ready themselves for the next installment in Eastwood's war cycle — "oneself as the other" — in *Gran Torino*.

Gran Torino

You may have heard of *Gran Torino*. It's the movie that everyone was waiting for: Dirty Harry #6. For months I waited, enthralled by the trailer that advertised the movie for months before it opened in December 2008. I guess Eastwood couldn't help making another Dirty Harry revenge movie, I thought. He has so many children to support. But what a pity that would be! Eastwood has spent the past thirty years acting in and sometimes directing movies with lots of audience appeal, such as all five Dirty Harrys and *Every Which Way but Loose*. He has alternated the big-box-office movies with the "personal," little-seen movies that he directed and funded himself, such as *Honkytonk Man* and *Bronco Billy*. *The Outlaw Josey Wales* in 1976 and *Bridges of Madison County* in 1995 had a little more traction at the box office, partly because he was still the number-one actor in the world. But he didn't begin to get major press for his directing until *Unforgiven* in 1992, and then again for *Mystic River* in 2003. Since then, it has been one brilliant movie after another, including *Changeling* (2008). So why, I asked myself, was he doing another Dirty Harry?

As it turned out, he wasn't. Not that the Man With No Name, Dirty Harry, the Stranger, and the Preacher have gone away, replaced by the gentle and sympathetic Robert Kinkaid in *Bridges of Madison County* and the vulnerable and affectionate Frankie Dunn in *Million Dollar Baby*. They are all there in the movie's first half, like the ghost of a good old buddy, all wrapped up in the figure of Walt Kowalski (Eastwood), the movie's central character. But they are there to be dealt with nonetheless.

The mythic apparatus of the superhero is present in Walt's acid one-liners and in the giant gun he stashes not too far out of reach. Although the one-man American superhero model hasn't worked out too well — we only have to look at Iraq and Afghanistan — isn't vigilante justice still a hot topic in some circles in 2011? Think of the Minutemen "guarding" the border between Mexico and the United States. I had to wonder what Eastwood would do with the vigilante response in *Gran Torino*. He had been rejecting that model for a long time in his "personal" films, but audiences and the press mostly just didn't get it when awards season came around. They were stuck back in the 1970s and '80s.

Let me give you a quick summary of the plot. The "story world" is set in a formerly booming but now rundown American industrial city, Detroit, with formerly all-white neighborhoods overtaken by waves of immigrants. Walt, the protagonist, embodies the dreams of a better life of one immigrant strand, the Polish. He worked on a Ford assembly line for his whole life, and he took pride in his craft and his tidy home. He is now retired. Blacks and Hispanics have drifted into his neighborhood, and now, heaven forbid, an extended Hmong family has moved in next door.

In a painfully timely movie, Eastwood links depression and spiritual uncertainty to a history of violent acts, associating markers of personal disintegration with larger economic and social instability that is indirectly or directly caused by war. In this chapter I will explore the terrain on which Eastwood examines such spiritual and social dislocation: Walt and the war memories that poison his life; the collapsing city within which he lives; his Hmong neighbors, who have been displaced by the Vietnam War and relocated in another kind of war zone; Walt's rebirth through the embrace of Sue and Thao, his new neighbors; and the fashioning of a wider human community.

The movie has two overarching themes: isolation and reconciliation. The first half anticipates events and persons in the second half in rhythmic, ritual antiphony: call and response, with a meal as the pivotal point. Funeral echoes funeral; meal scenes in one section return in another with startling variations; buried secrets surface unexpectedly and yet, in the movie's elaborate structure, fit inexorably into the larger redemptive scheme. In the first part, Walt is newly widowed, and his really jerky sons and grandchildren seem to inhabit the world of commedia dell'arte — fools galore — or at least are playing in a different movie from what we've expected from Eastwood since *Mystic River* and *Million Dollar Baby*. Walt hates dirt, shoddy workmanship, laziness, immigrants, and the world in general. His flag flaps crazily outside his porch, where he sits most of the day and drinks beer from his cooler, alone with his regrets, whatever they are. Isolation is established visually and thematically as surely here as in the beginning of *Flags of Our Fathers,* where a young soldier stares desperately around him, unmoored in a gray and pitted battlefield.

Gran Torino begins with alienating devices that anticipate its later exposure of buried secrets. A long God's-eye sweep of the camera alights on a modest church building surrounded by grass and cement. The camera dips inside to investigate the building's interior, where a massive organ fills the sanctuary with solemn music. It's a funeral, but for whom? It might as well be for the tall, gaunt man standing beside the coffin, a poor creature whom the camera isolates as it begins to rove around the gaping spaces trying to catch a snarl here, a yawn there, or a few words of irreverence or kindness.

With economical whispered dialogue, we learn that the funeral is for the man's wife; yet we hear his sons scorn him, and his grandchildren admit that they feel no sense of gravity or loss at their grandmother's death. One friend, Al, comes forward to console the bereft man, whose name is Walt. Otherwise, he stands alone — comfortless. Rather than the classic organ background that plays at the funeral, the film could have opened with "I'll Walk Alone," the wrenching period song that underscores the beginning of Eastwood's antiwar movie *Flags of Our Fathers* (2006). Instead, we are face to face with the deep wounds that scar a former soldier and the isolation he suffers even within his own family.

In Eastwood's previous two movies, *Flags of Our Fathers* and *Letters from Iwo Jima,* he engages the horror and senselessness of war through the eyes of two innocent conscripts (Doc Bradley, the student, and Saigo, the baker). One is American, the other Japanese, and each is haunted by what he saw and did during the war. *Gran Torino* signals the thoughtful director's further reflection on "what war does to men's souls," as he told interviewer Terry Gross.[1]

Even more, Korean War veteran Walt, Catholic and Polish, seems to embody one of the "hard-working white Americans" targeted in the 2008 election by presidential candidate Hillary Clinton; he is clearly one of the "real Americans" targeted by vice presidential candidate Sarah Palin and presidential candidate John McCain during the long summer and fall campaigns of 2008. Throughout Walt's emotional and spiritual journey, however, director Eastwood underscores the continued need for all Americans to welcome their new immigrant neighbors and revitalize the ideals

---

1. Interview with Terry Gross on *Fresh Air,* January 10, 2007.

of a nation founded on equality and opportunity for all persons. By the calculations of race-baiting election strategists, the good folks of Indiana, Pennsylvania, and, yes, Michigan, should have chosen "one of us" over "one of them" ("them" being nonwhites) as their president. Coded language about race was designed to reanimate fears that had been successfully stoked in earlier elections. In 1988, for example, Michael Dukakis's bid for the presidency was derailed by the infamous "Willie Horton" television ad, which implied that he was "soft on (black) crime." Nonetheless, Indiana, Pennsylvania, Michigan, and even Virginia and North Carolina voted for Barack Obama and his message that welcomed blacks, Hispanics, and immigrants instead of excluding them from the American — and the human — community.

The artistic and theological agenda of Eastwood's long career as a director has stimulated filmgoers to see through the eyes of the other person, the forgotten ones. As Jesus says in Matthew 25, when we serve the hungry, thirsty, and imprisoned, we serve God.[2] We read in this passage: "Verily, inasmuch as ye have done it unto one of the least of these my brethren, ye have done it unto me" (Matt. 25:35-46, KJV). Like confession, practical acts of mercy and love draw us closer to the divine, while hate speech and hate acts alienate us from God and each other. Eastwood the director defies the rhetoric of passionate screeds that aim to divide Americans from each other by opening his cast of characters to women, the poor, the oddballs, and minorities, and — with *Gran Torino* — marginalized immigrants such as the Hmong.

Catholics were themselves regarded as thoroughly foreign in the largely Protestant America of my childhood: witness the hysteria that surrounded the Kennedy-Nixon election in 1960, with fear-mongers shouting that the pope would take over America if we elected a Catholic president. (Even my saintly grandmother told my aunt that if a boy who picked you up for a date had a statue of the Virgin Mary dangling from his dashboard, you should jump out of the car and run the other way.) The Irish — and other ambitious if desperate immigrant groups — were regarded as threats to men and women whose American roots may have been barely decades old when the Irish arrived.

A country with its human and economic resources depleted by World

---

2. See Dorothée Sölle, *Silent Cry: Mysticism and Resistance,* trans. Barbara and Martin Rumscheidt (Minneapolis: Fortress, 2001). During a talk at Northwestern University, Sölle said, "God has no hands other than our own."

Walt (Eastwood) enjoys a tasty meal with his new Hmong friends.

War II should have welcomed the newcomers. But our government repeatedly tried to shut out nonwhites and non-Christians. Walt's string of insults for racial and ethnic groups may offend contemporary ears, but they voice a persistent anti-immigrant sentiment that was openly expressed without reproach until a few years ago, and they are still often voiced today, in 2011, with damaging effects to our economy and our sense of dignity as a civilized nation. Almost immediately in *Gran Torino* there is a challenge to xenophobia, which remains a simmering sore in a country that professes to be a righteous nation. Eastwood uses edgy humor to tackle the bigotry reflected in his central character's racial insults. Toxic shame, as Robert Jewett has written, emanates from hatred for others and pollutes its speaker. Nontoxic shame that listens to conscience can cleanse the heart in confession by word and begin to heal a community by deed.[3] And healing is on Eastwood's mind in *Gran Torino,* aided by a sharp script by first-time writer Nick Schenk.

Film critic Manohla Dargis nails the multiple layers of our pleasure when we watch *Gran Torino:* the movie delivers "enjoyment [that] can be likened to spending time with an old friend — Dirty Harry is back, in a way, in 'Gran Torino,' not as a character but as a ghostly presence. He hovers in the film, in its themes and high-caliber imagery, and of course most obviously in Mr. Eastwood's face."[4] Whereas Walt's age seems to rule out

3. Robert Jewett, presentation at a conference on American theology, Lincoln, NE, October 2010.

4. Manohla Dargis, "Hope for a Racist, and Maybe a Country," *The New York Times,* December 12, 2008, C1, 14.

the possibility of a romantic second act, the narrative focuses on Walt's empty heart and his abandonment of life itself. Scene after scene reveals the absence of generativity, what psychologist Erik Erikson calls care for others and contribution to the good of society.[5]

The funeral meal for Walt's wife illustrates the absence of life. Its flat, brown components lie inertly on his dining room table; the guests, uncomfortably crowded into the space, don't seem to belong (a visual effect emphasized by foreshortening). Walt's sons engage with him only to recycle their childhood antics. They leave the heavy lifting to him (the folding chairs) and abandon him when he and the guests need help (the jumper cables). His grandchildren, romping around in the basement, know nothing of their grandfather's life history or even any basic geography or history. "Korea? Where's that?" The granddaughter, a tartish register of a contemporary female consumer, nails the generation gap with her belly rings and mobile phone: "This ghetto is a dead zone for my cell, and I'm bored."

Sitting on his porch after the funeral dinner, Walt stares at a wedding photograph of himself and his wife, Dorothy. Walt sighs to Daisy, his beloved dog: "We miss Mama, don't we?" This cannot end well. The last time we saw an Eastwood character look at a photo of his dead wife was 1992, when Will Munny gazed at a portrait of his wife, Claudia, before he began to prepare his tired body for a bounty hunt that got really, really out of control. (The visual redoubling, a reference to a movie whose vigilante violence was severely critiqued, further confuses the viewer. Will this movie prove that violence is good after all?)

What is at stake here? Walt has refused to go to confession, which his dead wife wished he would do. Is he suffering from an empty heart? Death and abandonment? Ungrateful children? The plot summary recalls *King Lear,* or at least hints at a setup for movie redemption, or possibly even a real resurrection, given the right narrative setting. But will the movie allow this? Or, more importantly, will Eastwood's die-hard *Dirty Harry* fans allow it? It's Detroit, after all, riven by racial tensions and economic collapse (at least according to Rudy Giuliani's snide references at a fundraiser for Michael Bloomberg).[6]

---

5. http://www.learningplaceonline.com/stages/organize/Erikson.htm. See *Childhood and Society* (1950) and *Young Man Luther* (1958).

6. See Bob Herbert, "We Know What He Means," *The New York Times,* October 23, 2009, A19. In a speech in support of Mr. Bloomberg's reelection, Giuliani tried to ratchet up racial fear among New Yorkers by saying that without Bloomberg as mayor, New York City could decline "like Detroit."

You can hardly blame fans for expecting Eastwood to somehow rekindle the old magic of the Spaghetti Westerns or somehow revive the long-dead *Dirty Harry* franchise. Manohla Dargis observes, however, that "Mr. Eastwood is an adept director of his own performances and, perhaps more important, a canny manipulator of his own iconographic presence. He knows that when we're looking at him, we're also seeing Dirty Harry and the Man With No Name and all the other outlaws and avenging angels who have roamed across the screen for the last half-century."[7] The producers certainly encouraged this misconception with their *Dirty Harry*–style trailer for *Gran Torino:* Eastwood threatening the movie's miscreants with his rifle and his growling threats.

But healing, not vigilante justice, is on Eastwood's mind in *Gran Torino.* Eastwood the director is not to be equated with the character Dirty Harry, played by an actor, Clint Eastwood, who in the past has also played director John Huston (flamboyantly), photographer Robert Kinkaid (romantically), and boxing coach Frankie Dunn (gently). He is Eastwood, one of the finest movie craftsmen working in America today. A moviegoer who has never seen *Bird* or (unforgivably) *Unforgiven* or *Mystic River* or *Million Dollar Baby* would hardly be prepared for the director's daring exploration of theological resonance, much less for his stringent criticism of American civil religion (violence run wild; American exceptionalism and imperial ambitions; hatred of outsiders). Therefore, they might initially be fooled into taking *Gran Torino*'s first events at face value — as "realistic": Walt threatens the gangs; he uses both a pointed finger and thumb in mock gunshot, and he has real guns; he insults everything and everyone in sight. But if they took those events as realistic, they would miss the film's theological undercurrents: the social and political critique and transformation at work in the film. They would miss Walt's regeneration.

Who are the Hmong who move in next door to Walt and slowly become his extended family? The ethnic group Walt initially despises as "chinks" and "gooks," like the ones he "used for sandbags [in Korea]," came to this country when the Americans abandoned their allies at the end of the Vietnam War despite the Hmong's faithful, decades-long protection of the American military throughout Vietnam and Laos. When the Communist government began a program of systematic extermination of the Hmong, groups like the Lutheran Church arranged sanctuary for the survivors.[8]

---

7. Dargis, "Hope for a Racist," C1, 14.

8. After massive campaigns of repatriation and persecution from Thailand to Laos,

"Hmong is not a place, it's a people," explains Sue, Walt's feisty cultural interpreter. The Hmong are a people that American administrations from Nixon to Clinton did not consider important enough to rescue.

As a consistently surprising director, Eastwood has tackled war ethics since the beginning of his career, making a disturbing Civil War tale, *The Beguiled* (codirected with Don Siegel), in 1971, and *High Plains Drifter* in 1973. His other westerns, *The Outlaw Josey Wales* (1976), *Pale Rider* (1985), and *Unforgiven* (1992), revolve around the search for community in the haze of the Civil War, a bloody conflict that continues to hold American culture in its grip. *Gran Torino* seems to ask: For our nation, will vengeance or reconciliation prevail? Will we actively cultivate respect for other cultures and welcome new Americans such as the Hmong? Will we undertake programs that stimulate economic growth with fresh ideas and enhanced entrepreneurial spirit, or will we lapse into parochial stagnation, goaded by deregulation and license to exploit our country's most vulnerable citizens?

War takes the young men (and now young women) from our country's margins and promises them glory, prosperity, safety, and happiness. War also steals our national treasure — funds that should be spent on education, roads, bridges, job creation, health care and rescue — and leaves behind the wasteland shown in *Gran Torino*.[9] Walt Kowalski is more than a retired Detroit autoworker whose sons and their families have become casualties of consumerism run wild.[10] He tries to live close to the earth, making and fixing things with his hands, looking for the centered life he never grasped when he was young. He tries valiantly to hold together a life that was shredded fifty years ago by yet another war undertaken for less than noble reasons. As in the invasion of Sicily in 1943,[11] and the Vietnam War

some Hmong were allowed to immigrate to America after 1975, and now large communities exist in California, Wisconsin, Minnesota, North Carolina, Rhode Island, Pennsylvania, and Massachusetts. See Jane Hamilton-Merritt, *Tragic Mountains: The Hmong, the Americans, and the Secret Wars for Laos, 1942-1992* (Bloomington: Indiana University Press, 1999; first published in 1993).

9. Our bridges collapse; health care is in shreds; schools don't educate — and yet the Bush government paid out $31 billion to contractors for reconstruction of Iraq, a country the United States had illegally invaded and bombed. Furthermore, much of the reconstruction has proven shabby and dangerous. *The New York Times,* May 4, 2009.

10. The original location was Minnesota, where the Hmong population is particularly high. Eastwood changed the location to Detroit to take advantage of massive tax rebates for filmmaking: http://latimesblogs.latimes.com/the_big_picture/2008/11/rookie-screenwr.html.

11. In Andrew Roberts, *Masters and Commanders: How Four Titans Won the War in the West, 1941-1945* (New York: Harper, 2009), details emerge about the Allied armies and com-

Walt (Eastwood) begins life anew with the young folks.

in the 1960s, the United States entered the Korean War with little planning and almost no military equipment.[12] Promoted as a "police action," the war swept up American young men and sent them unprepared to kill other young men at close range.

In *Gran Torino,* Eastwood confronts a host of individual and systemic troubles brought on by the contemporary crisis of the failing auto industry — all coalescing in Walt's aging body. His trim frame straightens itself with great effort; he coughs blood; and he doesn't eat. Like Frankie Dunn in the early segments of *Million Dollar Baby,* he has lost his appetite for life. Walt has become detached from the social and economic needs of the world that lie beyond his well-kept front yard.

Walt, the director's character, caricatures Eastwood the actor's laconic wise-cracking self, the one he shows in *A Fistful of Dollars* and *The Good, the Bad and the Ugly,* or as the enraged seeker of cosmic justice in the intense *Dirty Harry* franchise. Here he presents a compendium role of the loner with no family, no communal bond, and a deeply buried past. In refusing to acknowledge the past even to his parish priest, Walt reminds the viewer of Doc Bradley and the hidden medal in *Flags of Our Fathers.* Both men reject their medals and refuse to be called heroes. War made Walt a

---

manders' "caution and bungling" at Salerno, which encouraged the Germans to return troops from the Russian front to defend Italy. This in turn put the Western front — Britain, France, Belgium, etc. — at renewed peril.

12. The war began on June 25, 1950, and concluded in July 1953. The loss of life was astonishingly high: more than 50,000, with one source noting that 20,000 of these were accidental deaths.

killer, and killing ironically turned him into a hero, which he rejects with all his heart. Now he barely keeps the nightmares and the violence at bay, scarcely able to control the urge to take rapid, swift vengeance against "anything that walks or crawls," as Will Munny mumbles in *Unforgiven*'s climactic scene.

As the sole survivor of his company in Korea, Walt is "no longer alive."[13] War fosters bitterness on the inside and creates hatreds on the outside, as newcomers to great urban areas find that no jobs or educational opportunities await them when they attempt to settle in and assimilate. The Hmong gang members who harass Walt's neighborhood and his new neighbors live in a parallel universe that resembles a wartime black market — with no goods for sale (except possibly drugs), with only empty days and nights, and vague images of nineteenth-century mythologies of the western cowboy vigilante to sustain them. The Hispanic and Hmong teens seem to have nothing to do but drive around the neighborhood brandishing guns, and the black teens we see in this Detroit have nothing better to do than bother young Hmong women and their boyfriends. We laugh when the two cars of guys wave their guns at each other — relatively harmlessly. The play-acting is funny in a juvenile sort of way. We never see young males at any kind of job, and no one reads or attends school except Thao. No beauty stimulates their senses. It's all concrete and potholes — all the time.

Eastwood's use of Detroit as a location signals a deeper social and economic dislocation in the underbelly of American society, one that has emerged more tellingly since the recent shattering of the world economy and the collapse of the auto industry. Settled long before white colonists assumed control of Native American lands in Michigan in 1830, the city flourished through manufacturing, particularly the auto industry.[14] In 1920 it was the fourth-largest city in the country, attracting whites and blacks to its robust factories. But by 2007 it was ranked as the "Poorest Big City in America," with poverty, job loss, and denial of home ownership affecting blacks disproportionately due to discrimination in lending, hous-

13. W. G. Sebald, *On the Natural History of Destruction,* trans. Anthea Bell (New York: Random House, 2003), 163.

14. Gloria Albrecht, "Detroit: Still, the 'Other' America," *Journal of the Society of Christian Ethics* 29, no. 1 (Spring/Summer 2009): 2-23. See also "G.M., Detroit, and the Fall of the Black Middle Class," *The New York Times Magazine,* June 28, 2009, pp. 30-47, for an in-depth study of one family who left the South in the 1960s for Detroit's promise but may have to return simply to survive.

ing, and jobs. (The G.I. Bill of Rights, which allowed so many young [white] men to reclaim their lives after World War II, was written to exclude blacks from many of its benefits.)[15]

Once a hands-on producer of a much-desired commodity, the American automobile, Walt is now castoff goods to his family and a consumerist society. He is both healer and killer. A hope-filled twenty-year-old when he landed in Korea, Walt was turned into a twenty-three-year-old spiritual corpse by the killing, like the Stranger in *High Plains Drifter*. Eastwood captures this duality of Walt's life through the chiaroscuro lighting that has been his trademark from *High Plains Drifter* to *Unforgiven* to the recent war movies. *Gran Torino* saves its darkness for the film's ending, as Walt ponders a morally just response to the violation of his adopted daughter, Sue.[16]

Halfway into the movie, light bursts into Walt's life. Up to that moment in the film, the audience has been reveling in its comic overdrive — squints, snarls, and one-liners. Walt has seen and rejected his new neighbors; he has discovered young Thao (the family's son, played by Bee Vang) about to steal his precious Gran Torino, exquisite symbol of a lifetime working on the Ford assembly line; he has threatened a gang of Hmong thugs; and he has met the sassy Sue, Thao's sister (played by Ahney Her). His own sons continue to plague him. One calls only if he wants a favor, and the other does a pitch-perfect comforting job on Walt's birthday with a large-dial phone, a cake that looks like a plastic prop, and a pile of retirement-home brochures. It's been a full sixty movie minutes, and the end of the movie's first half leaves Walt sitting on his porch alone.

Sue invades his space and his life, beckoning him toward the wider human family. His porch cooler empty, he steps off his own lawn and onto hers. Sue, superbly self-confident, and Thao, who needs a mentor, will become the beloved children of Walt's heart in ways his sons never could be.

---

15. Note that while the three young black guys hector Sue and her dopey boyfriend, Trey (played by Eastwood's son Scott Reeves), they are neither armed like the Hmong and Hispanic gangs nor violent — only irritating and parochial. The violent attack on Sue comes from within her own family.

16. As Rachel Koontz notes, "This reminds me of *Changeling* — the intense rain of the young boy's confession scene, and that terrifying, impenetrable darkness in the cages on the farm which the young boys have been locked in: the fan in the window, dusty light spilling through and being whirred around the room — and then the contrast of the bright white room where the murderer is hung at the end." Rachel Koontz, conversation with the author, Summer 2009.

They will help him confront the demonic memories that have haunted him for more than fifty years and have drained his life of joy.

Walt walks off his porch into a real birthday celebration, built visually and thematically on the blessing of a new baby by the community's shaman earlier in the film. Within minutes, Walt has patted a child on the head and looked everyone in the eye, not realizing his cultural blunders. Nonetheless, with the help of Sue's friendly patter about assimilation, he begins to feel comfortable in the gathering. Fresh from baptizing the new baby, the shaman moves in on the other birthday child, Walt, ripe to be reborn. He asks to "read" Walt, and the latter, surprisingly, consents.

Thus is launched the second half of the movie, one marked by a shift in sound, light, and rhythm, *son et lumière,* as in a French cathedral, antiphonal and moody, like a religious ritual. As light and darkness alternated earlier in the movie, when Walt caught Thao trying to steal his Gran Torino, the four scenes in Thao and Sue's house reveal changing lighting temperatures that help interpret this sudden shift in the direction of the plot. All the senses are activated once Walt enters the house with Sue, unlike the parallel funeral meal in the movie's first half, where the lighting is harsh and senses are flattened.

The shaman wastes no time getting down to an Erik Erikson–style analysis of a withered life. "The way you live, your food has no flavor. You're worried about your life. You made a mistake that you're not happy with," he announces, as though it's a weather report. After a series of shot-countershots in medium range that swing around to include both Walt and the shaman, the camera moves in to a close-up on Walt's face. The shaman continues (through Sue, the interpreter): "You have no happiness in your life. You're not at peace." This segment unfolds largely in real time, embracing two characters in verbal exchange that is punctuated by reflective silence.

Gran Torino is rich with such exchanges, which unspool slowly and sweetly as in a well-spiced meal: the conversation between Sue and Walt in his pickup truck; Walt and Thao's counseling session in the back garden, shot with an overcast sky that allows the hectic green of the basil to pop out visually; the two barbershop sequences; and the picnic for Thao and Youa ("Yum-Yum") in Walt's backyard.

The shaman somehow has intuited Walt's grief in a flash — in counterpoint, one might note, to the painfully long time it takes Sue to joke Walt out of his misery or the time it takes Walt to jolt Thao into maturity. Walt, stricken with the truth of the holy man's words, retreats to the bath-

Thao (Bee Vang) and Walt (Eastwood) stock up on tools.

room upstairs where, coughing up blood, he confesses to his image in the mirror: "I have more in common with these gooks than I have with my own spoiled rotten family." While script purists may have preferred the viewer to infer this similarity rather than hear it, Walt's words set up the film's shift from bitterness, loneliness, and anger toward an embrace of friendship and community.

The shaman's analysis (a shock for the viewer as well as for Walt) echoes the young parish priest's pleas in the first part of the movie for Walt to come to confession. Walt refuses, which is part of the dialectic between call (an invitation to enter others' lives) and response (a refusal or acceptance of the invitation) that characterizes the film from start to finish.

The peaceful, not violent, confrontation with a holy man from another tradition begins Walt's transformation. The face, the "essential object of inter-individual seeing," reveals Walt and the shaman to each other. The spiritual leader dominates the seated Walt, just as Walt's 6-foot 4-inch frame dominated the far shorter Hmong guests earlier in the sequence.[17] Looking at himself in the mirror, he voices a connection of "being": "They are like me; to judge resemblance, I have to move outside visible appearances." The light shines directly on his face, clarifying his reflection. In an earlier scene there is also a reflection of Walt's face in his back window when he spots the intruder in his garage. Now the image reflects dawning self-knowledge rather than the fear and anger of the earlier reflection.

17. David Frisby and Mike Featherstone, eds., *Simmel on Culture* (London: SAGE Publications, 1997), 113.

Exiting the bathroom, Walt meets a worried Sue, and together they compose a two-shot as he crosses the threshold and enters even more deeply into her world. The transition, the *peripeteia* of the narrative and the *metanoia* of Walt's spiritual journey, is effected efficiently through a number of devices. Light symbolizes fruitfulness and the promise of re-generation, and the soft, diffuse light that floods Walt's lawn and garden, full of giant basil plants and tenderly mulched flowers, is very different from the harsh lighting that distorts the faces and spaces whenever Walt is with his sons. The same soft light penetrates the windows of the Hmong house next door when a reluctant Walt, encouraged by Sue, eases himself into the role of needy and hungry single man surrounded by attentive older women and bowls full of tasty food. Rachel Koontz has observed: "A little light is let in and sneaks its way on screen. Might such moments sig-nal morality and spirituality and transcendence trying to make their way in, but they aren't fully present because the characters are struggling to grow and change?"[18]

And rebirth is indeed on its way. The sequence that follows the sha-man's analysis reveals a smiling Walt seated in the kitchen among mothers and daughters, as the women pile his plate. "This food is wonderful. You ladies are really good," he says. Soft light shines through the two broad windows behind the table, enlarging the space and baptizing the area with a glow that recalls the warmth of Francesca's kitchen in *Bridges of Madison County* or the embrace of the evening light when Josey Wales dances among his new family at the Texas ranch.

Earlier, Walt had commented to Sue that the food looked good — "smells good, too" — and now he tucks into the third sensory element, taste. The shaman's comment about the absence of flavor in Walt's food resonates with his empty refrigerator (exposed by Sue) and his diet of beer. (It was, after all, the empty beer cooler that initially drew him to Sue's place.) But the loss of a sense of taste and smell is a mark of depression and decline, as recent research has indicated.[19] And apart from trouble with his back, Walt seems fit enough. Threatening him more than age are loneliness

18. Rachel Koontz, conversation with the author, Summer 2009.

19. Smell loss is well documented as one of the early and first clinical signs of Alz-heimer's and Parkinson's, according to University of Pennsylvania School of Medicine re-searchers in 2004, a hypothesis followed up at Northwestern Memorial Hospital and North-western's Feinberg School of Medicine in 2009: http://www.sciencedaily.com/releases/2004/03/040312090410 .htm and www.healthjockey.com/ . . . /does-loss-of-smell-indicate-onset -of-parkinson.

and self-inflicted isolation — an isolation Sue is determined to crack. She draws Walt away from the bountiful table down into the basement teen hangout, where a version of Walt's young self, Thao, sits by himself, prime for Walt's peculiar brand of dating advice once they are left alone to talk.

Walt leans against the dryer, smiling for the first time in the movie and observing the teens whom Sue wants him to get to know. On familiar turf with a lopsided dryer, he repairs it quickly, then resumes his survey of the room. Unlike Walt's low-ceiling dark basement with the secret trunk and sad memories, this basement radiates young energy — the crowd on the couch and a young girl's frank assessment of the odd visitor. What is happening here, with light coming in from all directions — though Thao sits in a corner brooding — is that love is in the air.

So is truth-telling. The young woman, Youa, voices a repeated theme throughout the movie: "What are you doing here?" Walt is at least fifty years older than anyone else in the basement hangout; he's also white, and a stranger. He has been unpleasant to his Hmong neighbors up till now, even when they brought him gifts of food. He's not a convivial kind of guy. These are Walt's own words earlier in the film: "What's with kids these days?" "Get off my lawn." He's not alone. The black guys who harass Sue and Trey are also strong on turf: "What're you doing in our neighborhood? Go back to your own." And so on.

It isn't too long after the basement sequence, though, that Thao and Youa are sitting in Walt's backyard beside the Gran Torino, and Walt allows them to take his precious possession out on a date. So begins the friendship between Thao, a teenage boy under siege by local gang members, and Walt, a victim of a long-past U.S. war who desperately needs to be reborn. Eastwood does much more than throw one-liners and comedic scenes at us. He undercuts everything with these rich and complex characters interacting in community.

Walt's transformation, then, begins with a meal and begins to heat up with the matchmaking he does with Thao and Youa, whose relationship mirrors his own with his wife, Dorothy. The Hmong women have brought the unhappy stranger into their midst for a real birthday celebration. (Even better, the event itself — a ritual celebration — offsets the depression that often afflicts elderly immigrants in America. So it's a twofer!)[20] Even more pertinent to *Gran Torino*'s redemptive movement, the meal follows Walt's

---

20. Patrick Leigh Brown, "Invisible Immigrants: Old and Left with 'Nobody to Talk To,'" *The New York Times*, August 31, 2009, A1. See also Ang Lee's *Pushing Hands* (1992).

recognition of what he holds in common with the Hmong, the "equality" that meals in the early church fostered: the "real identity" created among believers by the mystical partaking of the (symbolic) body and blood of Jesus Christ. Shared being is reinforced by the shared meal.[21]

The camaraderie of the meal challenges theories of "fixed human nature." At the beginning of *Gran Torino* we witness what Walt believes he "is," or rather, what he has become because of his experiences and the sorrow he bears. When he crosses the threshold of Sue's house and enters into a relationship with the Hmong, Walt shifts from a stagnant person into Nicodemus, someone ready to be reborn into the lives of Sue and her family in a forward-moving journey toward confession and release. As Wayne Meeks has written, "character takes shape . . . within a social process."[22]

The actor Clint Eastwood has played a lonely man without a sweetheart many times before. Despite the presence of strong women in many of the movies he has directed (e.g., *The Gauntlet*'s Gus, *Unforgiven*'s Strawberry Alice, *Gran Torino*'s Sue), the iconic Eastwood that is enshrined in the public imagination for good or for ill slinks through his roles, big gun or not, with a dead or estranged wife in the background. Eastwood's assorted characters, from the Man With No Name in *A Fistful of Dollars* onward, carry around loss as part of their persona. "I once knew someone like you. No one was around to help," the Man says to the Mary figure he has rescued from sex slavery in *Fistful.* There were also Dirty Harry, Josey Wales, Will Munny, and the protagonists in *True Crime* and *Blood Work.* Rootlessness may add to his appeal, or it may signal the end of the isolated hero-savior as a life model. As Eastwood told Michael Henry Wilson in an interview, "You can only go so far with a solitary hero. If you create family connections for him, you give him a new dimension."[23] And Walt Kowalski does build family connections in *Gran Torino.* But it takes a world of time — 115 minutes in the course of this movie — for a damaged man to emerge from depression and isolation.

Gran Torino has given director/actor Eastwood yet another chance to rescue the forlorn man without a family in his other films: Josey Wales, with flames of loss imprinted in his dreams; Will Munny, with only a

---

21. Frisby and Featherstone, *Simmel on Culture,* 134-35. Simmel goes several steps further by saying that the table ranks higher than the food itself: food is material, but the gathering elevates all those who sit down together.

22. Wayne Meeks, *The Moral World of the First Christians* (Philadelphia: Westminster, 1986), 12.

23. Michael Henry Wilson, *Clint Eastwood* (Paris: Edition Cahiers du Cinéma, 2007), 47.

Walt: Drive my Gran Torino! Don't take the bus!

photo to sustain his sense of rightness with God and the social order; Charlie Parker, a black man adrift in a white world and his own demons; Frankie Dunn, keeping vigil at his surrogate daughter's bedside. Furthermore, the movie's emotional landscape cannot be divorced from its political and ethical message. Its deeply humanistic tenor emerges organically from Eastwood's nearly forty years of criticism of America's failure to love. "Blessed are the poor," the rabbi Jesus preached, one of the thousands of biblical references — in the Old Testament and the New — exhorting us to take care of the needy among us. Eastwood has mobilized another story, another set of characters, a transformed version of all his former selves to open America's mind and heart. And he does it in the most unexpected way — self-sacrifice, which is the special domain of the powerless female in millions of story lines. Here weakness is strength, as the teachings of Jesus and the prophets of old remind us.

The dark night sky shrouds Walt's figure as he emerges from his house with a shotgun early in the film, as ready as Dirty Harry, it seems, to take swift action against the murderous Hmong gang's threats. "Get. Off. My. Lawn," he growls in that raspy low voice we know all too well. Significantly enough, Walt ratchets up the action both here and in the sequence where three young black men mock-threaten Sue and her boyfriend, Trey. Walt first pulls a mock gun, his cocked finger, and then a real one. The confrontations are all so silly that we are shocked when first Sue, then Walt, are actually harmed.

The darkness at movie's end, however, signifies something rooted in a deeper emotion than anger or despair. It signals the warm embrace of a death that comes before new life can begin, a warmth conveyed by the soft light and full score in the ending frame sequence in *Unforgiven,* or in the "Eastwood shots" of two people connecting their lonely lives in *Million Dollar Baby, Bridges of Madison County,* and *Breezy* (1973).[24]

Unlike the unkempt professional killers who slept in their clothes and looked it (the Man With No Name, for instance, and the Stranger), Walt Kowalski prepares for this latest showdown by getting a haircut and a shave, mowing his lawn, crafting a new will, buying a tailored suit (left back in his closet), and making a gift of his beloved dog to his irascible female counterpart, the Hmong grandma. He has prepared to sacrifice himself in a radical, reconciling response to the violent assault on and gang rape of the redemptive and life-giving figure of Sue, another surrogate daughter for the Eastwood persona. Sue has been sacrificed to all the violence in the unstable, cruel, and tragic world of an economically ravaged city in which hatred and fear have trumped welcome.

The two kinds of sacrifice call for differing reactions from viewers. Sue exists in the relational dimension of *Gran Torino:* she is shown as sister, daughter, granddaughter, cousin, neighbor, and girlfriend in extended conversations with her family, Walt, and the thugs who hang around the adjoining neighborhood. Her violation has nothing of the abstract about it. Sue possesses a centered sense of herself and her ambitions ("Hmong girls go to college," she tells Walt), and in one scene after another she shows uncanny insight and maturity. Nonetheless, as a woman and a minority in a decayed part of an American city, she is unprotected. In thematic solidarity with the millions of women throughout our troubled globe, she suffers the most from the war that America has waged on its marginalized citizens and that the displaced citizens have waged on each other: sexual violation.

Walt, however, gives up his life voluntarily. Critic Karina Longworth comments that the film's "fairy tale" ending would never solve the problems shown earlier in the film, "ever." But the film's ending reaches for a mystical and spiritual response to violence: to derail retribution in order to allow agents of law and policy to address the serious social problems the film shows so graphically. In some of Eastwood's earlier films, such as *The Gauntlet, Pale Rider,* and *Million Dollar Baby,* the main characters absorb the violence of the life around them with compromised hope for a better world. In *Gran Torino, Flags of Our Fathers,* and *Letters from Iwo Jima,* the

---

24. Idea from "Critics Roundtable," discussion recorded on Youtube, Part 3, on "Shots in the Dark: The Eastwood Look": http://www.youtube.com/watch?v=gWun9zSQYvg.

characters and fabrics of the films achieve transcendence and point toward a reconciled world free of war and war's memories. *Gran Torino*'s core story, for instance, far surpasses the petty and mean-spirited emptiness of Walt's clueless sons and their wives and children, who consider Walt as an easy source of favors like Lions tickets (now) and of money (once he's dead) — a nuisance to be warehoused, not cherished. As he has done throughout his career, Eastwood goes for the jugular: an apocalyptic wasteland (the war zones on Iwo Jima and in urban Detroit); a brutalized innocent (Sue, Ira Hayes, Shimizu, and Saigo); the financial risk (Eastwood the producer's possible economic ruin by making *Letters*); and Walt's death.

At its magnificent end, justice and peace prevail in *Gran Torino* through Walt's intentional martyrdom. When Sue is finally released, bleeding from every opening in her body after the Hmong gang members have raped her, one might think of Bess McNeil in *Breaking the Waves* (Lars von Trier, 1996), who submits her body to be raped and beaten to death as she — believing in the efficacy of sacrifice — seeks to bring about her husband's healing through magic and miracle. In *Gran Torino*, though, it is the male who offers his body in sacrifice to save the lives and salve the pain of those he has come to love.

Rather than continually patrolling the crumbling neighborhood's outer edges in the white pickup, Walt and Sue have transformed it. The distinctive truck not only serves as the contemporary equivalent to the Pale Rider's white horse but also functions as a metaphorical companion to "Dirty Harry" Walt's Gran Torino.

When Walt appears, the lights in the windows of the buildings that surround the gang's house brighten and drumbeats begin to thunder under the images. Eastwood's cinematographer has lit the entire neighborhood to allow light to etch Walt's figure when he arrives in front of the gang members' house to face the gang and their guns, defining the iconic gunfighter of old. He stands on one leg, as Eastwood the actor had done in the Spaghetti Westerns, and witnesses (including a Hmong policeman and the parish priest with whom Walt has battled throughout the movie) peer out to observe, record, and later testify. He looks as though a gun belt could be strapped tautly across his hips in the practiced gunfighter's style.

But Walt does not have a weapon. "Gotta light?" he asks as he holds up one of his coffin nails, a cigarette. "I've gotta light." Saying his Hail Marys, he pulls out the lighter he has preserved since his war days, which is etched with the insignia of his lost battalion. Instead of a .44 magnum, the most powerful pistol on earth, Walt clasps the lighter that had sparked the millions of cigarettes that consumed his lungs. But now, as Alex Schwarm has observed, it points his way toward escape.

Bullets rip through Walt's body, just as they must have torn the Preacher's flesh in *Pale Rider*. He dies blasted by gunfire, exactly as he had killed the young Korean soldier, who "could have been [my] brother," fifty years before. He is murdered by Asian boys loaded with too many weapons, as he once murdered other Asians. He falls in slow motion into a messianic death pose. "As he bleeds to death on the lawn, the camera slowly pans out, revealing Walt framed as if he were Christ himself, arms outstretched with blood trailing down his wrists," Danny Fleishman has written.[25]

We are a far cry from *Shane*'s deliberate savior-lighting, wound in the side, and its hero's blond hair a golden halo around his angelic face as if to obscure the violence that charred his lifelong journey. The light changes its direction as we see Walt's body laid out prayerfully, recalling yet another body, the young Japanese soldier from *Flags of Our Fathers* with a bayonet sticking through his chest, etched in a harsher light than this but evoking similar sorrow at a life lost.

In keeping with the earlier Eastwood films that emphasize witness (*High Plains Drifter, Unforgiven*), the innocent onlookers can no longer turn their faces away from the degraded condition of their neighborhood. They cannot save Walt, but they may be able to save others. The passivity of the nighttime crowd in *High Plains Drifter* has been reimaged in *Gran Torino*, not as vigilante justice but rather as the orderly investment of citizens, however diverse their background, in the stability of the rule of law and the health of their neighborhoods.[26]

Sue and her family, resilient even in their sorrow, arrive at Walt's funeral arrayed in ritual garb to celebrate his life and honor him in death. Their numbers nearly fill the previously empty cathedral, the symbol of a church that itself can be revitalized by including new neighbors. In final thematic echoes, the limping elders from the opening scene are now inter-

25. Thanks to Alex Schwarm and Danny Fleishman, Northwestern University Eastwood class, Winter 2009.

26. Thanks to my class on Eastwood at Northwestern University during the Winter 2009 session, whose members provided perceptive insights into Eastwood's accomplishments in this movie: the metaphorical significance of the white truck; the creation of inclusion and community — "from lone man to family man"; Walt's ritual preparations for death; the parallel confessions; and the complementary elements in *Unforgiven* and *Gran Torino*, with each film exploring the outer edges of human nature.

spersed with young and old, all with their differing life stories. The young priest's sermon counters his earlier platitudes about "death is bittersweet for us Catholics" with words that he now speaks to his new extended family, who lie outside the narrow bounds of doctrine.

Thus *Gran Torino* responds to the ethical and theological questions about justice that have motivated much of Clint Eastwood's filmmaking from the beginning of his career. Walt Kowalski, American male war hero, veteran of the great American auto industry, has been coaxed into new life by Sue and Thao and his own better nature as much as by the young red-haired priest (his name, Janovich, suggests a Croatian ancestry) to whom he refuses to offer confession. Walt — and Eastwood — gives us a meditation on the best way to confront the legacy of violence that all immigrants to America have carried across the oceans in their escape from home-grown genocides, famine, and abandonment.

Gran Torino boldly asks us this: In what ways can you shape a wise, ethical, and just response to a hideous and violent crime against a dearly beloved friend? The assault on Sue recalls the lynching of Ned in *Unforgiven,* which called down the fury of the angel of death on a saloon full of violent men, and took lives for a life, not simply an eye for an eye. It also reminds the viewer of the wrenching ethical decision that Frankie Dunn contemplated in *Million Dollar Baby.* Like Josey Wales and the protagonists of the Dardenne brothers' award-winning movie *The Son,* Walt chooses life, not death. His action, the unarmed and willing sacrifice of his life, will bring about impartial and legally sanctioned justice on the predators without staining "the soul" of young Thao or reverting to the murderous nightmare of the battlefield. Walt has sought to end the neighborhood's isolation (a community banished to the edges of the American dream) and weave its diversity into a new communal fabric.

Invictus

Invictus, the coda to Clint Eastwood's war cycle, seizes the moment when a colonized, brutalized, and strife-torn nation holds its first multiracial, democratic elections and then asks, "Now what do we do?"

"Live with it" was the sage existential response the Stranger delivered in *High Plains Drifter* (1973) as he rode off into the mists whence he came. In *Invictus* (2009), director Eastwood delivers a social, political, and ethical response to the classic *jus post bellum* question that hovered in the background of all his war movies. After the war is done, how can we pick up our lives again?

In *High Plains Drifter,* the savior figure vanishes, and his female truth-telling partner leaves town. Josey Wales rides off into the sunset, gravely wounded; the peace he has crafted with the Comanche chief will dissolve before the ferocious assault of westward settlement. *Heartbreak Ridge* ends as the disillusioned sergeant and his estranged wife walk offscreen, the camera uncomfortably following their receding forms as flags fly and horns blare in the foreground to celebrate a phony war. The truth lies in the telling with *Flags of Our Fathers* and *Letters from Iwo Jima.* Sixty years after the western and eastern fronts closed on the tales those films revealed, Western powers find themselves still enmeshed in eternal bloodshed — only now in Iraq and Afghanistan and Libya. Peace comes to Korean War veteran Walt Kowalski only after fifty years.

Yet storytelling continues to offer us an emotional and imaginative arena in which to explore alternative endings and new beginnings. In *Invictus,* a surprisingly undervalued movie, Eastwood shows his continuing commitment to the dialectic between hard-edged retributive justice and reconciliation, legalism and agape love, despair and hope. He cross-fertilizes the historical and the imaginative — what was and what yet might be. It is strange to watch a movie with two parts, where neither involves violence or bloodshed; where "color" means more than the temperature in which the scenes are shot; where borders, fences, and lines are dissolved through the astute manipulation of symbols and rituals — a cup of tea, a song, and a series of games; where the entire film is played virtually and actually on a blood-soaked rugby pitch instead of a battleground. But that's what it is: a tour de force by cinematic gamesman Eastwood, as eager a champion for peace as the great Nelson Mandela himself, whose miraculous diversion of murderous postconflict impulses into the national sport of rugby Eastwood celebrates in *Invictus*.

When Mandela (Morgan Freeman) was elected president of South Africa in 1994, he took carefully measured steps to ensure that the postconflict time ("live with it") would mean a stable, humane democracy and not more warfare. Only someone who has experienced violence can understand it enough to transcend it: he knows the marks and the moments of slippage. "Violence is not the way," he tells his skeptical, frightened followers when he takes office. He did not want to repeat the mistakes of the past but rather to move forward.[1] After all, he knew his enemies: they were men and women "who came out of the womb with guns in their hands," as the movie has it. "I had to know my enemy before I could prevail against him."

And, indeed, he did know those enemies. He studied their language in prison and befriended them even as he pondered the thinkers — Martin Luther King, Jr., Gandhi, and Dietrich Bonhoeffer — who taught him to love and affirm the enemy. How else could he move past the terrible injustice and cruelty of twenty-seven years in prison?[2] Through his charisma and wisdom, which he had bitterly won from his experience of state violence, he found the political insight and creativity to search for the right ritual form for national reconciliation. As an underground freedom fighter and prisoner, he knew how much he had learned from and forgiven his jailors, and they had taught him that an integral key to their hearts could be found in the game of rugby. On the largest stage possible, the World Cup, he would promote an intercultural idea of "the good" — not a perfect world, a

---

1. Martin Luther King, Jr., *Stride toward Freedom* (New York: Harper and Row, 1958), 82.
2. Thanks to writer/editor David Jones for the insightful language.

utopia laced with the self-righteousness of the pure, but a transformed society.[3] *Invictus* pays homage to Mandela's historic accomplishment.

Once again Eastwood has taken the pulse of the times, as he did with *Mystic River* (child abuse), *Million Dollar Baby* (assisted suicide), and *True Crime* (capital punishment). Not only did our divided nation, the United States, elect a black president in 2008; South Africa was also back in the news when Eastwood the director shot the movie. Excluded from the Olympic Games from 1970 until 1991, during which time the world had taken a stand against its apartheid policies, South Africa was allowed to host the World Cup rugby matches in 1995 after apartheid was defeated. In 2010 they would play host again for the FIFA World Cup (soccer). The latter event focused world attention on the country's current economic, racial, and health crises and spotlighted its continued poverty and devastating AIDS epidemic.[4]

Invictus flows naturally from Eastwood's other personal movies, particularly *Gran Torino,* where another man shifted from embittered warrior to peacemaker for an embattled community. As filmmaker and critic Michael Smith has written, with an auteur like Eastwood, each film takes its place in an overarching pattern and rhythm of the director's work. "*Invictus* could only have been made after *Gran Torino,*" he observes.[5] The celebration of nonviolence fittingly concludes Eastwood's three-film revelations of human beings at war with their mirrored selves.

In *Invictus* we witness the disbelief of whites and blacks alike when, instead of exacting revenge for more than a century of unthinkable violations of property, liberty, and life, Mandela chooses not only to weave the

3. King, *Stride toward Freedom*, 82.

4. In sad synchronicity with the film's release was the death of South African educator and poet Dennis Brutus, a lifelong activist who spent sixteen months at Robben Island prison in the cell next to Mandela's. Like Mandela, he had been hounded by authorities since he began to openly oppose apartheid in 1959. The apartheid regime stalked, shot, and imprisoned him. Brutus helped found the South African Sports Association, which lobbied all-white sports organizations to change their racial policies. The South African Non-Racial Olympic committee, formed in 1962, met with more success. But, like Mandela, Brutus was never safe until the regime fell. See article entitled "Dennis Brutus, 85, Fought Apartheid in Sports," *The New York Times,* January 3, 2010, p. 22 (the article mentions *Invictus*).

5. Michael Smith's full text reads: "Each film in a director's career should ideally play like a single scene in one overarching movie. In other words, the movies must show consistency from one to the next (in terms of style and themes), but there must also be a crucial sense of *evolution;* Eastwood's filmmaking career has this satisfying kind of evolution, more so than most other great filmmakers." Email message to the author, December 24, 2009.

Mandela (Morgan Freeman) hands Springboks captain Pienaar (Matt Damon) a cup of tea. First tea, then reconciliation.

old regime into his new one but also to embrace the country's rugby team and keep its name and colors. Mandela understands the power of sight and language, the synecdoche that symbolizes the unstated yet keenly felt whole. The green and gold team colors, the proud (or despised) name of the Springboks, and the mostly blond Afrikaner Springbok players themselves symbolized what the world was late to recognize as apartheid. Mandela's own chief of security could not stand the sport of rugby because he, like many black South Africans, saw it as a whites-only sport. Yet, though rugby was, as South African expert William Beinart writes, "largely a white sport, the event [the rugby World Cup] was specifically used by Mandela as an arena to emphasize reconciliation and shared values."[6] If Mandela was going to refuse vengeance and transform the tortured past into a positive future, what more economical symbol could he choose than to turn green and gold from colors of blood into colors of unity?

Rugby? How foolish! Is this simply a sports movie told by an old athlete, as one of my friends fretted? But rugby as a sport, and the World Cup tournament in particular, indexes the full range of brutal conflict and oppressions under which black South Africans had struggled for centuries. The contrast of cultures produced by colonial rule and apartheid — white privilege and black destitution — is imaged in the opening minutes of the

6. William Beinart, *Twentieth-Century South Africa* (Oxford: Oxford University Press, 2001), 302, 341. Beinart notes that Mandela wanted to win over the armed forces, since he was worried about a possible power base in the military. Beinart is Rhodes Professor of Race Relations at St. Antony's College, Oxford.

film in overhead shots that expose the nation's deep divisions. On a lush green pitch, a team of ruggedly buff men (all white with one black man, known as Chester) practice rugby, "a hooligan's game played by gentlemen," as the men put it. Across the road and surrounded by a tattered wire fence that cordons off one side from the other, dozens of black adolescents kick away at a soccer ball on a dusty dirt field, their efforts no less earnest than the white men's but the more wrenching when we see the children's underfed bodies and lack of sports uniforms. They play soccer, "a gentleman's game played by hooligans." The painful dichotomy, revealed for a few minutes and passed over, is reprised later in the film when the white men (whom we soon discover belong to South Africa's beloved rugby team, the Springboks) are assigned to put on clinics in the black townships as part of their training for the World Cup. The townships, the viewer has since learned, are the ghettos to which former residents of South Africa, with its bountiful resources, were confined by the apartheid government — far from jobs, far from city centers, far from life.

Those watching *Invictus* for the first time may have forgotten the details of apartheid, if they ever knew them. The destructive racial policies, institutionalized officially in 1948, were even more unthinkable at the time, since the Allies had so recently defeated the Nazi regime in Europe. The all-powerful South African National Party resembled Hitler's Third Reich in religious justification, laws, and actions. To telescope a long and bloody history, in 1838 the Afrikaners (descendents of Dutch settlers and only one of several contending colonial powers) took a vow to conquer a land they viewed as being designated theirs by God. Even in 2010, a group of settlers' descendents celebrates the Day of the Vow to commemorate the beginning of the Great Trek north from Pretoria to conquer the entire country. As one of their current leaders, Lukas de Kock, told a reporter from *The New York Times* recently, "We believe it was God's will to have Christians lead the way in this land. . . . On that day, the Day of the Vow, God made a clear statement that this was his will for South Africa."[7]

As we know from American history, those who imagine God's blessing on their own invidious land acquisition often hide murder behind pious language. The Dutch were not the first colonizers of South Africa; the British had imposed their own systems of exploitation and repression before the Dutch arrived. But the Afrikaners, fortified by the entrenched Dutch

---

7. Lukas de Kock, quoted in "Holiday of White Conquest Persists in South Africa," *The New York Times*, December 17, 2009, A10.

Reformed Church, imposed unbelievable suffering on people who had inhabited the land for millennia before they arrived.

By movie logic (as in, for example, *Taken, The Gangs of New York,* or *Oldboy*), anyone who takes your land, your possessions, your children, or your life, "deserves" to die. The Afrikaners feared bloody reprisals for their stealing of the land and resources from the region's many tribes, for systematically brutalizing the people, and for sequestering the survivors in prison camps. Mandela, Thabo Mbeki, Steve Biko, and the African National Congress, who initially followed the mandates of Reinhold Niebuhr, felt justified in resisting so great an evil, as the Allies had resisted the Nazis and the Empire of Japan.[8] History has validated them. But moral victory did not mean license to continue to kill once the rebels had gained power.

If Eastwood made a timely film in *Invictus,* he also made a bold one, seeing that his first proposed audience, American viewers, was steeped in the rhetoric of retaliation since September 11, 2001. They would recognize the warped logic of movie buff and academic commentator Stanley Fish:

> [A]s the [wronged] hero's proxy, the audience enjoys the same justification for vicariously participating in murder, mayhem, and mutilation. . . . You can almost see the director calculating the point at which identification with the hero or heroine will be so great that the desire to see vengeance done will overwhelm any moral qualms viewers might otherwise have.[9]

Rather than giving Fish the gory, butt-kicking thrill ride he apparently desired, Eastwood gave us a film about forgiveness, regeneration, and reconciliation, which is as radical in the movie world as in the world of conflict around us.

8. Thanks to Kenneth Vaux, conversation with the author, December 2009. Brothers H. Richard and Reinhold Niebuhr explored just-war ethics in correspondence during the 1930s, which was published as "An Exchange between Brothers" in *The Christian Century.* Reinhold took a "realist" position: there is evil in the world that must be combated. Richard, a pacifist and pragmatist, argued that war never solves anything; it only leads to more war. Both were professors of Christian ethics at the time, H. Richard at Yale University, and Reinhold at Union Seminary in New York. Presidents Carter and Obama have been greatly influenced by the later writings of Reinhold Niebuhr: http://books.google.com/books ?id=nH3lHfXFUwgC&pg=PA216&lpg=PA216&dq=richard+niebuhr+letters+Christian +Century&source=bl&ots=EF5x.

9. Stanley Fish, "Vengeance Is Mine," *The New York Times* online, December 28, 2009. Fish completely misreads both *Gran Torino* and *The Outlaw Josey Wales.*

"We need inspiration, François."

Raw vengeance may be fleetingly sweet for the wronged and vicariously cathartic for a prominent moviegoer like Fish, particularly if that critic allows himself to be swept up in the passive consumption of the images on screen. But for a thoughtful audience, vengeance movies beg for analysis, not consumption, and a political-vengeance script — the recipe for endless reprisals, perpetual warfare, and the unaccountable deaths of innocents — eventually must beg for one person or group to rise up and say, "The killing stops here."

What really lies at the seething inner heart of *Invictus*? Absent a traditional revenge or romantic story, what keeps us glued to the movie's surface and sucked into its core? I suggest that the absence of violence in the history-telling first half of the film works as a vortex, a calm before the storm, its bound-up energy driving the narrative forward. All the swelling political passions and all the blood that Mandela pointedly does not spill across his beloved country are released through the intensity of sport in the World Cup action scenes that make up the movie's second half. To keep intensity high (and simulate warfare), Eastwood choreographed the rugby match much as he filmed the battle scenes in *Flags of Our Fathers*. Furthermore, the film's first half is steeped in muted tones — grays, browns, and blues — while the second half (after the pivotal tea party to which Mandela has invited Springbok team captain François Pienaar) is bathed in warm greens and golds to reflect Mandela's words to his followers: "Forgiveness liberates the soul."

The message of reconciliation and the means to achieve it are transmitted visually between Nelson Mandela and Pienaar (Matt Damon) in a remarkable afternoon tea conversation at the presidential palace midway through the film. White furniture gleams in the room; white light spills through the spacious windows behind Mandela. The latter pours tea (a holdover from the country's former British colonial masters) for Pienaar, who is seated in the sunny window of Mandela's spacious office. Time stands still as two men from opposing sides of a bitterly divided country sip the warm, sweet beverage. "We are one country now" is at the core of the conversation, dense with meanings that lie beneath every word, every gesture, and every social formality. When Pienaar responds to Mandela's query that he tries to lead by his own example, he is defining what the film shows to be Mandela's profound genius for leadership. Mandela does far more than seduce Pienaar with sweet words (the poem "Invictus," with its inspiring message of leadership and self-sufficiency). He is preparing the young man, the viewer, and his country for the greatest ritual of all, the World Cup.

Rugby becomes a symbol of healing, not violence, as Mandela and his staff peek through the windows of their office and see his bodyguards, black and white, playing on the front lawn of the palace. Whereas the boxing matches in *Million Dollar Baby* had functioned as symbols of greed and ambition — a scrappy poor woman and a bloodthirsty gambling crowd — the stakes are set much loftier for these World Cup rugby games. In *Invictus,* Mandela sets up expectations about the Cup to deflect the whites' urges toward defensive violence and to divert the blacks from riotous reprisals. Mandela was simultaneously a political pragmatist and an idealistic humanist. The ritual of reconciliation he envisioned through the sporting event was intended to create the national solidarity necessary for the political and economic life of the new South Africa to flourish.

François Pienaar is stirred by Mandela, first to train his team to win games and then to internalize his leader's mission in part through taking his team to visit Robben Island, where Mandela had been held so many years. He experiences an epiphany as, touching the walls of the narrow cell, he sees a vision of the young Mandela before him on the rocky beach performing the endless tasks his jailors demanded of him. Over the course of the film, the young man sheds his symbolic identity as heir to entrenched white racism (as a child of racist Afrikaner parents) to become a symbol of the virtues of cultural pluralism. Just as leaders in a violent society manipulate language, actions, and symbols to perpetuate injustice, just as the apartheid regime attempted to justify its murderous grip on millions through the use of religious language, so do Mandela and Pienaar use propaganda tools to shift the underlying understandings of the ways people can and should live together.

But Pienaar must soften his team members as well as his own hard heart. In a beautifully staged scene in the Springboks locker room, François hands his teammates sheets of paper with the words to the national anthem of the new South Africa that they must sing at the beginning of their historic final match. The anthem blends black and white hymns together to represent national unity, but the men on the team scorn it, crumpling and discarding the sheets like schoolboys. François shouts back, "The words mean 'God bless South Africa,' and Lord knows, we need some of that now." In the progression of the movie's final scene, the camera sweeps across their intent faces as they belt out "Nkosi Sikelei Afrika" with fierce conviction:[10]

> God [Lord] bless Africa
> May her glory be lifted high
> Hear our petitions
> God bless us, your children.

In the second half of *Invictus,* a unified and newly purposeful Springboks team progresses up to the top of the competitive rugby ladder, to face their archrival in the finals, the New Zealand All Blacks, the fearsome and nearly undisputed international rugby kings throughout their long sports history. Not only is rugby New Zealand's national sport, but the team members also magnify their potency by performing the *haka* (Maori war dance) before every game, a terrifying sight to behold. Mandela (and Eastwood) could not have planned a more perfect ritual game: the All Blacks' painted faces and massive bodies are all fanned out on display and geared up for man-to-man warfare. They are the "other" who "deserve" hatred and violence, indexing the wider history of "othering" blacks during apartheid. Mandela, however, was determined not to allow a new majority black nation to turn the whites into the new "others." He was determined, as leader of this new nation, to find modes of reconciliation — even the superficially simple mode of the secular ritual of a rugby match.

The long close-up shots of the brutal and bloody embrace of the rugby

---

10. A heartfelt counter to the negative criticism of *Invictus* is posted on the web at: http://blogs.creativeloafing.com/dailyloaf/2009/12/22/cry-freedom-the-story-behind-invictus/. YouTube rendering at http://www.youtube.com/watch?v=H8iZ8jIqrQo.

scrum display corded, muscular human flesh desperately clinging to the equipoise of the civilizing goals and rules of professional sport. So taut does the animal tension in the scrum become that the clawing of a finger or the jiggle of a patch of exposed rough flesh shakes the screen. The shots of the rugby scrum image human conflict in its most primal form. This is most definitely some kind of warfare. The Springboks and All Blacks ritually enact displaced war between the ascendant black South Africans and their white former oppressors. Mandela had worked hard during his final years in prison to craft a policy of "reconciliation and of cultural pluralism," with Bishop Desmond Tutu as his guide, and had "championed national unity" together with former president de Klerk.[11] Mandela now sits contentedly in the stands as a spectator to witness the "game of the century," as sports announcers like to say. He might well have been barricaded in his palace instead, watching out the window as blood-soaked, violent sacrificial warfare between his own citizens unfolded — "inevitably," as many had said — and he knows that.

Mandela's campaign to prevent eternal war and promote the dawn of peace plays out on the pitch before him, as young men of an age to go to war play enemies who want to kill each other over a ball (a displaced diamond, one might say). South Africa's potential ongoing tragedy, the strife that had rent other countries on the Continent since colonial occupation, is recast as François's impassioned words to his weary teammates: "This is our destiny." But the word "destiny" now has lost its implication of civil war; it now means unity. It means a communal fabric woven from the threads of the past. And it means spiritual victory.

Historically speaking, the World Cup match launched a bloodless transition to democracy. Instead of uniting temporarily against an external enemy — perhaps another country, such as Russia, which wanted its diamonds — South Africans unite to oppose a great symbolic enemy, the New Zealand rugby team. With the victory, the spectators hug each other in the stands. The creeping affection between the little black child and the white cops who listen to the match on the car radio, shown with almost comic brio, humanizes all of them. Black and white, male and female eyes watch television in integrated bars, and black and white ears listen to the radio broadcast of the game. These small gatherings are not displayed for sentimental effect. This is a globally expansive version of what happens in the streets, taverns, and stores of cities in the United States when their team

11. Beinart, *Twentieth-Century South Africa*, 289; introduction.

wins the World Series, the Super Bowl, or the NBA championship. There is much less at stake in those championships in the larger picture, but there is the same sense of mass civic euphoria that is shared among strangers and former enemies.

And when the ritual warfare has ended — when the ritual gathering has worked its magic — the players of the two warring teams, bent on mutual destruction only moments before, regard each other with warmth, admiration, and affection. May it always be so.

PART IV

Hereafter: Eastwood and the Reconciling Community

Hereafter: Beyond a Perfect World?

In the preceding three sections I offer meditations on Eastwood's ethical vision from a nontraditional perspective: ways in which his personal films not only challenge the gunslinger icon that has obscured his artistic imprint but also continue to enhance his philosophical (some would say theological or religious) meditations on human life. Although his foundational westerns anticipate the devastating social insights of *Mystic River*, *Million Dollar Baby*, and the war movies, each of the films discussed in this book reveals a keen sensibility to individual and societal suffering and pleads for empathy with and care for other human creatures. Eastwood's most recent film, *Hereafter*, fits easily (though not entirely self-evidently) within a career of a director who plays with mysticism and the possible existence of a life beyond this one *(High Plains Drifter, Pale Rider)*, and who alludes to a "paradise" or "perfect world" that the characters dream about and long for (e.g., in all the westerns, in *The Gauntlet, Bird, A Perfect World*, and *Million Dollar Baby*). Wars, collapsing urban spaces and shrinking rural ones, hunger, homelessness, and the constant indignity of marginalization pervade most of the spaces in Clint Eastwood's films.

For Eastwood, such misery must continually be placed against a vision of a perfect, if not a better, world — one of the themes of this book. What forces, teachings, or persons can bring a world of poverty, or a war-stricken country, back to life? In mythology, the lone savior, the "hero" (whether a god or a gifted human), saves the day. Eastwood's films question the wisdom of depending on the heroic strong man. His heroes are often wounded healers whose journeys bring them into community with others (e.g., Josey Wales and Walt Kowalski). Robert Jewett is correct: the idea of a single, mighty, exceptional, gun-blazing savior can neither save a wounded individual nor permanently heal a fragmented community. *Hereafter* alludes to the power of narratives (visual and verbal) to transform its audience: to melt the hardened heart and to write the law (of love, justice, and charity) on the human heart, as Jeremiah has written (Jer. 31:31-34).

Attentive Eastwood watchers will also remember how conflicted his heroes have been, and how murky are the lines between the rule of law and lawlessness, from *High Plains Drifter* through *Bird* and *White Hunter, Black Heart,* and from *Unforgiven* to the great meditative phase that began with *Mystic River* in 2003. Along with the liminal and ontologically uncertain Stranger and the undead Preacher in *Pale Rider,* who returned from the other side to judge this world, every iconic Eastwood movie has explored its stories from the perspective of eternity with a moral fervor that never assumed that "justice" came cheap or that religious doctrines of any stripe magically transformed the human heart. Instead, Eastwood audiences have found themselves thrust into ethical dilemmas in medias res, where the only constant is that cruelty toward other human beings is unacceptable. A vision of an ethical "ought" (the ways humans should behave toward each other) emerges via patient storytelling.

It may seem an odd time to write about a perfect world, or "paradise," and the "hereafter," words that smack of spiritual isolation in this world and the unknowable in the next. But Eastwood questions — he does not endorse — isolation from the chaos of a world sorely in need of healing. Politicians stoke the fires of ethnic violence by way of their toxic rhetoric and insistent hawking of hatred. *Unforgiven,* the war diptych, and *Changeling,* among others, place in the foreground ways that the rhetoric of leaders and their media outlets connect directly with suffering. *Flags of Our Fathers* and *Letters from Iwo Jima* show political leaders hawking hatred via the ubiquitous shrill radio broadcasts and newspapers that blast into Japanese and American homes as dime novels once spread their wild mythologies all over the nineteenth- and early twentieth-century western territory.

Eastwood, working through the equally powerful medium of film, teaches viewers to long for and work toward a more just and peaceful world, and through narrative to value others cast aside by the dominant culture. As human beings continue to live "amongst physical evidence," as Kent Jones puts it, they need to be stimulated to wish for the physical, emotional, and social health of each other, particularly to confront well-financed media outlets that thrive by demonizing the poor, immigrants, women, and children, and by equating differing religious practices as evils to be marginalized, even eliminated. In a perfect world, then, seasoned by light from the hereafter, individuals' actions in their private and public lives can reflect their belief in the goodness of the earth and all its creatures.

High Plains Drifter expresses Eastwood's scathing criticism of the disconnect between private professions of faith and public acts in almost every scene. When it comes to painting the town of Lago red, priming it for purifying fire and destruction, the Drifter specifies "especially the church." The "God-fearing" townsfolk had colluded in the town's string of crimes and participated almost to a person in the murder of its young lawman. The director's searing criticism of social and religious hypocrisy appears in almost every one of his iconic films.

Hereafter, Eastwood's most recent (though not his last) movie, has struggled to find an audience. It is not difficult to guess why. Its title suggests a religious film, a horror movie, or a fantasy flick — all movie genres that have long and in a few cases distinguished pedigrees. Despite disappointing the die-hard Dirty Harry fans, *Hereafter* does contain all the elements of a good story: danger, death, and grief; appealing, even winsome, characters; and a gentle, quiet, hope-filled ending with the promise of romance. But, like *Gran Torino* and *Invictus* in the opening months after their releases, it has suffered the misfortune of coming to American screens at a time when violence and fear of "others" coincide with the increasing availability of guns.

Hereafter braids together three narrative strands: the near-death and complete spiritual transformation of a lovely French media star, Marie LeLay (Cécile De France); a lonely young man, George Lonegan (Matt Damon), whose brain, disturbed by disease, allows him to cross into the world beyond; and a young boy, Marcus (Frankie McLaren), who wants to connect with his beloved twin brother, Jason (George McLaren), who has been killed. The movie follows each story strand as it begins to interweave with the others. The "hereafter," as an imaginative construct and (possibly) a knowable reality, inserts itself into every segment. In addition, along with the three main characters' increasing interconnections, the film slowly reveals — almost as throwaway scenes — layers of a commercialized "hereafter" industry: peddling George's skills as a medium; disdain for Marie's personal encounter with death, even as her television station sells images of disaster like lollypops; and dozens of fraudulent mediums whom the young boy locates on the Internet and experiences in public séances.

Hereafter raises this question: What if the future entered the present, as happens with the "ghost of Christmas yet to come" in Charles Dickens's *A Christmas Carol*? Ebenezer Scrooge is transformed spiritually by what the ghost reveals will happen to him if he does not change the ways he behaves toward other people. A parallel character in Eastwood's work is Walt Kowalski, who confronts his poisonous memories to cleanse his guilt by giving his love and his life to his new friends, the outcast Hmong family. The young priest who stalks him (and becomes his friend) offers confession and communion — that is, to participate in the blood sacrifice of Jesus Christ — as a way to release his toxic memories. Walt refuses that gift up to the time of his redemptive relationship with the Hmong.

The near-death experience of Marie in *Hereafter* teaches her a new way to live, the premise on which Dickens (George's much-loved author) built his greatest works. The artistic work wrenches truth from falsehood, stripping away layers of image from consumerist contemporary life: as in *Amores Perros* and *Red*, where heavily marketed women's images on billboards correspond to emotional and physical collapse, the giant billboards bearing Marie's image are removed as soon as she is no longer a salable commodity.

Charles Dickens makes a fitting visit to and becomes a silent partner in Eastwood's concept of the hereafter. Dickens struggled with many of the themes we have seen emerge in Eastwood's iconic work: the tension between a dark, unforgiving world of poverty, social isolation, and grief; and the wish for renewal, welcome, and joy. Whereas his early novels imagined that paradise or a perfect world might be realized through the love of one person for others (*Pickwick Papers*, for instance), as Dickens's career unfolded, the worlds became bleaker; the power of (specifically Christian and romantic) love became less efficacious; and the small cottage surrounded by a verdant terrain became less fully embraced.

A Christmas Carol plunges into the heart of evil, identifying ignorance and poverty as the death-dealers of the society Dickens's readers knew. But the story ends with Scrooge's journey toward a chance for a new life. The instrument of his transformation? Spirits guide him to tap into the restorative past, immerse himself in the horrific present — in which most English men, women, and children lived out their miserable days — and glimpse into life after death, life without metanoia, life without a softening of his hard heart.

Eastwood's *Hereafter* suddenly leaps from its three interwoven narrative strands toward the central characters' grasp of moral, spiritual, and emotional strength. The three narrative strands join as the once-restless hands of George and Marie touch each other, and a happier Marcus, now friends with both, reenters a family life. The characters no longer need the certitude of knowing what lies on the other side of death. They have opened their hearts to the world around them.

The Gathering, the Meal,
and the Reconciling Community

I n the summer of 2004, my husband, Ken, and I participated in a remarkable re-creation of the feeding of the five thousand (recorded in
Luke 9:10-17). We could have been anywhere: perhaps beside the Sea of
Galilee, where a few loaves and fishes, it is written, expanded to feed everyone in the hungry crowd who had come to hear Jesus preach. Perhaps on
the shore of the North Sea, where we spent one wet, gray Christmas with
our daughter and husband before their baby was born. But we were in
Spain, where a dozen tents, stretched along the edge of the Mediterranean
Sea, opened their golden doors to the sun.

It was summer in the city of Barcelona. We had traveled from Oxford
to Antwerp to Paris to Spain to experience the World Parliament of Religion festival's wild mix of songs, rituals, study groups, and camaraderie.
Every religion in the world (or so it seemed) gathered for private or public
celebration during the week, culminating in the luminous evening concert
presented to thousands in front of the city's famed Gaudí-designed *Sa-
grada Família*. The Sikhs had set up camp just outside the bounds of the
Parliament, which included cots for anyone who needed a place to crash
during the week-long extravaganza. The Sikhs had trumped everyone:
they announced on the first day of the Parliament that they would feed
anyone who was hungry — free of charge.

A few adventurous souls — a hundred or so — wandered over the first
day. On the second day, Ken and I ventured over to find that the numbers
had swelled to many more. We took off our shoes inside the door and offered our hands to be washed; we covered our heads. The elders motioned

toward an inner area of the canvas hall and instructed us to sit cross-legged to avoid disrespect toward others. After yogurt soup, flatbread, lentils, and rice, followed by a strong, sweet tea, we quietly contemplated before rising to leave.

By the seventh day of the meeting, nearly ten thousand people had poured into the Sikh tent to be fed, now lavishly. The servers had embellished the original simple fare with cauliflower and potatoes, spiced vegetables, and sweets. As the lines snaked their way into the tent's corners, more and more vats of food appeared from the makeshift kitchen nestled just inside the canvas walls. Although a benefactor had underwritten the entire venture, volunteers showed up to help the old men prepare and serve the food. Strangers reached across the aisles to share news from their country and congregations and to express their worries about a world destabilized by the recent U.S. invasion of Iraq. Surrounded by new friends clad in garments of every color of the rainbow, I listened to the warming hum of dozens of languages.

I reflected that, only a few years earlier, the armies of many of these guests were slaughtering each other, playing out the theater of violence set into motion by their ancestors. In Bosnia, Palestine, Israel, and Rwanda, in the former colonies of Belgium, Portugal, England, France, the Netherlands, or Germany — and now in Iraq and Afghanistan — bloodshed had begotten bloodshed, and it was never resolved, never reconciled. Reparations were too little, too late, or they were rejected out of pride, for the loss of one's children or parents or one's land or livelihood can never be repaired. With mass violence in particular, as Martha Minow has written, "[t]here is no punishment that could express the proper scale of outrage."[1] In the earthly chaos after Babel, men armed with stones, swords, machetes, bows and arrows, bombs, drones, land mines, guns — always guns and more guns — stormed toward the final apocalypse.

But collapse can eventually yield to the impulse to begin anew. In our time, almost miraculously — and with the help of their former enemies — the nations of Germany, Japan, and Vietnam have been rebuilt. In moments of hope after world wars, the world's nations convened or organized the League of Nations and the United Nations to discuss ways to live together in peace. Tribunals were summoned (South Africa's Truth and Reconciliation Commission, as echoed in Rwanda and Bosnia) in an effort to

---

1. Martha Minow, *Between Vengeance and Forgiveness: Facing History after Genocide and Mass Violence* (Boston: Beacon Press, 1998), 118-21.

call perpetrators to account, while also achieving a balance between remembering and forgetting, between an acknowledgment of suffering and a movement toward the future. Minow continues: "What's needed is a process for reinterpreting what cannot be made sensible, for assembling what cannot be put together, and for separating what cannot be severed from both present and future."

It is the perpetual threat of carnage (endlessly mythologized in our culture), which is resumed in tension with the potential of healing through the creation of a new, restorative narrative, that Eastwood engages throughout his movies. In this chapter I want to explore the search for a spiritual balance in Eastwood's movies — a mythopoeic "gathering" of opposing forces.

The Barcelona gathering — like the Johannesburg rugby World Cup recorded in *Invictus* — might well have erupted in riot. The dark avenger or lone gunman celebrated or bemoaned in thousands of Hollywood movies (and repeatedly critiqued in Eastwood's) might have stayed buried in his past as an angel of death, endlessly reenacting the original wrong he never could quite make right as he wandered the earth, like Shane or the Man With No Name or a parade of contemporary superheroes, such as Batman, Spiderman, or Iron Man. Unnamed, known among mere humans as the Stranger or the Preacher, he could summon past witnesses to his unjust death to observe and give evidence of the terrible vengeance he exacts on those who murdered him in his past life. (Witnesses are crucial to Eastwood's critique of the failed community, as we have seen in *High Plains Drifter* and *Unforgiven,* just as they are essential to rebuild a healing community, as we have seen in *Gran Torino* and *Invictus.*)

Eastwood the director could have remained in the past, recycling Dirty Harry or reinventing himself as Count Dracula or as Lord Voldemort in the Harry Potter franchise — or seizing the role of Batman, as rumor had it he might in about 1997.[2] His gatherings could focus on "meals that went wrong," like the welcome-home banquet in *High Plains Drifter,* which ends up in flames; the mockery of the Last Supper in *Fistful of Dollars,* which would have made Luis Buñuel (director of *Viridiana*) proud; or the dyspeptic funeral meals in *Mystic River* and *Gran Torino.* Eastwood's movies could have featured an aging Dirty Harry watching yet again — in a ceaseless loop — as the waitress pours too much sugar in his coffee (Harry's clue in *Sudden Impact* that a robbery was going down).

2. This tidbit came from Christopher Deacy, in correspondence with the author, 2010.

Instead, the director has stepped up the intensity of the "reconciling" movies he has made in the last twenty years and has further developed the experiential magic of *the meal* as healing element that he began with *The Outlaw Josey Wales*. The gathering, particularly "the meal" — so often the site for confession in Eastwood — becomes the place where traumatic events are both remembered and forgiven, and where reconciliation begins. In this perspective, gatherings take on distinctly ritualistic form and rhythm, much like the practice of remembering in the Seder, the Mass, Ramadan, and Communion (among other religious celebrations), all of which allow recitation of past events as a method of commemoration as well as a means toward a liberating catharsis. All these gatherings allow the participants not only to own their past but also to move out of it. Significantly, in recovering the original meaning of the Lord's Supper, Robert Jewett has shown that the outgoing message of the Supper was not forgiveness of sins but reconciliation with God and each other, and a fresh start with fellow humans.

For Eastwood, the number and variety of gatherings in his movies have increased over the years, even as he has deepened the dialectic between conflict and harmony that occurs in any social gathering: massive, as in a soccer stadium; large, as in a family meal; or smaller, as individuals experience it in the intimacy of the confessional or in the front seat of a car or pickup. The expectation of sharing and solidarity for meals, for instance, can be crosscut with the dynamism of discord and antagonism played out in the ritualistic transparency of false, hollow reasons for the gathering itself. Indeed, many meals have "gone wrong."

The dialectic, rhythmic antiphony in ritual lies at the heart of Eastwood's narrative art. It provides a technique that reveals the character of individuals as we watch their behavior in a gathering. For instance, Walt Kowalski (in *Gran Torino*) initially breaks a number of rules of social conduct when he first enters the home of his Hmong neighbors. But he soon picks up the signals and defuses potential conflict — in contrast to his open belligerence at the dinner after his wife's funeral. Sitting alone on his porch with his dog and his beer cooler (a "movable feast," David Jones has suggested), Walt embodies all the lone-man characters since Leone's Man With No Name: essentially homeless, violent, detached, and sad, without friends or nourishing food. But once he recognizes his past trauma, he begins the long path toward wholeness. As he participates in the euphoria of a Hmong meal, the gathering becomes his baptism into new life.

Two features of Walt's meal with his new Hmong neighbors reflect

Robert (Eastwood) and Francesca (Meryl Streep) prepare a home-cooked meal.

biblical wisdom. Wayne Meeks has observed that, in addition to the connection between the bread and wine as substantive memorials, the rituals of communion repeat some of the language and ideas of the ritual of baptism. The shared language signals initiation into new life.[3] Furthermore, as both Meeks and Jewett note, the apostle Paul is concerned that the rich and the poor see themselves as a new being in Christ, not separated by social class and wealth but rather united as the "new human."[4] "The agape meal is law's fulfillment," as is summed up nicely in Paul's exhortation: "Owe no one anything, except to love one another, for he who loves his neighbor has fulfilled the law" (1 Cor. 13:1-3; Rom. 13:8-10).[5]

However, gatherings (whether they involve a meal, sports event, or confession) are never falsely romanticized in Eastwood's iconic movies.

3. Wayne A. Meeks, *The First Urban Christians: The Social World of the Apostle Paul* (New Haven: Yale University Press, 1983), 157-59.

4. Meeks, *Urban Christians*, 161.

5. See Robert Jewett, *Romans: A Commentary*, Hermeneia Critical Commentary Series (Minneapolis: Fortress, 2007).

The possibility of dissolution always lurks beneath the surface. The peace and reconciliation that emerged so powerfully in *Gran Torino* and *Invictus* gain urgency from the possibility that new tensions might have arisen during the meals, the ceremonial tea, or the rugby game: what could have been social exclusion and conflict rather than inclusion and solidarity; renewed violence, not the rechanneling and taming of aggression; fear of the stranger and the other, far from the welcoming of new neighbors. As the "bread of life" is no mere grain, the *meal* in these movies is never hollow artifice, an empty exercise of manners. The characters know that they gather together for good and necessary reasons.

The same spirit I experienced at our magical seaside week in Barcelona hovers over many of Eastwood's films, in the attention he lavishes on the rituals of gatherings, particularly eating and drinking — as remedial to isolation, loneliness, and bitterness. *Gran Torino* highlights the meal that recent widower Walt shares with his Hmong neighbors in all its attendant sweetness as a marker of inclusion, welcome, healing, and restoration.

But *Gran Torino* is hardly the first of his movies to link the meal with possible spiritual, communal, and physical redemption, key ingredients in the building of a welcoming community. Scenes that reflect on the customs of gatherings belong to a succession of films that engage ferociously divisive ethical dilemmas under cover of humane inclusion: capital punishment, end-of-life issues, law enforcement, treatment of juveniles, war marketing, women's rights, immigration, education, urban decay, and *Invictus*'s stirring reconciliation of warring peoples.

Eastwood's films look beyond hunger itself, a physiological need easily satisfied by picking up a *wafel* at a Belgium waffle stand, a *burek* at Deta's café in Chicago, or a peanut-butter sandwich in your own kitchen at midnight. Apart from providing a time and a space for conversation, the meal has social value in itself: it is a gathering of family or friends; an attempt to counter the hostility of enemies; a time to narrate the stories of the past. Laying out the meal offers a chance to include the stranger, as in the story of Abraham and the three angels (Gen. 18:1-16), the wedding banquet, and various "banquets with the bad," such as the wedding at Cana (John 2:1-11) and Jesus' dinner with the tax collector (Mark 2:13-17).[6]

---

6. From Ben Witherington III's lecture, October 19, 2009, conference on "The Bible and the American Future." Witherington's full discussion of Christianity and culture appears in *Cultured Pearls: Changing the Future of America as an Exercise in Culture-Making* (Eugene, OR: Cascade Books, 2009), pp. 237-65.

And meals index not only social life but also moral and ethical health in all their dimensions. What happens during the meal preparations? What is revealed about a community's social hierarchy as preparations begin? Who prepares the meal and for whom? Who's welcome? Who or what motivates the gathering, or the performance of ritual, to honor a guest, to show wealth or status? What's on the menu?

Does the meal take place to welcome the dawn? To feed the workers at midday? To include the children before they go to bed? Or at the reasonable and fully pleasing hour of nine o'clock p.m., with candles, wine, fresh-caught fish, and breezes off the sea? We could, after all, remain islands unto ourselves as we eat our TV dinners on coffee tables, fork in one hand and remote control in the other, or cradle our drive-through burgers on our laps as we speed off to our next appointment. Instead, human beings do often choose to gather with friends or mates, neighbors or the ritual community — as on Thanksgiving in the United States, Harvest Sunday in the United Kingdom, or the feast of Eid in Muslim households — with communal emphasis on sharing with the stranger and asking neighbors for forgiveness.

Eastwood extends the meal to other modes of meeting, perhaps the most disputable feature of my analysis. He observes the ways people come together around a table, in a stadium, in an automobile, or in trading posts, stores, or diners. What do the men and women, players in their own life dramas, bring to the gathering from their differing lives? Will the reunion (especially a meal) heighten already smoldering resentments, or will it offer a site for confession, peacemaking, and reconciliation?

How, exactly, does reconciliation emerge from conflict in the sites and moments of meals and other social gatherings? Furthermore, in what ways might a lone charismatic individual use the sites and moments of gatherings to create solidarity and reconciliation by transcending expectations of social conflict, such as when Nelson Mandela, in *Invictus,* challenges both African National Congress and Afrikaner expectations of a bloodbath after the fall of apartheid?

And what situational social traps await the naïve peacemaker? The barbershop, restaurant, and general store in *High Plains Drifter,* sites of discrimination and death, anticipate the destructive gatherings in *The Outlaw Josey Wales, Pale Rider, Bird, Unforgiven* (if you count Greeley's saloon), *A Perfect World, Bridges of Madison County,* and *Mystic River.*[7] As-

---

7. For a discussion of informal sites of healing and reconciliation, see Melissa Harris-Lacewell, *Barbershops, Bibles, and BET* (Princeton, NJ: Princeton University Press, 2006).

sassins converge; rapists close in on their prey; proprietary storekeepers discriminate against Indians, blacks, and escaped prisoners; waitresses and customers shun a woman who has flouted their moral code. The clearly framed and encoded gatherings provide easy visual transparency in which an artist can examine the rituals of inclusion and exclusion, as destructive parties enter, encounter, and exit — further embittered or forever transformed. As viewers, we are allowed to witness the magnification of everyday discrimination as it occurs, for example, in the rejection of the woman who has committed adultery in *Bridges of Madison County* (one of the saddest and most morally perceptive scenes Eastwood has ever filmed).

However, in the charged dialectic of Eastwood's movies between conflict and solidarity, apocalypse and peacemaking, I prefer to forget the tense, stifled gatherings in *Mystic River* (metaphors for cultural claustrophobia) that finish with death outside a diner. I choose to remember the warm darkness and slivers of light that illuminate the faces of Frankie and Maggie in the front seat of a car *(Million Dollar Baby)* or the transformation of the figure of *Mystic River*'s dark waterside diner into a space for communion, comfort, and lemon meringue pie as in Ira's Diner in *Million Dollar Baby*. The long drives through the American terrain in *Bronco Billy, Honkytonk Man,* and *A Perfect World* are a bit kooky as they are spun out in real time. We witness each of these scenes and listen to the confessions, the pacts made, the hopes voiced — all perfectly tuned to the magic of loving and innocent hearts. Who can resist the graceful life-sharing banter in the cab of a pickup truck *(Bridges of Madison County, Gran Torino)* or in a posse on the trail (riding through the ripened wheat in *Unforgiven*)? Who can forget the shared, redemptive dreams of the discarded misfits Gus and Ben in *The Gauntlet,* barreling down a highway in an old bus, dreaming of their future life together (a little cabin, appropriately) while 800 cops shoot at them?

In *Million Dollar Baby* the meal is initially associated with poverty and isolation. Maggie serves food to people who can afford to eat in restaurants. Like the woman in a tale I heard related from late in the German Nazi era, she takes people's leftovers home "for my dog." For Maggie, a meal means the poorest kind of leftovers, consumed alone and in silence. She survives on leavings that she scrapes off rich people's plates, as in the not too distant past slaves and servants were given the castoff bits of meat from their masters' tables: oxtails, chicken backs and wings, ham hocks.[8] Scrap's voice-over locates the shadow of Maggie's past (a dumpy, dilapi-

---

8. "The Question of Leftovers, Ever Fresh," *The New York Times,* July 8, 2009, D1, 5.

Butch (Kevin Costner) and Phillip confront death and new life.

dated town in Missouri). A shot that reveals her wrapping a bit of leftover steak folds into the next sequence, where harsh light illuminates first the piece of meat and her sports water bottle, then the jar of tips she's saving to pay her Hit Pit dues, and finally the mask of her intent face, chewing the precious food.[9]

As a first sign of her prosperity and Frankie's growing regard for her, Maggie and Frankie dine at a restaurant located oddly at ringside. Earlier in the film Frankie had bought her a cheeseburger, her first sign that the cheap old guy was up to no good (in this case, trying to pass her training off to someone else). But in the system of allusions that binds the differing levels of the movie together, the idea of the diner where Maggie and Frankie eat becomes central. The modest local eating place alludes to frontier times but also to the earthy and transforming lifestyle extolled by Barbara Kingsolver in *Animal, Vegetable, Miracle*.[10] The diner serves in

9. In *Cinderella Man* (Ron Howard, 2005), the boxer James J. Braddock (Russell Crowe) devours a bowl of food before his fight. He, too, is starving, but he must fight to feed his family. Later in the movie, he gives his meat to his son. (Thanks to Rachel Koontz for this reference.)

10. Barbara Kingsolver, *Animal, Vegetable, Miracle* (New York: HarperCollins, 2007). See esp. the chapters on eating and family, the family dinner (142 ff.), and the connection between Thomas Jefferson, democracy, and farming. Kingsolver's book, respectful of the fruits of the land and the bonds between people, could have been written by my father and mother, with their tightly packed yet abundant garden and their door open to strangers.

part as a space where Maggie has known love (first from her father, now from Frankie), in part as a place of gathering regardless of race, education, or social class, and in part as a mirror of the space to which Maggie wants to retreat with Frankie to cook for him — the clay-and-wattles cabin imagined so lovingly in Yeats's poem "The Lake Isle of Innisfree," which lies at the heart of *Million Dollar Baby.*

Time moves slowly in Eastwood's eating scenes, with the action often shot in real time. In *Gran Torino* the rhythm of cuts shifts from brief, brittle bursts of surrounding minidramas to a more leisurely style that lets the connections between people develop. The initial "false" funeral meal in *Gran Torino,* for instance, is filled with quick, acid one-liners from Walt, his son, and the ungrateful grandchildren. The meal at the Hmong home, in antiphony, answers the first meal's darkness with light. The sequence takes its time to unfold. We fully witness Walt's disastrous entry; the shaman's personality analysis; Walt's bathroom mirror self-revelation; the meal itself; and the basement standup comedy between Walt and the partying teens.

The speed with which scenes occur directly relates to Eastwood's use of time and space in laying out a "peace" message. Kent Jones and his fellow film critics have noted the care with which Eastwood sets up moments of human connection. His camera embraces two people in the same shot — sometimes bathed in warm lighting, sometimes shot in almost total darkness.[11] The meal may take place around a campfire with singing and dancing, as in *Josey Wales,* or at ringside, as in *Million Dollar Baby.* Confession belongs to such intimate environments, as with the unrushed dance embrace in Francesca's kitchen in *Bridges of Madison County,* which follows an evening of shared secrets.

In the intimate space of a car or a pickup truck, ordinary time and space vanish, and the veils of artifice drop away. Eastwood is not the first to imagine the front seat of a car as the equivalent of a traveling living room, a galloping steed, or a spaceship; in America a moving vehicle represents the endless freedom to explore a country without bounds. Eastwood's distinctive touch lies in the ways he seizes the car or truck mainly as a moving confessional — a meal on wheels. The car offers the setting and the leisure to freeze time and space in a series of moments when two or three beings confront each other heart to heart. In *Million Dollar Baby,* in a sequence miraculously lit by Tom Stern, light flips back and forth across the faces of

---

11. Online roundtable: http://www.youtube.com/watch?v=somtBpUjVRA.

Maggie and Frankie as they take the long drive home from a sad, abusive trip to Missouri toward a healing future. The car's darkness envelops them as Maggie rescues shards of happiness (memories of her father, memories of her old dog) from the wreckage of her past. A warm blackness covers their bodies as with a soothing balm, as though, from deep within a confessional, each had knelt before a priest.

Eastwood's gathering in cars and trucks may supplant the false premises of the meal that might be set at table. A premier example of this occurs in *Honkytonk Man,* when the family's grandfather is not allowed to retell his experience of the Oklahoma land rush while sitting at his son's table, even though it was the defining event in his life. Critical to the larger story world of the movie, the land rush itself led to ecological disaster, the devastation of the Dust Bowl, and the ruin of the descendents of the land-hungry settlers. Yet once Grandpa is on the road with Red (the country singer played by Eastwood) and his grandson Witt, he is transported back in time to 1893. He now travels with two people who cherish his suffering and his memories. He is free to journey forward to his anticipated death, the full freight of his story now told, appreciated, and passed along to a roaming country singer, to an adolescent on the cusp of self-discovery, and to us, the viewers.

In *Bridges of Madison County,* Francesca and Robert roam the back roads of Iowa in his pickup. Each conversation they share propels them closer in heart and body than either ever felt possible in a world imprisoned within convention. Eastwood makes the connection between the meal, confession, and the creation of a loving bond, as the lovers discuss the life of the "lonely man" versus the abundance available to the "family man."

A Perfect World contrasts the burlesque bus trip of the rangers, the federal agent, and the criminal psychologist to the metaphysical journey of Butch Haynes, locked up unjustly as a young boy, and his hostage, Phillip, as they journey toward an imagined new life. The cops eat T-bone steaks and "tater tots"; they spar, seduce, insult, and bungle their clumsy way toward murder — the subversion of trial by jury. Butch and Phillip, whose saga is the heart of the movie, eat mustard sandwiches and exchange questions and answers akin to confession and confirmation. In motion on the open road, they banter about parents and children, prison, religious faith and practice, justice, sex, and dreams — the whole nature of the Torah (the Law) mediated by Butch's natural kindness and good sense and Phillip's innocent honesty. Here again we have the intimate space of a car, truck, or bus used as a confessional booth, a vehicle suffused with treats, truth, and powerful dreams.

Whether allowing us to eavesdrop on his characters' conversations around a table or inside a car, then, gatherings are the places where Eastwood raises core questions about morality, justice, and forgiveness. Butch, rocking between his damaged past and his better instincts, represents a pivotal figure between the otherworldly angel of death, who metes out retributive justice in *High Plains Drifter,* and Nelson Mandela, the reconciling angel of peace in *Invictus.* This is midway, as it happens, between 1971, the beginning of Eastwood's directorial career, and the great Eastwood movies from 2003 forward. Though Butch, like Jimmy in *Mystic River,* has been severely damaged, his common sense and decency are still intact; Jimmy has simply been damaged beyond repair.

Conversely, Mandela upends the narrative device of the man with a dark past who must endlessly seek revenge. Prison does not poison him to seek vengeance for the waste of his young life; rather, it leads him, harshly or gently, to learn from his enemies and to love and forgive them. It leads him to move, as Martin Luther King, Jr., had done before him, to harness all his learning and energies toward remaking the country he would finally emerge to lead.

Eastwood's heart belongs to his flawed and vulnerable characters. This is the "table" where he finds his peace and his home, and the tablet on which he inscribes their tales. His realistic eye observes the desperate fugitive Butch and the little boy as they live their unfolding present on the road — "the only life you'll ever have, Phillip," as Butch puts it. He includes us "at table" with an escaped prisoner and a marginalized child with no money, no freedom, no future, and no part in the American dream. The mustard sandwiches that Phillip prepares in their getaway car somehow remain as vivid an image for me of the heavenly banquet as any in the Eastwood oeuvre.

Finally, though, we join Nelson Mandela, the former terrorist and ex-con, seated at tea with François Pienaar, son of hate-filled parents and a murderous land. We have tickets to the biggest worldly banquet of all, a packed stadium of rugby fans in 1995, where history meets hope in a rough but victorious scrum, where social tensions between whites and blacks are — for that moment and in that social gathering — transcended. Mandela, the man *with* a name and a country, the man with a vision of a new community, carries the day with his belief in the ritual power of a gathering to achieve reconciliation. And yet again, an Eastwood movie engages with the meal, the most critical of gatherings, in an age-old replay of the search to re-create original agape meals, the all-too-rare moments when human barriers fall away and historic tensions resolve.

To return to summer of 2004, while American bombs and rockets rained down on Iraq, the Sikhs were feeding thousands from their tent on the sparkling shores of the Mediterranean at Barcelona. That place and that historical moment opened up the possibility that all of us may pray for and work for "the dawn of peace." In the same shadowed valley of a dark and dangerous time, Mandela prepared a symbolic Lord's Table for all the world to witness and gather around in Johannesburg, South Africa.

We are fortunate, indeed, to partake in this meal via the welcoming and humanistic vision of a filmmaker as steadfast, richly spirited, and clear-eyed as Clint Eastwood. He calls us together in our theaters and our living rooms to help us see that the old table talk is ineluctably true. We cannot live by bread alone. Sometimes we have to go to the movies.

Another Clint

O ne fine afternoon way back in 1992, I packed up my husband, two sons, and two daughters and set off to see another "Clint": *Unforgiven*. My sons, already profound Eastwood enthusiasts, spoke on the way to the theater with great anticipation and authority, as if seeing "Clint" movies was what every red-blooded American citizen should do whenever possible. (Indeed, as I've been working on this book, their knowledge of the Eastwood oeuvre and trivia has proven invaluable.)

My theologian husband had managed to sidestep most of the major pop cultural events of the previous few decades, preferring to spend his time engrossed in medical ethics, theology, and sports. As for me, I remembered the undeniably adorable (if clueless) Rowdy Yates character from the TV series *Rawhide,* whom Eastwood played for seven seasons beginning in 1959; but graduate school and four children had cut down my TV and movie watching during the late 1960s and early '70s, the period of Eastwood's meteoric rise as a bankable international movie star. I mainly knew about Eastwood as an actor by way of my academic friends' snide (or adoring) references to Dirty Harry and his big gun.

Fortunately, the first Eastwood movie I saw from start to finish was the guy favorite but critical flop *Firefox* (1982). If I had seen *The Good, the Bad and the Ugly* or *The Outlaw Josey Wales* first, I might well have become a Clint Eastwood fan a good deal sooner. Instead, I turned up my nose at the simplistic Cold War plot and excessively dark visuals of *Firefox,* and somewhat haughtily advised my boys to watch *The Seven Samurai* (Akira Kurosawa's 1954 masterpiece, then out only on Beta) if they wanted some real visual and narrative excitement. In addition, no doubt, I delivered a motherly sermon on the perils of excessive weaponry in this world of ours.

Then again, if I had been hooked on Eastwood back in 1982, I might have missed out on a formative and fruitful decade studying the films of Robert Bresson, Carl-Theodor Dreyer, Krzysztof Kieślowski, and Andrei Tarkovsky — on torn and faded videotapes or dingy bootleg copies smuggled off Polish television. I might well have missed the multiple narrative and visual references that Eastwood the director continually makes to these directors' films, as well as to Kurosawa's *Seven Samurai,* one of Eastwood's all-time favorites.

Or perhaps not. Eastwood is full of surprises. His movies quietly but insistently invite meditation on human nature, history, and ethics — the strange ways that human beings organize themselves into social and political groups or divide themselves from the people and forces they fear. He explores the ways they polarize and publicize and distort truth and exclude those who are not rich, beautiful, or ruthless enough to ascend to power. From the first film of his career — when he was chosen by a famous Italian director to film a western in Spain with an international cast — Eastwood appears to have sided with the poor of the world, gathering all the rejects of humanity, even as he perfected his famous squint, his six-gun swirl, and his swagger. It's not that far a leap from loners Harry Callahan and the Man With No Name to Bresson's Yvon in *L'Argent* (1983). Nor are any of them far from the fragile family community built in *The Outlaw Josey Wales,* set in post–Civil War western America, or the anguished birth pangs of Poland after World War II, as it struggled to construct a new community after the war's catastrophic murders and betrayals — the basic story of Kieślowski's *Dekalog.* If I had watched carefully enough, it might have been hard to miss Eastwood's deeply articulated cinematic sense of history after all.

On that afternoon in 1992, the opening shots of *Unforgiven,* underscored by "Claudia's Theme," released a lifetime of memories of growing up in Indiana, daughter of an Indian historian and a schoolteacher mother who was reared in West Texas. Every summer when I was a girl, my family left our industrial town of South Bend, haven for Poles, Serbs, Montenegrans, Lithuanians, and all the other refugees from Europe's war-torn upheavals, and headed for a place in the south of the state that appeared to have changed little since cotton was king. While cotton was never actually grown in that part of southern Indiana, a peculiar sense of postbellum nostalgia still hung in the air. (One of my students remarked that while she was on a spring break trip in southern Indiana recently, she was struck by the presence of Confederate flags.) Wild dogs roamed the streets of towns. Methodism reigned here as though Billy Sunday or one of the other early twentieth-century revivalist preachers had just left town. Back then, as a child, I felt that I was living in the South, as though the Mason-Dixon line had slipped over the hills and stretched out surreptitiously across the fields just north of town. In fact, Martinsville, Indiana, once a home to virulent racists and a national seat of Ku Klux Klan activity, was just down the road, where (it was said) a good number of fine, upstanding local citizens had white robes in their attics, sinister testament to the heyday of the Klan in 1920s Indiana.

My dad and mother thoroughly schooled me in the prejudices of the locals: fear of blacks and Catholics; fear of non-Protestants and nonwhites in general; and the tricks and traps of trying to erase the Depression and its humiliations through joining exclusive, "restricted" social clubs. At the same time, they taught me the virtues of providing for the needs of other people. .

Best of all, during the long summers in America's South, I learned the solace and uplift that music can offer to hungry hearts, as snippets of opera arias seeped through the doors of the postwar military barracks that served as practice rooms for the local school of music. I was most intrigued by the luminescent escape from just about anything and everything at one of the four movie palaces in town — the Von Lee, the Indiana, the Princess, and the Harris Grand — where I first learned about American superheroes.

It took years before I connected my kind and generous-spirited parents with the history of this mysterious corner of the state or its situational similarity with their own birthplace, a northwestern Indiana farming community. Both areas were strangely sheltered from the wider world I had come to know by living most of the year among the immigrant populations of South Bend.

Before five minutes of *Unforgiven* had passed, though, I began to recall my dad's stories about the displacement of Indian tribes from rich Indiana farmland, the violence that inevitably followed in the wake of such a massive ethnic cleansing, slavery's seemingly unending legacy, and the lynchings that plagued southern Indiana and much of the rest of the country after the Civil War was over. As early as 1850, my father had observed, an entire new, casually racist genre of dime novels appeared that romanticized those bloody "western" times as somehow divinely destined and glorious.

In *Unforgiven,* Eastwood catches a contemporary viewer by the throat and thrusts her into the middle of a time only a dozen years after the Civil War, when men who had seen things never to be recalled or repeated roamed the country, wounded and feral, barely human animals, unable to stop killing or stanch their bloody nightmares. Enraptured by the movie, I could feel the terrible dislocation and fury of those years.

My father grew up listening to tales about the hideous devastation of the Civil War on the American population. No family was left untouched, even mine. My father's mother, Gear Anson, made a quilt in about 1900 with remnants of her uncle's Civil War uniform woven into bits of old blankets and women's capes from mid-century. She would tremble slightly when she stroked the pieces of wool that had covered the chest of a farm boy who had aspired to become a teacher, quoting poetry (she and my dad told me) to survive the days and nights soaked in mud and blood. That young man, it was said, related few of the horrors of close combat, but what he and others could not reveal, Clint Eastwood tells — and shows — on their behalf.

Yet, amidst the recounted carnage, what a lovely, loving vision of a better world Eastwood also gives us. The friendship of Will Munny and his former partner, Ned. The love the broken man feels for his wife and children. The faces and stories of the prostitutes in Big Whiskey, Wyoming, where most of the action takes place: plain human faces and stories rarely seen and heard in otherwise tarted-up, oversexed American movies. Eastwood offers up the stark juxtaposition of violence and hope, which he has caught through the sight of a sunset, or a bright snowy morning, or two battered faces that the camera caresses for a tender human moment.

As I think about Eastwood's movies today, I am captivated by the director's uncanny fixation on the balance between solitary and community lives, the solitary one endlessly celebrated in American cowboy mythology, even now (with Alaska as the "new west"), the community one too often denigrated as weak and suspect: the "moose hunter" versus the "community organizer," as current political jargon goes. During the months that followed my first revealing viewings of *Unforgiven,* the director whom I now know and love was to fully emerge: champion of the weak and forgotten in American society, enemy of racism, and staunch opponent of vigilante justice.

Eastwood's films are filled with a lyrical ache for the justice of cosmic closure. Perhaps I was thinking of all the vanished farmers and soldiers who populated my dad's and grandmother's storytelling lore when I saw

Eastwood as Will Munny, grizzled and worn down with poverty and memories and clear imaginings of impending death. Maybe his music drew me in.

Eastwood is certainly a musical omnivore: self-taught, he listened to his mother's jazz records, picked up the piano well enough to play in a club while he was still in high school, and soaked up the black jazz idiom of Lester Young and Charlie Parker and the white lumberjack's country music once he went out to work. His films are suffused with music from the very first years of his directing career. Two of them, *Play Misty for Me* (1971) and *Bird* (1988), are *about* the music, though they swirl in and around musical worlds of far different subcultures: cool jazz from the white California environs of Carmel, and dusky New York City of the 1940s, where a mixed-race couple drew icy stares, and a deep South, where a wolf whistle could — and often did — mean death. Eastwood sings in *The Beguiled* (1971), a little-seen movie he made with Don Siegel, and he composed and sang his way right through the end of the 1980s. He sings again at the end of *Gran Torino*.

However, given Eastwood's long-term and passionate devotion to jazz as the only indigenous American art form, *Unforgiven* is surprisingly barren of music. In fact, as I write, I have been searching to understand why I remember the film as being so musical. Perhaps Eastwood's opening melody, "Claudia's Theme," seized my imagination. Perhaps the rhythm of the movie's shots, as ritualistically prepared as for holy service, echoed with unheard tones. Certainly, the resonance of the individual speaking voices, carefully controlled by the director, punctuates the segments that go on just a beat too long, as Eastwood lets the human dimension of unfolding truths emerge.

Nonetheless, I kept waiting for a church bell to sound, as in the Spaghetti Westerns, or a honky-tonk piano to knock off the sassy tunes that somehow justified the absence of wives and the ubiquity of dancehall girls in almost every other western I've seen, for example, *Destry Rides Again* (George Marshall, 1939), with Marlene Dietrich as Frenchy and Jimmy Stewart as Destry, or Katy Jurado as Helen Ramirez with the good-guy marshal played by Gary Cooper in *High Noon* (1952).

Musically, however, Eastwood's soundtracks are not like John Ford's famous westerns *Stagecoach* (1939) or *My Darling Clementine* (1946), with their heady mixtures of heavily coded frontier, folk, or minstrel tunes popping up on- and offscreen to help the audience register fear or ethnic identity or romantic yearnings for the South or the Old West. Music conveys easily accessible messages and meanings, as Ford knew so well. As Kathryn Kalinak observes, Ford was well aware of the "linkage of Anglo American folk song and Protestant hymnody in the frontier community" when he organized his musical scores.[1] In *Unforgiven,* Eastwood avoids predecessors' musical backgrounds.

What kind of a "sound" movie, then, is *Unforgiven*? Music that is strummed by an acoustical guitar appears under the opening and closing frames. Snatches of what might be folk tunes briefly waft from the saloon, but only in the second chapter. Chords or bars of melody appear occasionally after that, whenever moments of human connection surface. Several bars of "Claudia's Theme" surface when Will looks out his window at his wife's grave, and again when his friends Ned and Sally spot him riding toward their home. When the prostitutes confront their tormenters soon after the start of the movie, the music starts low and circles desperately until it sinks in descending discordance. When Will lies dying and talks about the "angel of death," music starts in the lower register again — not to turn his frightened meditation into pathos with trembling strings, but discordantly, as if to mock the angelic trumpets.

Music returns under the images only when Will rides toward Greeley's saloon and spots his friend Ned's coffin. Strings imitate thriller music but quickly are punctuated by sounds of thunder, pelting rain, and barely audible voices offscreen. As Ned's body comes into full view, a growling cello and bass are joined by horns — low and ominous. The music is swallowed up, though, as the camera rushes toward the inside of the saloon. Cut to silence.

The much-debated killings pass with no sound except gunshots and exclamations. Not until the writer Beauchamp reprises the classic western question, "How did you know who t' shoot first?" does the music begin, as low strings disappear amongst the relentless rain. The notes circle aimlessly until Little Bill's gun explodes.

In a Ford movie, the hint of resolution would be triggered by the return of a folk tune or minstrel song played earlier in the movie. But Eastwood does not allow easy allusion. He nails the viewer/listener to the dusky claustrophobia of the death scene. Apart from one snippet of bar music in chapter two, we hear no cheerful "Lost Cause" banjo twanging, no Stephen Foster tunes romanticizing the Old South, no frontier folk

1. Kathryn Kalinak, *How the West Was Sung: Music in the Westerns of John Ford* (Berkeley: University of California Press, 2007), 81.

melodies, and certainly no minstrel tunes that would smack of racism. Ned has been associated with music off and on during the film, but as Will passes Ned's body once again and we are shown the beloved friend full-face, the orchestration runs toward what critics called "Sulspicien" (kitschy) in Bresson's earliest films: low melodic lines ascending and descending slightly, confused by discordant higher instrumentations into two separate tonal lines aharmonically intertwined. The music never advances. As Will heads out of town, the sound of rain (always amplified in the film) drowns out unresolved melodic lines.

The gaping absence of music in *Unforgiven* — and certainly the absence of the omnipresent song patterns of Ford's films — makes Eastwood's style even more distinct. The opening frame of the film introduces a clean guitar line that hints of immigrants' homesickness. Its singularity emphasizes the loneliness of the silhouetted man; its potential to become a song sung around a campfire does not appear until the closing frames of the movie, when, as the credits roll, the theme acquires a gentle harmonizing accompaniment. By the end of the credits, the quiet melody has become fully orchestrated, stark contrast (and uplift) after the convoluted musical accompaniment to Will's ride out of town or the theme's simple statement at the beginning of the film.

Pointedly amplified sound was not new to Eastwood with *Unforgiven*. He absorbed much from Sergio Leone: the latter systematically amplified sounds of hooves, gunshots, howls, and wind for operatic effect, as I have mentioned in the introduction.[2] Apart from the central role music and sound play in Eastwood's first directorial effort, *Play Misty for Me* (music as seductive and ominous), *High Plains Drifter* departs from standard western fare from the moment the Stranger rides into town, devoured by all eyes, and hears the crack of a whip. *Letters from Iwo Jima* captures the same shock with the suicidal grenade explosions of the trapped soldiers, and drumbeats accompany Walt Kowalski in *Gran Torino* as he goes to his final showdown with the Hmong gang. With that signal sound, the heavens part, and from then on the movie hovers perilously between reality and dream.

The Outlaw Josey Wales threads the ambivalent yet fetching song "Rose of Alabamy" to evoke sorrow for the death of young Jamie, Josey's fellow rebel, and regret for a lost childhood. But as the one song Josey remembers

---

2. Christopher Frayling, *Spaghetti Westerns: Cowboys and Europeans from Karl May to Sergio Leone* (London and New York: IB Taurus, 1981; paperback, 2006), 165, 168.

later in the movie, it also signals the birth of a new community; the tune is one of the few languages the outcasts in the film share.[3] As if to banish any nostalgia for the good old South, however, Josey's fellow vigilantes burn and murder to fife and bugle music, crazily amplified in volume and tuned in pitch to match Bresson's discordant bagpipe underscoring for the murders committed in *Lancelot du Lac* (1974).

Pale Rider opens to a sonic duet between a medley of life-affirming frontier melodies and the percussive thunder of horses' hooves. Throughout the movie, the machinery of hydraulic mining and the sounds of falling trees assault the senses in pounding counterpoint. *Unforgiven* suppresses any backdrop of familiar melodies, as might be deliberately chosen for historical and emotional resonance by John Ford, for instance. Eastwood goes for the unexpected: an elusive yet singable melody to accompany the movie's stately, sad bookends; the absence of melody for nearly the entire length of movie in part to allow selected sounds to resonate. The movie's relentless, theologically rich dialogues on cruelty, death, and the hereafter pop out of silence and darkness; a swelling orchestral score would trivialize them.

Again, Eastwood applies the practice of Bresson: darkness, absence, and silence summon the transcendent. The reign of darkness, so overwhelming when Will sees visions of death, recalls the night journey of Bresson's young priest in *Diary of a Country Priest*, as does the rain-pounded road when Will rides toward Greeley's at the end. The dying priest in *Diary* sees a vision of the Virgin Mary in the dark night, her hands cracked and bleeding from hard labor. Will sees his wife's face riddled with worms, yet recognizes the angel of God in the face of a scarred young prostitute. What could pat melody do but confuse the visual epiphanies such as these?

Eastwood has refused to view American history as all glory and glamour. Viewing *Unforgiven* again for its visual effects, however, I see that his

3. A website says that "Rose of Alabama," with its reference to a "Mississippi vale," has uncertain origins. The lyrics could indicate a minstrel background (the banjo) or alternately the love of a white man for Rose, the "tobaccy flower," or a black man for his sweetheart. Steve Hill notes that, like many minstrel songs, the references to the dark mistress could refer as well to her roots in Mexico.

> Oh fare thee well you belles of Spain,
> And fare thee well to Liza Jane,
> Your charms will all be put to shame,
> By Rose of Alabamy.

revolutionary approach to storytelling dwells on the faces and lives of women — discarded women, brought out to every western outpost as disposable goods. The prostitute with the heart of gold, who may own her own saloon (as in *High Noon*), decorates a good many westerns or provides morality points, as in *Stagecoach*. She lurks behind every man's respectable veneer as a necessity for capitalism to flourish, a throwaway idea that Eastwood thoroughly trashes in *High Plains Drifter*. She's the frontier Jezebel to the fair-haired schoolteacher from the East. In *Unforgiven*, by contrast, Eastwood makes the mutilation of a young woman, Delilah — bloody symbol of her chattel status — the motor for the male narrative. The camera's compositions, which place the women in the center of the frame, reveal Eastwood's ethical choices every time they appear onscreen.

The ironic use of the name Delilah evokes the biblical temptress who sheared the long locks of superhero Samson and caused his downfall. But even with this young prostitute, whose mutilation fuels the movie's plot, Eastwood does not revert to tired cliché. Rather, he establishes her as a saint — an innocent, a Sonia figure from Dostoevsky's *Crime and Punishment*. The other prostitutes, though, are in no way whitewashed. They are sad, certainly, and devalued (this much we know from their pimp Skinny himself); but they are eager to avenge Delilah's injuries, blows that have been struck at their own hearts. Most bitterly, the vengeance they unloose fouls the souls of these isolated women as thoroughly as it destroys the men around them. As in the massive conflicts that Clint shows us in *Josey Wales, Flags of Our Fathers,* and *Letters from Iwo Jima,* war defiles everyone who touches it.

Finally, though, the greatness of *Unforgiven*, and the distinctiveness of Eastwood's iconic films, lies in his confrontation with intractable subjects in American life — racism, sexism, poverty — that we must face, discuss, and understand if we are to live together, not with bloodshed but in harmony. *Unforgiven* exposes the deceptions that were fabricated about the west even as its era was being lived. "I was in the Blue Bottle Saloon in Wichita the night that English Bob killed Corky Corcoran," says Little Bill to Beauchamp, the dime novel biographer of the charlatan English Bob. The cascading deconstruction of myths, even from the film's opening frames, requires that we accept Little Bill at his word yet also distrust him. Was he really there, or is his folksy narrative one more cover to hide his own brutality? His putdowns of the "Duck of Death," after all, turn a dime novel formula story into a Socratic discussion: "You say that this is true. But consider what you think are facts from a new perspective — mine."

Unforgiven breaks down the myths we have memorized, layer by layer, challenging the ways we construct and perpetuate myths.

Alas, if the only perspectives we have on a history of our country are dime novels, pulp magazines, Hollywood glorifications of manifest destiny such as *Santa Fe Trail* (Michael Curtiz, 1940), dozens of throwaway samples of current Hollywood product, and increasingly incendiary speeches from political candidates — then we are still a troubled culture. *Unforgiven* arrived in 1992, when we needed to reexamine our foundational premises: justice and parity for all who have been continually and disgracefully betrayed by the fallout from slavery and genocide. After preemptive war, institutionalized torture, and a resurgence of racism, it is time to see *Unforgiven* once again and to listen to its sounds, attend to its silences and darkness, and know that apocalypse and ethics — our own actions in the perspective of eternity — are inextricably bound in its great cinematic depths.

Acknowledgments

I cannot finish this book until I acknowledge a long line of conversation partners. Henry Pommer, Charles B. (Brownie) Ketcham, and Marge and Herb Rhinesmith guided a hungry but untutored spirit during my years at Allegheny College. Without their encouragement and flood of intellectually stimulating ideas, I never would have studied in Edinburgh, Scotland, where I discovered that I had a hunger for knowledge and had acquired a taste for highly political conversation in dusky cafés, sharply focused research, and international travel. Sue Rhinesmith Momeyer, my constant companion in Mr. Ewart's boarding-house digs, in icy reading rooms, and in art galleries across Europe, modeled the well-equipped and disciplined mind.

Without my early mentors, I never would have met Jan and Ray Shepardson or attended the Unitarian Church in Scotland, where my ideas about a borderless and tolerant community began to solidify. I might have missed out on madrigal singing and one snowy Christmas night singing through the *Oxford Book of Carols* (my most treasured book apart from a first-edition copy of *Bleak House*) with the Edinburgh Bach Choir, high above the Royal Mile in a seventeenth-century house.

Nor would I have ever met my husband, Ken, who introduced me to theology (for good or ill) and to the joys and perils of totally unplanned travel, and who became my life partner in civil rights and antiwar activities.

Six years, three children, and five moves after I left college, I entered the PhD program at Rice University, where I encountered the brilliant and endlessly supportive Alan Grob and came to know Bob Patten, who guided

229

my dissertation and influenced the direction of my thought. I credit Alan and Bob with reviving my love for the life of the mind as well as leading me to discover religion and literature as a fertile area of intellectual exploration. Grob's meticulous methods of literary analysis and Patten's attention to Dickens's socially, politically, and religiously charged texts have seasoned my writing and teaching on film for the past two decades. Special thanks to Olive Ledlie, Eileen Coumont, and Catherine Veninga for intense and sustained debates about Shakespeare's sonnets, Dickens's novels, and the purpose of the intellectual quest altogether.

I spent many years outside the academy, sustained by conversation partners too numerous to name. Chief among them are: Caroline Allgood, Nancy Jircik, Vicky Watts, Camille Cunningham, and Mary Tobin; friends in Riverside, Illinois; Marianna Therstappen and Susie Spenner in Hamburg, Germany; Carol Hettinger in Watseka, Illinois; Joan and David Greenstone in Chicago. Philippa Berry and Lynn Pooler in Oxford and Geneviève Deschamps and Caroline DeNavacelle have accompanied me through the evolving stages of my vocation.

A decade at The University of Chicago and a dozen years at Northwestern University have seen the list of my film friends grow to include film critics Tom Gunning and Jonathan Rosenbaum, who heavily influenced the ways I look at the cinema now. Gaye Ortiz, Chris Deacy, and Rob Johnston anchor the dialogue between religion and film. Dan and Richard Kieckhefer have shared their own knowledgeable love of movies. Mike Smith, a talented Chicago filmmaker, has taught me (and my students) what the medium can accomplish in storytelling, cultural analysis, and visual beauty.

Judith McCue Kibblewhite and Sandy Lichty read early drafts of this book and a forthcoming book and continue to nourish me emotionally and intellectually. I have exchanged many thoughts about the anthropological wisdom manifested in the gatherings of Eastwood with Bill Murphy, who is well aware of the depth of my gratitude. Thanks to Dave Jones, Rachel Koontz, and Hayley Schilling, superb critics of language. And thanks to Dan Born, the meticulous editor of *The Common Review,* who taught me a great deal about good, clean language. Thanks to my students at Northwestern University, who have watched hundreds of movies — Eastwood's and others — with critical eyes and have rigorously disputed the many facets of film artistry. I owe some of my most salient points to their watchful words. (Ah, my colleagues in Northwestern University's Office of Fellowships: Steve Hill, Beth Pardoe, Brad Zakarin, and

Angela Johnson. I'd love to run this manuscript past your watchful editing eyes, but I fear that not much of it would remain! Yet just hanging out with you makes me write more cogent prose.) I must also acknowledge Deta, who feeds me whenever I show up at her café with a chapter and a red pen in hand.

My debt to Bob Jewett could only be captured in a Claire Denis–style documentary that tracked his fifty-odd years of jet setting through theology and biblical scholarship, touching down to talk movies whenever we met in Evanston or Chicago or Heidelberg. He, more than any other voice, has influenced the ways I view the intersections between film and religion, politics, and the social order, and the intensity with which I pursue this fertile field of study.

Thanks to my dad, who reveled in Ellery Queen and Raymond Chandler mysteries, sagely observing that since he didn't plan any murderous acts, he'd just settle down in an easy chair and read about them. And to my mother, a five-foot ball of fire, and to my brother, who soaked up the superheroes with me Saturday mornings in the movie palaces of Bloomington, Indiana.

My husband, Ken, and our children, Keith, Bert, Catherine, Sarah, and their partners and children come first in my heart even if last on this list. Their warmth and intelligence (and yes, their feistiness) may have made for a longer path from this book's conception to its finish, but without their critical voices the project would not have taken flight at all.

And, of course, thanks to my editor, Reinder Van Til.

Appendix A

Dulce et Decorum Est

Bent double, like old beggars under sacks,
Knock-kneed, coughing like hags, we cursed through sludge,
Till on the haunting flares we turned our backs
And towards our distant rest began to trudge.
Men marched asleep. Many had lost their boots
But limped on, blood-shod. All went lame; all blind;
Drunk with fatigue; deaf even to the hoots
Of tired, outstripped Five-Nines that dropped behind.

Gas! Gas! Quick, boys! — An ecstasy of fumbling,
Fitting the clumsy helmets just in time;
But someone still was yelling out and stumbling
And flound'ring like a man in fire or lime . . .
Dim, through the misty panes and thick green light,
As under a green sea, I saw him drowning.

In all my dreams, before my helpless sight,
He's at me, guttering, choking, drowning.

If in some smothering dreams you too could pace
Behind the wagon that we flung him in,
And watch the white eyes writhing in his face,

His hanging face, like a devil's sick of sin;
If you could hear, at every jolt, the blood
Come gargling from the froth-corrupted lungs,
Obscene as cancer, bitter as the cud
Of vile, incurable sores on innocent tongues, —
My friend, you would not tell with such high zest
To children ardent for some desperate glory,
The old Lie: Dulce et decorum est
Pro patria mori.

                                                    Wilfred Owen

Appendix B

L ast night I read through a friend's transcription of her father's narrative of his experiences as a British operative dropped into southwestern France in 1944 to support French Resistance efforts. I was reminded of Eastwood's advance "border-crossing" mission in the war diptych. The story is astonishing in its own right: the operative's firsthand reports lay hold of the pride and terrors of a mission undertaken out of equal measures of necessity and bravado. But the impact of this narrative — some forty single-spaced pages — resonates further with the interlacing of its text with the daughter's contemporary reflections. She writes as though she were the daughter in *Bridges of Madison County,* who has opened her dead mother's trunk and, with it, her heart's secrets:

> I believe it [her father's wartime journal] was written in October 1945. I found it in my mother's attic — I never knew of its existence. I read it for the first time on D-Day+50.

Her father was parachuted into France in March 1944 to "help organize *maquis* activities in the Toulouse area." He writes with the aplomb of a journalist of the thirties: breezy, a bit dismissive, and occasionally sardonic about the training he received and the extreme dangers he faced during the two months of his underground activities and one year's imprisonment. The tone seems perfectly fitting. After all, once he landed in France, he lived the life of an outlaw, with a new French identity, forged papers, and a seemingly endless store of excuses he had for traveling (on his way to see his girlfriend, on the way to Mass, etc.) to escape the scrutiny of the many layers of watchmen — the security stops and identity checks, the French police, the Vichy state police, and the Nazis. Any misstep — or the ill temper of the hired assassins, or simply chance — could have caused his instant death, or even worse: extreme torture and a slow death in a faraway camp.

The account contains an abundance of detail about secret firing ranges, abduction and release by partisans, and the destruction of rail access to a coal mine the Nazis needed, all of which would have been good material for a heroic movie in the vein of René Clement's *La Bataille des Rails* (1946). But self-styled heroism is not the aim of his memoirs. After he is captured in one of the Nazis' random sweeps, the tone deepens. The hospitality he was shown by the villagers when he first arrived was heartening but somehow expected: a British officer who offered his life to sabotage the Nazi occupation merited the best food and shelter poor citizens could find, even if their own lives were threatened in doing so.

But then, caught and imprisoned with twelve hundred other men, he found himself at the edge of death, starved, without shelter, and relentlessly interrogated. A witness to inhuman brutality all around him, he was sure that he, too, was threatened with death in a German concentration camp. Instead, he and an assortment of prisoners of many nationalities were sent to factories in Germany under the Gestapo's tight control. To his own surprise, he did not attempt to escape but rather endured "the hard daily labor, the continual hunger, the cold," focusing on his daily effort simply to survive.

In Dostoevskian anguish, the man reflects on the plague of loneliness and his long, slow slip away from a stable identity forged and constructed within a chosen community. His narrative exposes the terrible depth of that isolation, but it is also seasoned with hints of new, if fleeting, communities being born. He becomes obsessed with the householders in France who sheltered him when he was free, even though he was under cover. He now adds concern for new friends who tried at great risk to send him packages, and for an old Pole and his wife and three children who welcomed him into their one-room house. He speaks of a young Polish woman who fed him news from the outside world, and of a doctor who gave him sickness passes to keep him from being sent to a munitions factory.

The revelation of this hidden hospitality of strangers, even under threat of death, is set against the terrifying background of mass evacuations all over Europe (the evacuations of the 1940s are captured vividly in

Clement's *Les Jeux Interdicts* [*Forbidden Games*]). As Janet Vaughan wrote about that time, the suffering inflicted by the Nazis "could never be realized in its full horror unless one had seen and heard and smelt it."

Unlike the undercover agent who never shared his memoirs with his daughter, Vaughan, as president of Somerville College, Oxford, spoke publicly of the "cost of war in death and suffering," and also of the "distortion of the human spirit and the breakdown of conscience and moral feeling [that] was the greatest of all perils facing humanity."

I originally read this prisoner's tale with an eye toward weaving it into the chapter on Eastwood's use of "the meal," a time-honored narrative setting for confession and reconciliation, and, in these memoirs, an emblematic rite of sacrifice that salves the wounds of the stranger. After all, among the thousands of anguished moments the prisoner suffered during those harrowing months, he repeatedly emphasizes the fact of an alien or a foreign agent sharing scarce bread with him — an unknown stranger from far beyond his hosts' kinship boundaries. But since "bread" is "the Word" in a scriptural sense, it seemed to me that the hidden, secret words that Eastwood based his stories on provide food enough for meditation.

The story that this World War II veteran wrote and then concealed seems now to resonate even more with Eastwood's repeated use of secrets to conceal the spiritual meanings of dark events. If no sounds, words, or images can ever fully replicate the sounds, words, and smells of slaughter, then what can? The trunks in *Flags of Our Fathers* and *Gran Torino* and the buried cache of letters in *Letters from Iwo Jima* clutch the violent memories that paralyze human lives and mute their voices, choke their souls. The survivors of these terrible wars have all been prisoners of their own shredded psyches, their stifled spirits kept as poisonously silent as letters and journals growing moldy as they decompose in a trunk or disintegrate under volcanic ash.

Once the trunks have been opened, and once the prisoner's clandestine story is revealed to the world, the viewer/reader, like a cosmic detective, can — if only for a few screen moments — peek behind the veil that conceals all secrets. This tiny glimpse, this mustard seed of truth, promises to set the prisoner and us forever free.

Eastwood Filmography

Films Directed by Clint Eastwood

Play Misty for Me (1971)
High Plains Drifter (1973)
Breezy (1973)
The Eiger Sanction (1975)
The Outlaw Josey Wales (1976)
The Gauntlet (1977)
Bronco Billy (1980)
Firefox (1982)
Honkytonk Man (1982)
Sudden Impact (1983)
Pale Rider (1985)
Heartbreak Ridge (1986)
Bird (1988)
The Rookie (1990)
White Hunter, Black Heart (1990)
Unforgiven (1992)
A Perfect World (1993)
The Bridges of Madison County (1995)
Absolute Power (1997)
Midnight in the Garden of Good and Evil (1997)
True Crime (1999)
Space Cowboys (2000)

Blood Work (2002)
Mystic River (2003)
Million Dollar Baby (2004)
Flags of Our Fathers (2006)
Letters from Iwo Jima (2006)
Changeling (2008)
Gran Torino (2008)
Invictus (2009)
Hereafter (2010)

Films by Other Directors Cited in the Text

3:10 to Yuma (James Mangold, U.S., 2007)
The African Queen (John Huston, U.K., 1951)
All Quiet on the Western Front (Lewis Milestone, U.S., 1930)
Amores Perros (Alejandro Gonzáles Iñárritu, Mexico, 2000)
Apocalypse Now (Francis Ford Coppola, U.S., 1979)
L'Argent (Robert Bresson, France, 1983)
L'Armée des ombres (Army of Shadows) (Jean-Pierre Melville, France, 1969)
The Assassination of Jesse James by the Coward Robert Ford (Andrew Dominick, U.S., 2007)
Bastogne (Battleground) (William Wellman, U.S., 1949)
La Bataille des Rails (René Clement, France, 1946)
The Battle of Algiers (Gillo Pontecorvo, Italy/Algeria, 1966)
The Beguiled (Don Siegel, U.S., 1971)
Big (Penny Marshall, U.S., 1988)
The Big Red One (Samuel Fuller, U.S., 1980)
The Birth of a Nation (D. W. Griffith, U.S., 1915)
Bob le Flambeur (Bob the Gambler) (Jean-Pierre Melville, France, 1956)
Breaking the Waves (Lars von Trier, Denmark, 1996)
Brokeback Mountain (Ang Lee, Canada/U.S., 2005)
Broken Blossoms (D. W. Griffith, U.S., 1919)
Casablanca (Michael Curtiz, U.S., 1942)
Le Cercle Rouge (The Red Circle) (Jean-Pierre Melville, France/Italy, 1970)
Chariots of Fire (Hugh Hudson, U.K., 1981)
Children of Men (Alfonso Cuarón, U.S./U.K. 2006)

Cinderella Man (Ron Howard, U.S., 2005)
The Circus (Charlie Chaplin, U.K., 1928)
Cries and Whispers (Ingmar Bergman, Sweden, 1972)
Day of Wrath (Carl-Theodor Dreyer, Denmark, 1943)
Days of Glory (Rachid Bouchareb, Algeria/France, 2006)
Dead Man (Jim Jarmusch, U.S., 1995)
Dekalog (Krzysztof Kieślowski, Poland, 1989)
Destry Rides Again (George Marshall, U.S., 1939)
Diary of a Country Priest (Robert Bresson, France, 1951)
Die Hard (John McTiernan, U.S., 1988)
Dirty Harry (Don Siegel, U.S., 1971)
The Diving Bell and the Butterfly (Julian Schnabel, France/U.S., 2007)
Do the Right Thing (Spike Lee, U.S., 1989)
Doubt (John Patrick Shanley, U.S., 2008)
East of Eden (Elia Kazan, U.S., 1955)
Elevator to the Gallows (Louis Malle, France, 1958)
Every Which Way but Loose (James Fargo, U.S., 1978)
The Exterminating Angel (Luis Buñuel, Spain/Mexico, 1962)
A Fistful of Dollars (Sergio Leone, Italy, 1964)
For a Few Dollars More (Sergio Leone, Italy, 1965)
The Fugitive (Andrew Davis, U.S., 1993)
The Full Monty (Peter Cattaneo, U.K., 1997)
Gangs of New York (Martin Scorsese, U.S./Italy, 2002)
The Gleaners and I (Agnès Varda, France, 2000)
The Good, the Bad and the Ugly (Sergio Leone, Italy/Spain/West Germany, 1966)
Goodfellas (Martin Scorsese, US, 1990)
The Green Zone (Paul Greengrass, U.K., 2009)
Hang 'Em High (Ted Post, U.S., 1968)
Harry Potter and the Order of the Phoenix (David Yates, U.K., 2007)
High Noon (Fred Zinnemann, U.S., 1952)
A History of Violence (David Cronenberg, U.S., 2005)
The Hurt Locker (Katherine Bigelow, U.S., 2008)
It Happened One Night (Frank Capra, U.S., 1934)
It's a Wonderful Life (Frank Capra, U.S., 1946)
Les Jeux Interdits (Forbidden Games) (René Clement, France, 1952)
Jezebel (William Wyler, U.S., 1938)
L.A. Confidential (Curtis Hanson, U.S., 1997)
Lancelot du Lac (Robert Bresson, France, 1974)

A Man Escaped (Robert Bresson, France, 1959)

The Man Who Shot Liberty Valance (John Ford, U.S., 1962)

The Matrix (Andy and Lana Wachowski, U.S./Australia, 1999)

Men in Black (Barry Sonnenfeld, U.S., 1997)

The Messenger (Oren Moverman, U.S., 2009)

Miracle on 34th Street (George Seaton, U.S., 1947)

My Darling Clementine (John Ford, U.S., 1946)

My Name Is Ivan (Andrei Tarkovsky, Soviet Union, 1962)

No Country for Old Men (Ethan and Joel Coen, U.S., 2007)

North by Northwest (Alfred Hitchcock, U.K., 1959)

Nosferatu, A Symphony of Horror (F. W. Murnau, Germany, 1922)

Oldboy (Chan-wook Park, South Korea, 2003)

On the Waterfront (Elia Kazan, U.S., 1954)

Ordet (The Word) (Carl-Theodor Dreyer, Denmark, 1955)

The Ox-Bow Incident (William A. Wellman, U.S., 1943)

Pandora's Box (Georg Wilhelm Pabst, Austria, 1929)

Pretty Woman (Garry Marshall, U.S., 1990)

The Promise (Le Promesse) (Jean-Pierre and Luc Dardenne, France/Belgium, 1996)

Psycho (Alfred Hitchcock, U.K., 1960)

Pulp Fiction (Quentin Tarantino, U.S., 1994)

Pushing Hands (Ang Lee, Taiwan, 1992)

Rambo (Sylvester Stallone, U.S., 2008)

Rebel without a Cause (Nicholas Ray, U.S., 1955)

Red River (Howard Hawks, U.S., 1948)

Rosetta (Jean-Pierre and Luc Dardenne, France/Belgium, 1999)

Round Midnight (Bertrand Tavernier, U.S., 1986)

Sabotage (Alfred Hitchcock, U.K., 1936)

Le Samouraï (Jean-Pierre Melville, France/Italy, 1967)

Santa Fe Trail (Michael Curtiz, U.S./Hungary, 1940)

Saving Private Ryan (Steven Spielberg, U.S., 1998)

Schindler's List (Steven Spielberg, U.S., 1993)

The Searchers (John Ford, U.S., 1956)

The Seven Samurai (Akira Kurosawa, Japan, 1954)

The Seventh Seal (Ingmar Bergman, Sweden, 1957)

Shadows (John Cassavetes, U.S., 1959)

Shane (George Stevens, U.S., 1953)

The Silence of Lorna (Le Silence de Lorna) (Jean-Pierre and Luc Dardenne, Belgium/France/Italy/Germany, 2008)

The Son (Le Fils) (Jean-Pierre and Luc Dardenne, Belgium/France, 2002)
Stagecoach (John Ford, U.S., 1939)
Stalker (Andrei Tarkovsky, West Germany/Soviet Union, 1979)
Star Wars (George Lucas, U.S., 1977)
The Steel Helmet (Samuel Fuller, U.S., 1951)
Sunrise (F. W. Murnau, Germany, 1927)
Superman (Richard Donner, U.S., 1978)
Taken (Pierre Morel, France/U.S./U.K., 2008)
The Terminator (James Cameron, U.K./U.S., 1984)
The Thin Red Line (Terrence Malick, U.S., 1998)
Three Kings (David O. Russell, U.S./Australia, 1999)
Tightrope (Richard Tuggle, U.S., 1984)
Tombstone (George P. Cosmatos, U.S., 1993)
A Touch of Evil (Orson Welles, U.S., 1958)
Vertigo (Alfred Hitchcock, U.S., 1958)
A Very Long Engagement (Jean-Pierre Jeunet, France, 2004)
The Virginian (Victor Fleming, U.S., 1929)
Walk the Line (James Mangold, U.S., 2005)

Clint Eastwood: Select Bibliography

[Note: The books and articles listed below do not represent all the works I consulted as I prepared this book. Rather than presenting a compendium of secondary material on any single movie, this bibliography offers a close look at the texts of Eastwood's iconic films — how their "language" functions, what ideas they generate, and so forth. An extensive bibliography can be found online at: http://www.imdb.com/name/nm0000142/publicity.]

Allison, Deborah. "Clint Eastwood." *Senses of Cinema* (July 2003): http://www.sensesofcinema.com/2003/great-directors/eastwood/.

BFI Companion to the Western, The. Edited by Edward Buscombe and Richard Schickel. Cambridge, MA: Da Capo (Antheneum), 1991.

Bingham, Dennis. *Acting Male: Masculinities in the Films of Jimmy Stewart, Jack Nicholson, and Clint Eastwood.* New Brunswick, NJ: Rutgers University Press, 1994.

Buscombe, Edward. *The Searchers.* London: British Film Institute (BFI Film Classics), 2000.

———. *Unforgiven.* London: British Film Institute (BFI Film Classics), 2004.

Cohan, Steven, and Ina Rae Hark. *Screening the Male: Exploring Masculinities in Hollywood Cinema.* London and New York: Routledge, 1993.

Frayling, Christopher. *Spaghetti Westerns: Cowboys and Europeans from Karl May to Sergio Leone.* London and New York: I. B. Tauris, 1981. Revised paperback edition, 2006.

———. *Clint Eastwood.* London: Virgin Publishing, 1992.

Frodon, Jean-Michal. "Au coeur et dans le ventre, critique de Lettres d'Iwo

Jima." *Cahiers du Cinéma* 620 (Fevrier 2007): 38-40. (This issue of *Cahiers du Cinéma* contains four different articles, including an interview with Eastwood, about the war diptych.)

Jewett, Robert, and John Shelton Lawrence. *Captain America and the Crusade against Evil: The Dilemma of Zealous Nationalism.* Grand Rapids: Eerdmans, 2003.

Jones, Kent. *Physical Evidence: Selected Film Criticism.* Middletown, CT: Wesleyan University Press, 2007.

Kalinak, Kathryn. *How the West Was Sung: Music in the Westerns of John Ford.* Berkeley: University of California Press, 2007.

Kapsis, Robert E., and Kathie Coblentz, eds. *Clint Eastwood: Interviews.* Conversations with Filmmakers series. Jackson: University Press of Mississippi, 1999.

Kitses, Jim. *Horizons West: Directing the Western from John Ford to Clint Eastwood.* Film Classics. New York: Palgrave Macmillan, 2008.

Knapp, Laurence F. *Directed by Clint Eastwood: Eighteen Films Analyzed.* Jefferson, ND: McFarland and Company, 1996.

Lawrence, John Shelton, and Robert Jewett. *The Myth of the American Superhero.* Grand Rapids: Eerdmans, 2002.

McBride, Joseph. *Searching for John Ford: A Life.* New York: St. Martin's Press, 2001.

O'Brien, Daniel. *Clint Eastwood: Film-maker.* London: B. T. Batsford, 1996.

Saunders, John. *The Western Genre: From Lordsburg to Big Whiskey.* (Short Cuts) London and New York: Wallflower Press, 2001.

Schickel, Richard. *Clint Eastwood: A Biography.* New York: Knopf, 1996.

Simsolo, Noël. *Clint Eastwood: Un passeur à Hollywood.* Paris: Editions Cahiers du Cinéma, 2006.

Smith, Paul. *Clint Eastwood: A Cultural Production.* Minneapolis: University of Minnesota Press, 1993.

Wilson, Michael Henry. *Clint Eastwood: Entretiens avec Michael Henry Wilson* (Interviews with Eastwood). Paris: Cahiers du Cinéma, 2007.

Wright, Will. *Six Guns and Society: A Structural Study of the Western.* Berkeley: University of California Press, 1975.

Index